K. Kamaraj

K. Kamraj

Series Editor
Dr. M.H. Syed

Editor
Anil Kathuria **Bharat Singh**

Himalaya Books Pvt. Ltd.
'Ramdoot', Dr. Bhalerao Marg, Girgaon, Mumbai - 400 004
Tel : (022) 23863863, Fax : (022) 23877178
Email : himpub@vsnl.com

First Edition : 2010

Published by : H.B.P.L.
"Pooja Apartments", 4-B, Murari Lal Street, Ansari Road,
Darya Ganj, New Delhi-110 002
Phones : 23270392, 23278631 Reliance : 30180392 to 396
Fax : 011-23256286 Email : hphdel@vsnl.com

Sole Distributers : HIMALAYA PUBLISHING HOUSE PVT. LTD.

Branch Offices

Mumbai : "Ramdoot", Dr. Bhalerao Marg, Girgaon, Mumbai-400 004.
Phones : 23860170/23863863 Fax : 022-23877178
Email : himpub@vsnl.com
Website : www.himpub.com

Nagpur : Kundanlal Chandak Industrial Estate, Ghat Road, **Nagpur 440-018.**
Phone: 2738731, 3296733 Telefax : 0712-2721215

Bengaluru : No. 16/1 (Old 12/1), 1st Floor, Next to Hotel Highlands,
Madhava Nagar, Race Course Road, **Bengaluru - 560 001.**
Phone : 22281541, 22385461, Telefax: 080-22286611

Hyderabad : No. 3-4-184, Lingampally, Besides Raghavendra Swamy Matham,
Kachiguda, **Hyderabad - 500 027.** Phone: 040-27560041,
27550139, Mobile:- 09848130433 Telefax: 040-27560041

Chennai : No. 85/50, Bazullah Road, T. Nagar, **Chennai - 600 017.**
Phone: 044-28344020, 32463737, 42124860

Pune : No. 527, "Laksha" Apartment, First Floor, Mehunpura,
Shaniwarpeth, (Near Prabhat Theatre), **Pune - 411 030.**
Phone: 020-24496323/24496333/32326733

Lucknow : Jai Baba Bhawan, Near Dr. Sanjiv Awasthi, Church Road,
Kurshi Road, Aliganj, **Lucknow - 226 024.**
Phone: 9305302158, 9415349385

Ahmedabad : No. 114, "SHAIL", 1st Floor, Opp. Madhu Sudan House, C.G.Road,
Navrang Pura, **Ahmedabad – 380 009.**
Phone: 079-26560126, Mobiles: 09327324149,09314679413

Ernakulam : No. 39/104 A, Lakshmi Apartment, Karikkamuri Cross Rd.,
Ernakulam, **Cochin – 682011**, Kerala.
Phone: 0484-2378012, 2378016, Mob.: 09344199799

Bhubaneswar : 5 Station Square, **Bhubaneswar (Orissa) - 751 001.**
Mobile: 9861046007, E-mail:-orissa@himpub.com

Indore : Kesardeep Avenue Extension, 73, Narayan Bagh, Flat No. 302,
IIIrd Floor, Near Humpty Dumpty School, Narayan Bagh,
Indore (M.P.) 452 007 Mobile: 09301386468

Kolkata : 108/4, Beliaghata, Main Road, Near ID Hospital, Opp. SBI Bank
Kolkata - 700 010. Mobile: 09910440956

Printed at : H.S. Offset Printers, Daryaganj, New Delhi-110 002

Preface

Biography, is now a form of literature, very much in vogue. In fact, biography is a description or account of someone's life and the times, which is usually published in the form of a book. A biography is more than a mention of personal facts (life, education, work, relationships and death), it also portrays the subject's experience of events. Technically speaking, a work is biographical, if it covers, all of a person's life. Biography writing has a long history. A biography is real. Ancient Greeks developed the biographical tradition, which we have inherited, although until the 5th century AD, when the word 'biographia' first appeared, in Damascius' "Life of Isodorus," biographical pieces were called simply "lives". It is quite likely that the Greeks were drawing on a pre-existing eastern tradition. Certainly Herodotus' "Histories" contains more detailed biographical information on Persian kings and subjects. The earliest surviving pieces, which we would identify as biographical are Isocrates' "Life of Evagoras" and Xenophon's "Life of Agesilaos," both from the fifth century BC. "Parallel Lives" by Plutarch, a Greek writing under the Roman empire, is a series of short biographies of eminent men.

The Golden Age of English biography emerged in late eighteenth century, the century in which the terms "biography" and "autobiography" entered English lexicon. The classic works of the period were Samuel Johnson's "Critical Lives of the Poets" and James Boswell's "Massive Life of Johnson". Generally American biography followed English model. By World War I, cheap hardcover reprints had become popular. The decade of the

1920s witnessed a biographical 'boom'. Later, biographical writings developed a lot and today biographies are written and compiled in the finest form of the genre. In India too, biography, as a form of literature has been evolved, cultivated and polished over the years. Here is an effort to promote this tradition further.

This series of biographies of great men, great women and celebrities in all walks of life is an adventurous academic endeavour, in its own right. A team of researchers and compilers has worked for a good period of time to accomplish the project. For this purpose, hundreds of books by eminent authors and editors have been consulted and referred to. We have benefited from various works, liberally, in order to illustrate and enrich this effort of ours. Present book is devoted to the great personality of Kumaraswamy Kamaraj.

Kumaraswamy Kamaraj better known as K. Kamaraj was an Indian politician from Tamil Nadu, widely acknowledged as the Kingmaker in Indian politics, during the 1960s. He was the Chief Minister of Tamil Nadu and later a Member of Parliament. He was known for his simplicity and integrity. He was involved in the Indian independence movement. As President of the Indian National Congress, he was instrumental in bringing to power two Prime Ministers, Lal Bahadur Shastri and Indira Gandhi. In Tamil Nadu, his home state, he is still remembered for bringing school education to millions of the rural poor by introducing free education and the free Midday Meal Scheme, during his tenure as Chief Minister. He was awarded India's highest civilian honour, the Bharat Ratna, posthumously.

This is a compact and comprehensive account of the above mentioned great life, which is bound to attract the attention of scholars, researchers, students and the general readers alike. Let's hope this humble effort would receive a warm welcome and due applause.

— ***Editors***

Contents

1

An Illustrious Life

King maker of his times, Kumaraswamy Kamaraj, better known as K. Kamaraj was a great Indian politician widely known for his political intellect and strategic vision. He was widely known for his honesty, integrity and simplicity. He was involved in the Indian independence movement and was a close ally of Jawaharlal Nehru, the first Prime Minister of India. He was instrumental in bringing to power two Prime Ministers, Lal Bahadur Shastri in 1964 and Indira Gandhi in 1966. He was affectionately known as the Gandhi of the South, the Black Gandhi, and in Tamil Nadu, his home state he is still hailed for facilitating the spread of education to millions of the rural poor during the 1950s. He was awarded India's highest civilian honour, the Bharat Ratna, posthumously in 1976.

Kamaraj dropped out of school when he was in the sixth grade. When he entered mainstream public life he felt handicapped and realised the importance of a good education. He educated himself during his periods of imprisonment.

Early Life

Kamaraj was born on July 15, 1903, in a family of traders at Virudunagar. His real name was Kamakshi Kumaraswamy Nader but was affectionately shortened to Raja by his mother, Sivakami

Ammal. His father, Kumaraswamy Nader, was a coconut merchant. Kamaraj was enrolled at the local elementary school, the Nayanar Vidyalaya but was later shifted to the high school Kshatriya Vidyalaya.

Unfortunately his father died within a year of Kamaraj's enrolment in school. Kamaraj's mother sold all jewellery except her earrings and deposited the money with a local merchant and cared for the entire family on the monthly interest that the money earned.

Kamaraj was not a good student in school and dropped out when he was in the sixth grade. When he entered mainstream public life he felt handicapped and realised the importance of a good education. He educated himself during his periods of imprisonment and even learned English from his co-worker.

Kamaraj joined as an apprentice in his maternal uncle Karuppiah's cloth shop after dropping out of school. He would slip out from the shop to join processions and attend public meetings addressed by orators like Dr. Varadarajulu Naidu and George Joseph. His relatives frowned upon Kamaraj's budding interest in politics. They sent him to Thiruvananthapuram to work at another uncle's timer shop. Even there Kamaraj participated in the Vaikom Satyagraha led by George Joseph, of the Congress, against the atrocities of the higher caste Hindus on the Harijans. His elders had him called back home and pressured him to marry. Kamaraj resolutely refused to bow to the dictates of his elders.

At the age of 16, Kamaraj enrolled himself as full-time worker of the Congress. He participated in inviting speakers, organising meetings and collecting funds for the party. He also participated in the march to Vedaranyam led by Rajagopalachari as part of the Salt Satyagraha of March 1930.

Kamaraj was arrested and sent to Alipore Jail for two years. He was twenty seven at the time of arrest and was released in 1931 following the Gandhi-Iriwn Pact. Kamaraj was implicated in the Virudhunagar Bomb Case two years later. Dr. Varadarajulu Naidu and George Joseph argued on Kamaraj's behalf and proved the charges to be baseless. Kamaraj was arrested again in 1940 and sent to Vellore Jail while he was on his way to Wardha to get Gandhiji's approval for a list of satyagrahis.

While still in jail, Kamaraj was elected Chairman to the Municipal Council. Nine months later upon his release, Kamaraj went straight to the Municipality and tendered his resignation from his post. He felt that "one should not accept any post to which one could not do full justice."

Kamaraj was arrested once more in 1942 and sentenced to three years in the Amaravathi prison for spreading propaganda material for Quit India movement initiated by Gandhiji. While in prison, Kamaraj read books and continued his self-education.

Kamaraj's political guru and inspiration was S. Satyamurti, orator and parliamentarian. Satyamurti found in Kamaraj "an efficient, loyal, indefatigable worker and skilful organiser." Both developed a deep friendship and complemented each others' skills. In 1936, Satyamurti was elected President of the Provincial Congress and he appointed Kamaraj the General Secretary. Four years later they swapped positions. The party base was strengthened under their leadership. So deep was Kamaraj's devotion for Satyamurti that when India gained independence, he first went to Satyamurti's house and hoisted the Indian flag there. On his election as Chief Minister, Kamaraj went to Satyamurti's house and garlanded his photo and paid his respects to the leader's widow.

On April 13, 1954, K. Kamaraj reluctantly became the Chief Minister of Madras. To everyone's surprise, Kamaraj nominated C. Subramaniam and M. Bhakthavatsalam, who had contested his leadership, to the newly formed Cabinet. Kamaraj gave simple advice to his ministers, "Face the problem. Don't evade it. Find a solution, however small.... People will be satisfied if you do something." The State made immense strides in education and trade. New schools were opened, better facilities were added to existing ones. No village remained without a primary school and no panchayat without a high school. Kamaraj strove to eradicate illiteracy by introducing free and compulsory education upto eleventh standard. He introduced the Midday Meal Scheme to provide at least one meal per day to the lakhs of poor children. He introduced free school uniforms to weed out caste, creed and class distinctions among young minds.

Under his administration, a number of irrigation schemes were completed in record time. The Land Ceiling Act and the Tenancy Protection Act benefited small farmers and saved them from being exploited by landlords. Medium and small scale industries prospered in the midst of large industries making Madras one of the leaders in industrialisation. Nehru complemented Kamaraj for making Madras (later renamed State of Tamil Nadu) the best administered State in India."

Kamaraj remained Chief Minister for three consecutive terms. On October 2, 1963, he resigned to serve a greater purpose. Kamaraj noticed that the Congress party was slowly losing its vigour. He came up with a plan which was called the "Kamaraj Plan". He proposed that all senior Congress leaders should resign form their posts and devote all their energy to the revitalisation of the Congress. A number of Central and State ministers like Lal Bahadur Shastri, Jagjivan Ram, Morarji Desai and S. K. Patil followed suite and resigned from their posts. In 1964, Kamaraj was elected the President of the All India Congress and he successfully navigated the nation through the stormy years following Nehru's death.

On October 2, 1975, Gandhi Jayanti, Kamaraj awoke from his afternoon nap feeling uneasy. His housekeeper, Vairavan, rang up his physician. While he was on his way out, Kamaraj said, "Vairavan, put out the lights when you go out." K. Kamaraj died that day. He was honoured with the highest civilian honour, the Bharat Ratna, posthumously in 1976

Birth

"Public figures cannot afford private life", Jawaharlal Nehru is reported to have lamented once. But there was one figure in Indian politics in the recent past who willingly merged his private life into his public life. The former Chief Minister of Tamil Nadu and All-India Congress President, K. Kamaraj was one such personality. July 15, 2003 marks his birth centenary. A life-long bachelor, this freedom fighter had only aspired for his motherland's freedom from foreign rule and to serve its people afterwards.

Kamaraj's life story had been stranger than fiction for its unbelievable incidents and turn of events. Almost an illiterate with no formal education and born in a poor family in a remote village, he rose to great heights of eminence in the political arena.

K. Kamaraj was born on July 15,1903 to the couple Kumaraswamy and Sivakami in Virudhunagar, Tamil Nadu, in the southern-most part of India. His father Kumaraswamy had a small coconut shop to support his family. While Kamaraj was studying in the primary school, the family was struck with a misfortune. His father, the only breadwinner of the family, succumbed to a massive heart attack.

This put an end to the education of Kamaraj. He had to take up all kinds of odd jobs including that of a street vendor to support his widowed mother and sister. The Independence struggle was in full swing in the country at that time. Kamaraj was eager to contribute his mite to the freedom movement pioneered by Mahatma Gandhi. Inspired by the patriotic leader Satyamurthi's fiery oratory against British atrocities, Kamaraj plunged headlong into the movement. From then on there was no looking back for him. He became an able organiser in mobilising people for public meetings addressed by patriots. Appreciating his skill, Satyamurthi took him under his fold. In due course, Kamaraj, by his selfless devotion, rose in stature. Starting as Satyamurthi's personal assistant he ultimately rose to become the President of the Indian National Congress.

Education

Unfortunately his father died within a year of Kamaraj's enrolment in school. Kamaraj's mother sold all jewellery except her earrings and deposited the money with a local merchant and cared for the entire family on the monthly interest that the money earned.

Kamaraj was not a good pupil in school and dropped out when he was in the sixth grade. When he entered mainstream public life he felt handicapped and realised the importance of a good education. He educated himself during his periods of imprisonment and even learned English from his co-worker.

He joined as an apprentice in the cloth shop of his maternal uncle Karuppiah after dropping out of school. He would slip out from the shop to join processions and attend public meetings addressed by orators like Dr. Varadarajulu Naidu and George Joseph. His relatives frowned upon Kamaraj's budding interest in politics. They sent him to Thiruvananthapuram to work at another uncle's timer shop. Even there Kamaraj participated in the Vaikom Satyagraha led by George Joseph, of the Congress, against the atrocities of the higher caste Hindus on the Harijans. His elders had him called back home and pressured him to marry. Kamaraj resolutely refused to bow to the dictates of his elders.

Habits

Kamaraj proved himself as Chief of all the CMs in the country. He was the first CM who was in the post for a long period of 9 years, i.e. from 1954 to 1963 unless he resigned the post voluntarily he would have continued to be the CM.

He did his duty boldly and patiently without discourage. He listened the views of the opposite parties. He easily solved the political problems.

He attracted every one to his side. He listened others without himself speaking. He never concentrated on his food or dress.

Kamaraj honoured the news reporters. He affectionately moved with photographers. He never angered with anyone. Replied letters immediately. Listened the grievances and solved them immediately. He gave more data. Understood the problems easily and keenly studied the files. He did not like luxury, flattering and advertisement. He was very simple. He never uttered harsh words. Because of these habits he ornamented the CM's post. It would not be an exaggeration that the post got honoured through him.

The words of W. R. S. Sathyanathan were the evidence of the administration of Kamaraj. He served as Chief Secretary to the state under Kamaraj. He said that Kamaraj's efficiency made him to respect him. Kamaraj was fast and clean in finalising the things. He could judge people in a lightning speed who came to meet him. He can solve even a sophisticated big problem within seconds. He approaches the problem directly.

The judgement would be very clean. He detected the problems in an astonishing way. He used to read the files kept for his advice completely, then only he used to decide.

There was no village in the state which his feet never touched. Whatever the place whether Mountain area or river side he could explain with evidences about the climate of that region.

Politics

Kumaraswamy Kamaraj played a leading role in shaping India's destiny from the passing away of Jawaharlal Nehru to the Congress split in 1969. He was born humble and poor in a backward area of Tamil Nadu on July 15, 1903. He was a Nadar, one of the most depressed castes of Hindu society. His schooling lasted only six years. At twelve he was a shop assistant. He was barely fifteen when he heard of the Jallianwala Bagh massacre which was the turning point in his life. Two years later when Kamaraj saw Gandhiji at Madurai the path was chosen. He became a member of the Indian National Congress.

Kamaraj was content for years to remain a rank and file Congress volunteer, working hard for the cause of the freedom movement, unmindful of his personal comfort or career. He was eighteen when he responded to the call of Gandhiji for non-cooperation with the British. He carried on propaganda in the villages, raised funds for Congress work and took a leading part in organising meetings S. At twenty he was picked up by Satyamurthy, one of the greatest orators and a leading figure of the Tamil Nadu Congress Committee who was to be Kamaraj's political guru. In April 1930, Kamaraj joined the Salt Satyagraha Movement at Vedaranyam and was sentenced to two years his first term in prison. Jail-going had become a part of his career and in all he went to prison six times and spent more than 3,000 days in British Jails. Bachelor Kamaraj was forty-four when India became free.

Kamaraj was elected President of the Tamilnad Congress Committee in February 1940. He held that post till 1954. He was in the Working Committee of the AICC from 1947 till the Congress split in 1969, either as a member or as a special invitee. Kamaraj was elected to the Madras Legislative Assembly in 1937 unopposed. He was again elected to it in 1946. He was also elected to the Constituent Assembly of India in 1946, and later to Parliament in 1952. He became Chief Minister of Madras in 1954. He was perhaps the first non-English knowing Chief Minister in India. But it was during the nine years of his administration that Tamil Nadu came to be known as one of the best administered States in India. In 1963 he suggested to Nehru that senior Congress leaders should leave ministerial posts to take up organisational work. This suggestion came to be known as the 'Kamaraj Plan', which was designed primarily to dispel from the minds of Congressmen the lure for power, creating in its place a dedicated attachment to the objectives and policies of the organisation. The plan was approved by the Congress Working Committee and was implemented within two months. Six Chief Ministers and six Union Ministers resigned under the Plan. Kamaraj was elected President, Indian National Congress, on October 9, 1963. Twice he played a leading role in choosing the Prime Minister of India.

His defeat in Virudhunagar in 1967 considerably undermined his prestige. It was even said that he was a much disillusioned man. But the landslide victory at Nagercoil revived his political stature. However, the split in the Congress in 1969 (he remained in the Organisation Congress) and the General Elections of 1971 resulted in a set-back to his political prestige and authority. He continued to work quietly among the masses until the last. He was honoured posthumously by the award of Bharat Ratna.

Meeting with two Blossom Ministers

K. Kamaraj played an essential role in the meeting of India's two Blossom Ministers — Lal Bahadur Shastri in the gathering 1964 and Indira Gandhi in the period 1966. All throughout his dominion as chief minister of Tamil Nadu, K. Kamaraj strived to support aweigh meals and instruction to grouping. This was for the prime indication in the domain that a express like this was being executed in 1957.

Kumaraswamy Kamaraj, who is outmatch remembered as K. Kamaraj, was a strong Indian politico. He was regarded as the 'king-maker' in Amerind politics and was widely reputable for his traits of satinpod, unity and naiveness. During the try for Bharat's freedom from the Brits generalisation, Kamaraj was a enveloping person of Student Jawaharlal Solon, who was afterwards decreed as the opening maturity clergyman of the state. Read this story far to discover more most K. Kamaraj.

Kamaraj was titled king-maker because he played a pivotal persona in the appointment of Bharat's two First Ministers — Lal Bahadur Shastri in the 1964 and again Indira Solon in the period 1966. Thusly, grouping fondly called him the Solon of Southwesterly India or straight the Negro Solon. In his hometown Dravidian Nadu, the denizens plant assets him for wide breeding effortlessness to the thousands under the poorness reasoning.

All throughout the dominion of K. Kamaraj in Dravidian Nadu, he strived to wage disembarrass meals and pedagogy to people. And this was for the prototypical minute in the humankind that a step like this was being executed by K. Kamaraj in 1957. Due to his selfless maintenance for the peachy of the bad and the downtrodden in the lodge, the Regime of Bharat awarded him with the Bharat Ratna, posthumously in the period 1976.

Though K. Kamaraj's nurtured an diversion in opinion since immaturity, it was at the age of 16 that he linked the Indian Subject Legislature as a chockful term. His task was to bespeak speakers, make arrangements for meetings and collect finances for the Legislature circle. Kamaraj also participated in a gather to Vedaranyam spearheaded by C. Rajagopalachari as a endeavour of the restrainer Satyagraha. There were galore occasions when Kumaraswamy Kamaraj was put down the bars during the assay for India's city.

Daily Life

From his young age Kamaraj never liked luxurious life. He adopted simplicity in anything. His food, dress and speech were very simple. But he was not a miser. When he was CM he used to spend most of his salary for the poor who came to him for help.

A cup of coffee in the morning, lunch at 11.00 a.m. evening a cup of coffee and 2 Idlies and a cup of milk at supper were his daily food. His lunch was a simple vegetarian meal. Occasionally an egg would be added with his lunch. He never celebrated Hindu festivals. He used to get up from his bed at 7 a.m.

Kamaraj gave interview to all whoever came to meet him. He never sent anyone without seeing. He helped all as far as possible.

He never helped anyone on the basis of cast or creed. For genuine reasons he never hesitated to help. He used to read books before sleep, some times up to 22 o'clock in the mid night. Sometimes he used to discuss serious political problem upto 5 a.m. in the next morning.

He used to have a nap after lunch. Daily he received about 75 letters. But he never replied them. Just helped the needy ones. He never replied the letters from Virudhunagar. He never wounded anybody's feelings. He moved friendly with everyone without political enmity. He used to get angry at times.

Suppose if anyone confuses Kamaraj or tried to suppress the fact or telling the same matter repeated he gets annoyed. But that anger remains for a short period only. Later he forgets that and moved normally when he meets them next time.

Achievements

During British rule the education was only 7 per cent. But in Kamaraj's period it was 37 per cent. During Rajaji's period there were 12,000 schools in the state. Whereas it was 27,000 in the period of Kamaraj. Power supply in all the villages and industrial growth were there in the period of Kamaraj.

Tamils compared the education and knowledge to our eyes. Hence Tamilians were considered as genius. Kamaraj who hailed from this group made a revolution in education.

Kamaraj removed the system of communal education started by Rajaji. He ordered to reopen the 6,000 elementary schools closed by Rajaji. Moreover he opened 14,000 new schools.

During first plan schools which were about 21,500 in number had gone upto 26,750 during 2nd plan which crossed over 30,000 later. Likewise the admission of students also went up gradually from 25 lakhs to 33.8 and to 46.1 lakhs. During 3rd plan it was decided to admit 14 lakhs more students.

The result of his work was there for all to see. There was an all-round development with village as the nucleus. By inducting colleagues like Shri R. Venkataraman and C. Subramaniam in his Ministry he paved the way for the growth of industrial, agricultural and educational sectors. Tamil Nadu set itself as an example for other States to emulate.

Educational

There was the situation in the country that the construction of schools, serving midday meals, appointing teachers were the duties of the government. Kamaraj wanted to change this and started a great revolutionary plan.

Because of this plan every individual realised to think the education was his responsibility. That was the plan for growth of schools. Conference were conducted and donations were collected from public. About four crores of rupees were donated by public. Poor students were given free books and slates. Lakhs of poor students were benefited.

An important scheme for giving free uniform to poor children were organised and implemented. Kamaraj wanted to avoid the partiality between the poor and the rich students. Result was free uniform scheme. This stopped the inferiority complex among the students.

Kamaraj intended to give free education to all the students. He decided to give free education up to eleventh standard to all the poor students in the year 1960. The annual income of the parents of those students who get the concession should be less than Rs. 1,200. He modified this order in 1962-63. Children of the parents whose income was Rs 1,500 per annum could also get free education upto 11th Std., Apart from this order were issued that children of NGO's employees of Panchayat Unions may also get free education upto High School education.

To avoid illiteracy he formed compulsory primary education. He formed committee to make propaganda in villages about the importance of education.

Though compulsory and free education in schools were there was no proper response. Kamaraj seriously thought the reasons, therefore he meet the villagers and discussed with them. Found out the reason. He arrived at an solution.

How can a guardian parent who is lean bodied due to poverty, powerless eyes, scattered hair without oil and who struggles for at least one time food send his ward to the school. He will send his children to schools at least if they get one time food. Immediately Kamaraj arranged for this. Free Midday Meal Scheme made lakhs of students to come to school. Countries all over the world praised this. Nehruji was much pleased.

At first Midday Meal Scheme properly started in 1956. Over 14 lakhs students were benefited. This scheme got help from CARE OF USA in 1961-62. Milk powder, corn flour and refined vegetable oils were sent free of costs to schools from CARE.

Kamaraj who was deeply worried about the growth of education decided to induce the interest of public. The government took responsibility to govern, fulfil the schemes for the growth of education. These were intensified during Kamaraj's period only. But public did not show their interest and direct involvement.

Onwards from 1956-57 free education was given to the children of elementary school teacher, police constables, head constables and the lower grade employees of government. It came to know in the next year that only 17 per cent of students were not getting free education. To compensate this a scheme for free education to all was announced in 1962.

The revolutionary and progressive schemes and the services of Kamaraj in educational side attracted the public. Because of that there are no villages in the state without elementary schools. A high school for every 5 miles distance with modern amenities was constructed.

Apart from increasing and developing number of schools steps were taken to improve standard of education also. To improve the standard number of working day were increased from 180 to 200. Unnecessary holidays were reduced. Syllabus were prepared to give opportunity to various abilities.

Furthermore two session classes were started. 45 multipurpose schools were started. In the second plan 191 multipurpose schools came up. 286 double session schools were opened. Labourites with modern facilities and librarians were made available. Salaries of the school teachers were increased in order to improve there standard of teaching and to kindle their interest in teaching.

K. Kamaraj introduced a scheme providing pension, provident fund and compulsory insurance to teacher which were not their so far.

He had introduced this scheme for the first time in India. Along with this he introduced family pension scheme also to the teacher.

Scheme was also introduced to provide quarters to the teacher of village schools. Rs 25 lakhs were allotted to this scheme. Construction of 750 houses was planned.

Kamaraj also arranged to give interest free loans to the poor students of medical college, engineering college and agricultural college. This has improved in admission of Engg. College and Medical College in every year. Facility to train nurses in hospitals were also increased

Very number of Arts colleges were increased in the period of Kamaraj. 2 PT Colleges, 10 Teacher training colleges and 39 Teacher training schools were opened in his period.

His government made arrangement to open one more university in his period.

Industrial

Major irrigation schemes were planned in Kamaraj's period. Lower Bhavani, Mani Muthuar, Cauvery Delta, Aarani River, Vaigai Dam, Amravathi, Sathanur, Krishnagiri, Pullambadi, Parambikulam and Neyaru Dams were among them. The Lower Bhavani Dam in Coimbatore district was constructed with an expenditure of Rs. 10 crores. 2,07,000 acres of land are under cultivation.

About 45,000 acres of arable land are benefited through Mettur canal of Salem. Another scheme was Krishnagiri in the same district. Vaigai, Sathanur facilitate to cultivate thousands of acres of lands in Madurai and North Arcot districts respectively. Rs. 30 crores were planned to spend for Parambikulam River scheme in Kamaraj's period. This has helped for the development of Coimbatore district in agriculture field

In 1957-61 1,628 Tanks were de-silted under Small Irrigation Scheme 2000 wells were digged with outlets. Long term loans with 25 per cent subsidy were given to farmers. Apart from formers who are having dry lands were given oil engines, electric pump sets on instalment basis. 150 lakhs of acres of lands were cultivated during Kamaraj's period. One third of this, i.e. 56 lakhs of acres of land get permanent watering facility.

Major industries with an investment in crores of Rupees were started in his period. Neyveli Lignite Scheme, Raw photo film industry at Nilgri, Surgical instruments factory at Guindy, Sugar factories, Bi-Carbonates factories, Cement factories, Railway coach factory at Avadi, Mettur paper industry, were started only in the period of Kamaraj. These are the backbone of the development of the nation.

The result is that Madras state stood first in India in providing electricity to rural areas. About 13,300 villages were give electricity during 1955-61. Using electric power for agriculture purpose, Madras state stands first. Expense to improve electricity situation at Madras in 1959 was Rs. 2.71 crores. Hydro power station at Periyar was constructed at an expenditure of Rs. 9 crores. 1 lakh KW of electricity produced under this scheme.

Well-known Kunda Dam project was constructed at an expenditure of Rs. 3.5 crores. Nehruji inaugurated this project. It was completed in a very short period by over engineers which made foreigners to wonder. In 1958-59, the investment in electricity connection was 95 crores and the income increased to Rs. 12 crores.

In this context, Avadi Congress Conference was held in 20th January 1956. It was 6th Conference. Kamaraj constructed a city and named it as Sathyamoorthy Nagar. Kamaraj told to Mr. S. S. Vasan who took the responsibility of decoration that it was not important one to say that he had not seen such a decoration there before, but it was important that one to say that he had not seen such a beautiful conference even after 25 years.

Jawaharlal Nehru appreciated the decoration. Nehruji unveiled the statue of Sathyamoorthy. The Avadi Congress had increased the prestige of Southern people in Northern part of India.

Masses donated food grains for the meals. Kamaraj's mother came to Avadi Conference from Virudhunagar. Nehruji took photograph with his mother. In memory of Srinivasa Iyengar the AICC president his daughter Ambuja Ammal was nominated as the leader of reception committee.

Nation's newspapers wrote that Kamaraj was the main reason for the unforgettable Avadi Conference in the history of Congress.

Maulana Abul Kalam Azad proposed to form a society of equality in the action committee meeting. Kamaraj seconded the proposal. In the conference when all participated Nehru proposed this and Kamaraj seconded.

K. Kamaraj said, "Only hard labour will save people. Wealth should not be massed with one group. No violence is necessary to form equality in society. It is also not desirable. Gandhiji got the freedom in a peaceful way. Let us form this society in the same way."

When Nehruji came to Madras in 1936 Kamaraj joined with him in the tour. Since 1949 he attended the AICC meeting. Avadi Congress conference was a turning point to Kamaraj

Under Kamaraj's administration, a number of irrigation schemes were completed in record time. The Land Ceiling Act and the Tenancy Protection Act benefited small farmers and saved them from being exploited by landlords. Medium and small scale industries prospered in the midst of large industries making Madras one of the leaders in industrialisation. Nehru complemented Kamaraj for making Madras (later renamed State of Tamil Nadu) the best administered State in India."

Political

Since Kamaraj took charge as CM from 1954 he formed interim ministry and governed for 3 1/2 years. His record was appreciated d by all. Even opposite party people were afraid to blame his rule.

At this situation in the 1957 general election Congress won with an absolute majority, out of 205 seats Congress bagged 151. It astonished the whole India. For Madras state assembly Kamaraj won and became CM. He formed the second ministry.

Kamaraj submitted the list to the Governor A. J. John consisting the names of M/s M. Bakthavathsalam, C. Subramanian, A.

Manickavelan, P. Kakkan, V. Ramiah and Mrs. Lurdu Ammal Simon. His 2nd ministry took charge in 13th April 1957. Later R. Venkatraman was included in the ministry.

In 1957, general election Kamaraj was elected from Sathur Constituency. This election was a lesson to Kamaraj. Except Ananda Vikatan, the Tamil weekly, no paper or magazine supported Congress.

In general they were against Congress. Though Congress won in the election Kamaraj felt that there should be a newspaper for Congress.

According to his wish a Tamil Daily by name 'Thai Nadu' was proposed to be started in 1958.

But due to some delay in getting the machinery the daily could not be started. The registration of title was also expired.

In 1960 a daily by name 'Nava Shakti' was started. It was out and out for Kamaraj. The aim of it was to propaganda Kamaraj's view. In the 1962 election Congress bugged 139 seats and DMK 50. The communist who got 15 seats in 1952 election could get only 4 in 1957. Now it got only 2 seats.

Kamaraj was elected as CM for the third time. He sworn in as CM before the then Governor Vishnu Ram Methi on 15th March 1962. There were 9 persons including the CM in the ministry. It is to noted that it was only the smallest Cabinet in India.

Vinobaji toured Madras state (1956) only during Kamaraj's period. Kamaraj joined with him in tour and addressed the meetings. Vinobaji saw the affection of the public towards Kamaraj and said that he was only the true follower of Gandhiji.

Kamaraj was not only sitting in the fort where the flag was flying but he also was in the hearts of the public. He was the public and public was him. He was the only leader who constructed a bridge between the huts and the fort. He stood first in having a remarkable memory power in public life. Kamaraj was the main reason to forbid the red tapism in government.

Kamaraj remained CM for three consecutive terms. On October 2, 1963, he resigned to serve a greater purpose. Kamaraj noticed that the Congress party was slowly losing its vigour. He came up with a plan which was called the 'Kamaraj Plan'. He proposed that all senior Congress leaders should resign form their posts and devote all their energy to the revitalisation of the Congress. A number of Central and State ministers like Lal Bahadur Shastri, Jagjivan Ram, Morarji Desai and S. K. Patil followed suite and resigned from their posts. In 1964, Kamaraj was elected the President of the All India Congress and he successfully navigated the nation through the stormy years following Nehru's death.

Speech

Kamaraj delivered his speech on 9th January. amidst lakhs of volunteers to eradicate the poverty of 45 crores of Indians,. It was the place where Emperor Ashoka fought with his warriors against Kalinga's empire's lakhs of soldiers 2,500 years ago to establish Magada Empire. It was the place where Emperor Ashoka decided not to fight and preach peace. Two lakhs people heard his speech.

His speech at the conference was as under:

> "You have given me the responsibility to administer the INC by electing me to this highest post unanimously you, have exposed your affection towards me. I expect your full cooperation and enthusiastic support to execute my duty to the entire satisfaction of you all".

Kamaraj's speech had explained in a way about the steps to be taken to fight against economical conditions after paying homage to the departed freedom fighters and the soldiers who lost their lives in Indo-China war.

> "There are certain items in our economical conditions which worries us. I point out at first that massing of wealth with certain people. So there is monopoly in some trade. Tax evasion, black marketing of scare products. No honesty in trade, no regularity in trade. It is essential to take proper steps in this matter".

He further explained the procedures to be followed, "Since our aim is socialism we have to stop amassing of wealth with certain people and its hereditary continuance. If we allow this it will be hurdle for our development. At the end the rich will be more rich."

We have to see now whether the present laws and administration will fulfil our socialistic aims. INC should examine the developments in each state. Government should take action to stop monopoly and also they are to be examined. We have to develop new areas and start new industries. Districts should give free education upto secondary school education gradually.

Great Kamaraj

Just about three decades ago there lived here a selfless leader, an upright politician and a sacrificing son of the soil. Yet how many of us know of his greatness? It is to the credit of Ramana Communications that it has produced a film on K. Kamaraj, a diehard Congressman of the Nehru era. Making a film on the life of the distinguished personality, who remained a bachelor all his life and served the country till his last breath, surely allows no scope for any of the formula stuff that the filmgoer is so used to. And hence offers the investor absolutely no commercial guarantee. But undeterred by the risk, Ramana Communications has taken up such a venture.

Inspired by the Independence Movement and the Mahatma, the young, not very educated Kamaraj rises from humble beginnings to emerge as the Chief Minister of the State, a man of the masses and a king-maker of repute. His simple living and high thinking that ought to make each of us proud is presented with a visionary touch by director A. Balakrishnan. Kamaraj's corruption-free rule as Chief Minister, his sensitivity that made him do his utmost to educate the poor, his anger at injustice from any quarter, the elections in which the Congress was trounced, the period when Indira Gandhi declared a state of Emergency, and the effect that such events had on Kamaraj have been well brought out.

Besides documenting the life of the leader till the end, the film also traces the history of the nation and the State in an interesting manner. Kamaraj's interaction with his mother, the people who come to see him and the bureaucracy and his calm acceptance of the highs and lows of life are unforgettable facets of the film. And finally as you watch the funeral procession of the man, you are choked with emotion.

All the characters have been chosen to suit the roles they play. Thus, casting is a strong point of 'Kamaraj'. Richard Mathuram has done a neat job as Kamaraj. M. S. Bhaskar who has dubbed for him deserves special mention. The bright eyes of Sampathraj, the man who plays the young Kamaraj, is more an indicator of the kind of man he portrays.

Only the actor who plays Rajaji does not seem true-to-life in appearance and demeanour. Along with known faces such as director Mahendran, actors Vijayan, A. K. Veeraswamy and V. S. Raghavan, are Sumanth as Jawaharlal Nehru, Kovai Ramaswamy as Periyar, Aravamudhan as C. Subramaniam and Kanakaraj as Gandhiji. Well-known stage artiste, T. S. Anandhi is Indira Gandhi. The resemblance to the former PM, which is more because of her nose, makes her a reasonably right choice for the role.

The screenplay could have been moulded better and the sudden close-ups that come and go abruptly could have been avoided. Sembur Jayaraj and J. Francis Kripa take credit for the screenplay and dialogue. V. T. Vijayan has handled the editing. There are scenes that end too suddenly and thus give way to jerks in the narration. Rerecording is minimal in 'Kamaraj', and wherever it is heard, the maestro's touch is evident. The 'Naadu Parthathunda ...' number that Ilaiyaraja sings in the end makes a tremendous impact. Vaali's lyrics for the same moisten your eyes.

Presidential Address by Kamaraj

Even during the days of the freedom struggle, the Congress organisation had broadly indicated that the society which it envisaged after achieving independence was not the conventional type of society but a progressive one based on the modern concepts of social, political and economic equality and justice. The Indian National Congress, until Mahatma Gandhi assumed its leadership was confining its attention to political freedom. Mahatmaji not only spread the message of freedom to the farthest corners of India, but also devoted his attention to the eradication of poverty and misery among the masses. When the masses realised that the Indian National Congress stood for the betterment of their economic condition and their social progress, they joined the organisation in large numbers and gave them massive support.

Revolutionary Steps

K. Kamaraj reduced the ministry to eight from twelve. He included the supporters of Rajaji in his ministry. He also included C. Subramaniam who contested against him in his ministry. Bakthavathsalaam was also included one among the eight. The six person who opposed Rajaji were not included in the ministry.

At that time he thought that it would be better to include Vannian Community who opposed Congress. He included Ramaswamy Padaiaachi in the ministry who was the leader of opposite party and opposed Congress in the assembly. Hence there was no opposition for Congress from out side. He formed such a ministry and avoided the opposition from in and out of Congress. He took charge as CM on 13th April of 1954, the Tamil new year day. He was not a member in assembly nor a member in Legislative Council. He should become a member within six months from the date of taking charge in either of legislature.

It was quite easy to become a Member of Legislature Council. But Kamaraj did not prefer it. He had a strong belief for a healthy government one should be elected through assembly election only. Also he thought that he could understand the opinion of the public only if contest for the assembly election.

He was always elected from the Virudhunagar constituency. Suppose if he wanted to be elected from there the elected member of that constituency should resign. As always he did not want to create problem ever.

There was a vacancy in Gudiatham Constituency of North Arcot district. All wanted him to contest from there as the CM is common to the state and he contest from any constituency of the state. Finally he decided to contest from Gudiatham Constituency.

Kamaraj didn't belong to North Arcot which consist Gudiatham constituency. Even then he contested from there, except Communist party all other parties supported Kamaraj. Since the Dravidian parties did like Rajaji to become the Chief Minister again they supported Kamaraj and made serious propaganda for his victory. The Congress volunteers of all parts of Madras state invaded Gudiatham since Kamaraj decided to contest from a new constituency which neither was his native nor a place he dwelled. The Dravidian parties and Muslim league openly supported Kamaraj and hunted for votes. Gudiatham was flooded by party people. Public worked for Kamaraj. Kamaraj visited all the villages and addressed the mass. He won in the election. He thanked the people of that constituency.

Kamaraj didn't go for the post of minister. It came to him. The post which came to him in 1954 he resigned it 1963. He was the first Chief Minister who was in that post for such a long period.

Many ministries changed in other states of India because of Enmity, Plots, Jealous and for post but it was not in Madras state. There was no quarrel, enmity or jealous in the ministry of Kamaraj. After Kamaraj became Chief Minister the trend of Madras state was totally changed.

Kamarj's tenure was called as Golden Period. When he became Chief Minister he said, "People who works people as Maharajas and Lords who are lazy and live on other labours. I have become the Chief Minister only to wipeout the troubles of poor, else I don't want this post at all."

From that day onwards, all the poor had his portraits at their huts.

When he was the Chief Minister of Madras state he went in the path of Gandhiji and followed the principles of Nehru. He did what was Right. People respected him as a 'Model Man'.

Last Days and Demise

On October 2, 1975, Gandhi Jayanti, K. Kamaraj awoke from his afternoon nap feeling uneasy. His housekeeper, Vairavan, rang up his physician. While he was on his way out, Kamaraj said, "Vairavan, put out the lights when you go out." K. Kamaraj died that day. He was honoured with the highest civilian honour, the Bharat Ratna, posthumously in 1976

Birth Anniversary

Kamaraj birth anniversary has been declared as 'Educational Development Day'

Chief Minister M. Karunanidhi on Saturday announced that the State Government would enact a law in the forthcoming Assembly session to declare Kamaraj birth anniversary (July 15) as 'Educational Development Day.'

Launching the expanded nutritious noon meal scheme for school children on the 104th birth anniversary of Kamaraj, Mr. Karunanidhi said the day would also mark the celebration to perpetuate his memory by offering floral tributes to his portrait in all schools, besides expressing gratitude for his contribution to developing education.

Under the expanded nutritious noon meal scheme, eggs would be provided twice a week to the beneficiaries, he said.

Justifying the proposal to bring forward a Bill in the Assembly, rather than issuing a Government Order to celebrate Kamaraj's birth anniversary as Educational Development Day, he said the move would make it difficult for successive Governments to modify or abandon the scheme, as it would evoke stiff resistance from the Opposition in the Assembly.

He accused the erstwhile All India Anna Dravida Munnetra Kazhagam (AIADMK) Government of modifying or withdrawing many good schemes implemented by the previous Dravida Munnetra Kazhagam (DMK) Government. These schemes included the marriage assistance programme named after Moovalur Ramamirtham that had benefited about 2.50 lakh women and the scheme to provide eggs once in two weeks along with the nutritious meal, he said. It became possible for the AIADMK Government to abandon these schemes as they were implemented on the basis of GOs, he added. Tracing the evolution of the noon meal scheme, Mr. Karunanidhi said the programme was introduced after Kamaraj pointed out that it would be impossible for hungry children to attend school. The late Chief Minister M. G. Ramachandran converted it into a nutritious meal scheme implemented by the Government instead of leaving the responsibility to teachers.

The Government's decision to provide eggs twice a week would improve the health of the students, he said, adding that the expanded nutritious meal programme would reflect on their efficiency to learn.

Mr. Karunanidhi launched the scheme by serving eggs to 200 children at the Chennai Corporation Middle School in Chepauk constituency. He distributed prizes to the winners of oratorical, painting and essay writing competitions held by the school. He also handed over assistance to students and other beneficiaries under different schemes.

Social Welfare Minister Poongothai said the Chief Minister had added one more feather to his cap by implementing the scheme. Minister for School Education Thangam Thennarasu said the decision to celebrate Kamaraj's birth anniversary as Educational Development Day showed Mr. Karunanidhi's affection for the late leader. Whip of the Congress Legislature Party Peter Alphonse thanked the Chief Minister for his gesture. Chief Secretary L. K. Tripathy welcomed.

Nehru's Comments

Nehruji appreciated the services of Kamaraj as under:

> "It is impossible to find a person overcoming Kamaraj in public service. As a friend for several years I had a chance to know him. The value I had on him increased on and on whenever I moved with him. He is the CM to a government which is a example for efficient and good governance."

Husband of England Queen, Lord Eddianburro, congratulated Kamaraj and said that he should be the Chief Minister of Madras state during his next visit to India and Madras. Thus, Kamaraj ruled Madras State. As per the judgement of news reporters his way of ruling was a lesson to others and his service was an example to the post he held. S. Balasundrammal, wife of Sathyamoorthy said as under about Kamaraj:

> "Kamaraj served for the nation for more than 20 years along with my husband. During that time he had the sense of sacrifice and public service. He was best companion to my husband and worked without rest to strengthen the Congress in Madras state. His Chief Ministership was the evidence to the dream of my husband". Thus, the disciple made the dream of his leader alive.

2

Political Career

Rise in Politics

In Madras, Kamaraj succeeded C. Rajgopalachari, another great stalwart, as the CM of Tamil Nadu on April 13, 1954. Undoubtedly, this was a great achievement for him as he was the unanimous choice for the high office. He was honest and selfless to the core. Almost half a century has passed since he administered Tamil Nadu. But his pivotal role in the State's all-round development is still remembered.

Keeping pace with Nehru's visionary efforts at the national level, Kamaraj was instrumental in building many irrigation dams, linking the villages by all-weather roads and constructing hospitals in remote places. Today he is talked about for making primary education completely free.

Perhaps he might have felt that the asset of education which he was deprived of due to poverty should not befall similarly placed children. In fact, he felt that a major part of his life's mission was fulfilled by this one act. Kamaraj had also introduced the Midday Meal Scheme for the poor students at school. It helped arrest dropouts. It is now being replicated at the national level. Even the Supreme Court in one of its recent judgements has asked every State to implement the scheme besides instructing the Central

Government to release foodgrains from its godowns for this purpose. The President, Dr. A. P. J. Abdul Kalam, while inaugurating a similar scheme under 'Akshaya Patra' at a function in Bangalore recently, acknowledged the pioneering work done in this field by K. Kamaraj.

The result of K. Kamaraj's work was there for all to see and watch. There was an all-round development with village as the nucleus. By inducting colleagues like Shri R. Venkataraman and C. Subramaniam in his Ministry he paved the way for the growth of industrial, agricultural and educational sectors. The state of Tamil Nadu set itself as an example for other States to emulate.

Well impressed by the success achievements and acumen of Kamaraj, Prime Minister Jawaharlal Nehru felt that his services were needed more at the national level. In a swift move he brought Kamaraj to Delhi as the President of the Indian National Congress. That Nehru should have lent his ears to a little-educated leader like Kamaraj on party and national issues amazed everyone. Nehru realised that if he had wide learning and vision, Kamaraj possessed enormous common sense and pragmatism. This was amply proved when Kamaraj suggested to Nehru to seek the resignation of some of his senior Cabinet colleagues to draft them for party work. Kamaraj had realised that the Congress party was losing ground among the people due to the absence of dedicated leaders. Nehruji promptly accepted Kamaraj's suggestion and some of his Cabinet ministers resigned.

K. Kamaraj's political maturity came in full view when Jawaharlal Nehru died in 1964. How he settled the succession issue for the Prime Ministership was amply proved by his choice of L. B. Shastri and Indira Gandhi in succession.

Though later in life, K. Kamaraj had to lose his political power and sit in the opposition, he still remained a respected national figure both among his colleagues and opponents. He had no enemies in politics and remained endeared to the masses as before. This was evident when a multitude surged to bid the final farewell to Kamaraj on October 02,1975 after he died of a massive heart attack. Countless condolences came in from various parts of the country. But the one that came from Justice Krishna Iyer said it all: "A common man's man with an uncommon common sense".

Madras State

Asif Ali left for Bombay and met Sardar Patel and explained him the situation of Madras state. Then he left for Delhi and sent a telegram to Kamaraj asking Kamaraj whether he can have a conciliation with Rajaji as he has to handover the findings of enquiry.

Kamaraj's representative met Sardar Patel at Bombay and explained him the situation. Immediately Sardar Patel contacted Kamaraj and Rajaji.

Rajaji had a talk with Kamaraj. Kamaraj explained Patel that there should be 8 members in Parliamentary board and 3 from his group and 3 from Rajaji's apart from President and Vice-President. Rajaji accepted to this without any other go. It was the same thing what Kamaraj told right from the beginning. Finally Rajaji accepted the same. Patel too accepted to this on behalf of the Parliamentary board and informed to Aruna Asif Ali.

Eight members board for Madras State Congress Parliament was formed. Rajaji was not given a seat in this. Kamaraj, Rukmani Lakshmipathi, Muthuranga Mudaliar, Ramaswamy Reddiar, Avinashilingam Chettiar were on one side and C. P. Subbiah, Muthuswamy Pillai, Annamalai Pillai were on the other side representing Rajaji.

There was a political war between Kamaraj and Rajaji in Madras State. Rajaji had the support of Indian leaders at the beginning. But Kamaraj had a strong foundation and strong support of his followers. Hence no one could shake him.

Rajaji opinioned that Kamaraj was a sensible and honest man. He said it in 1966 June. Gandhiji presided the Silver Jubilee of Hindi Prachar Saba in January 1946 at Chennai. His arrival was kept secret as Gandhiji was unwell. Police took the charge of receiving Gandhiji.

Rajaji knew where Gandhiji would get down from the train. He did not inform this to Kamaraj. He took N. Gopalaswamy Iyengar and Sathyanarayana, Secretary of Hindi Prachar Sabha along with him without Kamaraj. When Kamaraj came to Hindi Prachar Saba he found that Rajaji and others went to receive

Gandhiji. He knew not the exact place of Gandhiji's arrival. He did not know what to do. At that time a news reporter by name Ganapathy came there, who like other reporting efficient in finding out the secrets like a brained detectives informed Kamaraj the exact location where Gandhiji would be invited and took to Ambattur railway station where Rajaji and others were waiting for Gandhiji's arrival. The special train in which Gandhiji was arriving came shortly. As a president of Madras State PCC Kamaraj first garlanded Gandhiji who accepted it palling the shoulders of Kamaraj.

Gandhiji stayed for a week at Madras. He left to Madurai on 1st of February. Kamaraj went along with him. He went to Madurai to worship Meenakshi Amman Temple and Palani. After finishing his tour in Madras state he left Madras. In February 10th of 1946, he started his newspaper of "Harijan" in which he praised Rajaji and his service to nation and Congress. It added fuel to fire to Kamaraj who felt very much.

Rajaji was strongly opposed in Parliament. But Gandhiji mentioned that as click.

Opposition of the public against Rajaji was mentioned as click by Gandhiji hurted Kamaraj. He decided to resign from the parliamentary board. He gave an announcement in 12th of February 1946. In which he said the parliamentary board meeting was conducted on the previous day. Gandhiji's article regarding Rajaji attracted the attention. After it the meeting was postponed. The information regarding Rajaji and the Madras state Congress appeared in "Harijan" gave shock to Kamaraj.

When Gandhiji toured Madras State Kamaraj was with him throughout the tour. But nothing was discussed about the Madras State Congress. But Gandhiji used the word of "Click". Since that hurted Kamaraj he was prepared to resign from the parliamentary board. This was conveyed to Gandhiji. Meanwhile Pattabi Seetharamiah explained Gandhiji about the position of Congress in detail.

The parliamentary board members other than Kamaraj accepted to sponsor nominees for 1946 election. The list was sent Sardar Patel. Bakthavathsalam and Mrs. Rukmani Lakshmipathi went to Bombay. Patel invited Kamaraj too. He went to Bombay on 18th February. But till the finalisation of the list he refused to meet Patel. He met Patel only after that and returned to Madras.

Though Rajaji included the names of his favourites he had no hopes of getting majority in the election. There was civil commotion at Madurai against Rajaji. As could not control the situation he resigned in March 21st. There was as problem in forming the Ministry. Kamaraj from Madras Prakasam from Andhra and Madhava Menon from Kerala went to Delhi, met Patel. But they were directed to Gandhiji. But Gandhiji did not like Prakasam to be the Chief Minister as Prakasam did not behave properly in Public Affairs. He did not want him to be even as ordinary minister.

Among Pattabi Seetharamaiah, Rajaji and Prakasam, name of Prakasam was eliminated by Gandhiji and he asked to select one out of the remaining two.

On April 10th seven leaders met Maulana Azad. He suggested to form a ministry consisting Prakasam, Rajaji and Pattbi Seethramiah. Pattabi Seetharamaiah did not accept to this. He met Gandhiji on 11th April.

Gandhiji invited Kamaraj consulted him and keenly noted the positions of Madras state and asked about the possibilities of wining if Pattabi Seetharamiah was nominated. Kamaraj wanted the Cooperation of Rajaji and Gandhiji gave his assurance for that.

Rajaji Came

When Rajaji was the CM he introduced the Communal Education System. One day morning around 7 a.m. Kamaraj was talking with Vincent of Tirupur about his dissatisfaction on Rajaji's educational policy. On that day he was unwell. He was in the upstairs with Vincent. Then his servant came and informed about the arrival of Rajaji to his house. Immediately he came down to invite Rajaji. Rajaji enquired about his health and they talked for about 10 minutes. Then Rajaji left Kamaraj went upto his car and gave a send off. Kamaraj never had hard feeling's upon Rajaji personally.

In the Life of Jeeva

Communist leader P. Jeevanandam was fighting for the issue of documents to the hut dwellers. Kamaraj was the CM then. Kamaraj went to Tambaram to open a school building. Jeeva's house was on the way. Kamaraj asked the driver to stop the car in front of Jeeva's house. It was dilapidated hut. Kamaraj saw that tears rolled down. He took Jeeva along with him to the function as the foundation stone to the school was laid by Jeeva. After sometime Jeeva's wife got a job. Kamaraj helped for that. He also helped Jeeva to stay in a good house. Jeeva was admitted in the General Hospital due to ill health where he died. Before his death he asked his nearby people to telephone to Kamaraj. Kamaraj was in the mind of Jeeva even at the time of his death. Because Kamaraj took the nation in socialistic way and he stood as an example for that.

One Day Chairman

Prior to his arrest, Kamaraj sent a notice that Janab Ubayathulla of Vellore should be the President of PCC Madras State.

As Virudhunagar Chairman Sankarapandia Nadar was also arrested Chairman's post was vacant. Regarding electing PCC Madras state president Ubayathulla sent a telegram to Dhanushkodi Nadar. But a reply was sent to him stating that the election of Chairman would be amicably settled.

R. Guruswamy the Vice Chairman fixed the date as 31st May 1941 for Chairman's election. Kamaraj who was in the prison at Vellore was unanimously elected as Chairman.

Before this 'Bengal Lion' Desabandhu Chittranjan Das was elected as Mayor when he was in the prison. Likewise Kamaraj too was elected as Chairman when he was in the jail. People were proud of this.

In the very first week of March 1942, a months after the Chairman's election Kamaraj was released. He came to Virudhunagar in the 2nd week. A warm welcome was given to him.

The municipal council's meeting was held on 16th of March under the presidentship of Vice-Chairman 90th item of Agenda was taken for consideration and recorded. Kamaraj as a Chairman came to the meeting and sat in the Chairman's chair. He recorded 91st item. He addressed to Councillors thanking them for having elected him as Chairman. But as he had some other important affairs to look after he was unable to continue as Chairman and tendered his resignation.

A nine months' Chairman who conducted the council meeting for nine minutes addressed like this "A person who holds a post even if it is a honorary one, should act properly. If he is not able to function properly he should not hold that post."

Prakasam became Chief Minister

On April 13th Kamaraj met Patel and informed about the discussions he had with Gandhiji. He informed Rajaji too about Gandhiji's decision. Rajaji opposed this as his name was not considered for Chief Ministership and refused to cooperate.

Since Gandhiji did not prefer Prakasam he supported Rajaji with a hope to get at least a post of minister. Due to this there was a split in the opposition group of Rajaji. There was change in Prakasam after his Delhi trip. He decided to contest for Chief Minister. As Gandhiji did not prefer Prakasam, Kamaraj refused to support him. He nominated Muthuranga Mudaliar against Prakasam expecting a support of Rajaji's group. Prakasam won by 7 votes. 33 members of Rajaji group supported Prakasam and got his victory.

Kamaraj was advised not to support the ministry of Prakasam but he refused. People from the group of Kamaraj were also in the ministry. Kamaraj wanted Mr. Madhava menon to be given a ministry post. But Prakasam made Raghava menon of Rajaji's group as a minister which resulted toppling down of Praksam's ministry.

Kamaraj did not take any step to topple down the ministry of Prakasam. At the house of Rajaji at Delhi a meeting was held for this toppling down. They decided to bring No Confidence Motion against Prakasam.

Rajaji recommended O. P. Ramaswamy Reddiar after Prakasam, meanwhile there was a talk for compromise too. Acharya Kriplani come to Madras from Delhi. Praksam pleaded to allow him as Chief Minister and elect any one as ministers. All accepted for this except Kamaraj. Kripalni compelled Kamaraj.

But Kamaraj did not go back from his decision. No Confidence Motion was brought in and passed. These incidents happened when Malabar and Andhra were with Madras as a composite state.

Peak Time

Presidentship of Kamaraj burnt the eyes of many. They wanted to remove him from that post. There came the election in May 16th of 1946. Rajaji's group worked vigorously to defeat Kamaraj. They asked Muthuramalinga Thevar to contest against Kamaraj. He refused. They approached S. Ganesan of Karaikudi and he contested against Kamaraj. Kamaraj won in the election and defeated his rival by a margin of 62 votes. He became as a President of Madras State PCC again.

After 1942 August revolution Indian National Trade Union Congress (INTUC) had the support of all the political leaders. They considered that as a bridge for freedom fight.

Leaders like V. V. Giri, N. G. Ramaswamy of Kovai took active part in Congress party an in INTUC. They considered as Independence as a weapon to remover poverty among labours.

There was a change in the unions under INTUC in 1942. Some unions started blaming others and betray the labours. Thousands of labours who were in jail in freedom fight condemned the behaviour of INTUC and wanted to form a separate union for them.

In 1945 Security Detunes and prisoners of independence were released in bunches. Congress prisoners who cam from the jail started a Congress union. Since PCC of Madras state was treated as against law on that period this union could not act under PCC. Muthuranga Mudaliar was in a key post. R. Venkatraman and late Rajagopalan decided to start Congress oriented union.

Congress Labours

Assembly election came in 1946. Four seats were allotted for the labours of Madras state. Buckingham Mill Labour Union, Coimbatore Cotton Mill Union, Workers of South Indian Railway and other factory workers of Madras were allotted those four seats.

The president and good administrator of INTUC P. Jeevanandam contest for INTUC. Congress wanted to nominate a poor labour so that through him Congress can have good growth. Kamaraj accepted for this proposal and Kanniappan was elected for the assembly.

Kamaraj handled any problems of labours personally. Being a president of PCC he liked to have his direct involvement. There was a strike at Coimbatore 30,000 labours participated in that. Kamaraj and R. Venkatraman met the mill owners and talked with them and consulted the ministry and reached for an amicable settlement, this confirmed Kamaraj as a friend to labour. Leaders of B&C mill unions used to consult Kamaraj for his advice. Labours of Madurai Harvey mill wanted Kamaraj to be their union leader.

Kamaraj helped a lot to form union for the Tea and Coffee plantation workers.

One Dr. Daniel a union leader of plantation workers said that had not there been the help and support of Kamaraj their union might have come to an end.

Narayanaswamy Naidu formed an union for agricultural labours in Madras state. But only Kamaraj gave all the right to that union. There was no security for peasants and labours in Tanjore. Kamaraj along with Narayanaswamy Naidu implemented the settlement arrived between Naidu and then Revenue minister K. N. Venkat Rao. He helped them a lot and they treated him as their godfather.

1500 Members

Problems faced by the employees of Simson group were solved with the help of Kamaraj.

He listened the grievances of labour with sympathy gave them the solutions and did the things that were to be done by the government. Labours treated him as their leader, godfather , friend and philosopher. Nathaniel the president Trivancore Dominion Madras State PCC met Kamaraj in 1946. He explained that they were being prevented to join with Tamilnad and of that position continues there won't be either Tamil or Tamilians. Hence the help of Kamaraj was very much necessary for this.

Kamaraj replied that due to wont of time and pressure of work he could not visit Trivancore though he received lot of letters and telegrams. As per that day's Congress committee formation they should join only with Kerala Congress Committee. Unless the law was changed there was no other go. But when the linguistic states were formed they could join with Madras state PCC. A resolution was passed in PCC working committee that places around Trivancore near Madras state should be permitted by AICC to join with Madras state for the work of congress.

Care taker government was formed in Trivancore in September 4th of 1947. Election was nearing with powers for aged to exercise their franchise. Tamils who went around with slogans for united Tamilnad were lathi charged by armed police. Lathi charge, oppression, false cases were the daily routines.

Tamils took oath to live with unity or to die. They sent telegrams to Kamaraj stating the dangers faced by them. Kamaraj left immediately. He met the people village by village and heard their problems. He had a talk with leaders of the Dominion Congress to safeguard the interests of Tamilians but was in complete. Before leaving for Madras he informed that he would invite Pattam Thaanuu Pillai and Nathaniel to Madras for a compromise. Pattam Thaanuu Pillai did not come to Madras at the appointed day. Election was conducted, all the Tamils joined together voted and won. The visit of Kamaraj induced for this victory.

Chief Minister of Madras

Since K. Kamaraj took charge as Chief Minister from 1954 he formed interim ministry and governed for 3 1/2 years. His record was appreciated d by all. Even opposite party people were afraid to blame his rule. At this situation in the 1957 general election Congress won with an absolute majority, out of 205 seats Congress bagged 151. It astonished the whole India. For Madras state assembly Kamaraj won and became CM. He formed the second ministry.

K. Kamaraj submitted the list to the Governor A. J. John consisting the names of M/s M. Bakthavathsalam, C. Subramanian, A. Manickavelan, P. Kakkan, V. Ramiah and Mrs. Lurdu Ammal

Simon. His 2nd ministry took charge in 13th April 1957. Later R. Venkatraman was included in the ministry.

In 1957 general election Kamaraj was elected from Sathur Constituency. This election was a lesson to Kamaraj. Except Ananda Vikatan, the Tamil weekly, no paper or magazine supported Congress. In general they were against Congress. Though Congress won in the election Kamaraj felt that there should be a newspaper for Congress.

According to his wish a Tamil Daily by name "Thai Nadu" was proposed to be started in 1958. But due to some delay in getting the machinery the daily could not be started. The registration of title was also expired.

In 1960 a daily by name "Nava Shakti" was started. It was out and out for Kamaraj. The aim of it was to propaganda Kamaraj's view. In the 1962 election, Congress bugged 139 seats and DMK 50. The communist who got 15 seats in 1952 election could get only 4 in 1957. Now it got only 2 seats.

Kamaraj was elected as Chief Minister for the third time. He sworn in as Chief Minister before the then Governor Vishnu Ram Methi on 15th March 1962. There were 9 persons including the Chief Minister in the ministry. It is to noted that it was only the smallest Cabinet in India.

Vinobaji toured Madras state in 1956 only during Kamaraj's period. Kamaraj joined with him in tour and addressed the meetings. Vinobaji saw the affection of the public towards Kamaraj and said that he was only the true follower of Gandhiji.

K. Kamaraj was not only sitting in the fort where the flag was flying but he also was in the hearts of the public. He was the public and public was him. He was the only leader who constructed a bridge between the huts and the fort. He stood first in having a remarkable memory power in public life. He was the main reason to forbid the red tapism in government.

As Chief Minister

On April 13, 1954, Kamaraj reluctantly became the CM of Madras Province. To everyone's surprise, Kamaraj nominated

C. Subramaniam and M. Bhakthavatsalam, who had contested his leadership, to the newly formed Cabinet. Kamaraj removed the family vocation based Hereditary Education Policy introduced by Rajaji. He reopened the 6000 schools closed by previous government for financial reasons and also added 12000 more schools. The State made immense strides in education and trade. New schools were opened, so that poor rural students were to walk no more than 3 miles to their nearest school. Better facilities were added to existing ones. No village remained without a primary school and no panchayat without a high school. Kamaraj strove to eradicate illiteracy by introducing free and compulsory education up to the eleventh standard. He introduced the Midday Meal Scheme to provide at least one meal per day to the lakhs of poor school children (first time in the whole world). Kamaraj introduced free school uniforms to weed out creed, caste and class distinctions among young minds.

Kamaraj remained CM for three consecutive terms. Kamaraj noticed that the Congress party was slowly losing its vigour. He came up with a plan which was called the "Kamaraj Plan".

On October 2, 1963, he resigned from the Tamil Nadu CM Post. He proposed that all senior Congress leaders should resign from their posts and devote all their energy to the revitalisation of the Congress.

In 1963, Kamaraj he suggested to Nehru that senior Congress leaders should leave ministerial posts to take up organisational work. This suggestion came to be known as the 'Kamaraj Plan', which was designed primarily to dispel from the minds of Congressmen the lure for power, creating in its place a dedicated attachment to the objectives and policies of the organisation. Kamaraj was elected President, Indian National Congress, on October 9, 1963.

Well impressed by the achievements and success of Kamaraj, Prime Minister Jawaharlal Nehru felt that his services were needed more at the national level. In a swift move he brought Kamaraj to Delhi as the President of the Indian National Congress. Nehru realised that if he had wide learning and vision, Kamaraj possessed enormous common sense and pragmatism.

Plan

Kamaraj remained Chief Minister for three consecutive terms. Kamaraj noticed that the Congress party was slowly losing its vigour. He came up with a plan which was called the "Kamaraj Plan".

On October 2, 1963, he resigned from the Tamil Nadu Chief Minister Post. He proposed that all senior Congress leaders should resign from their posts and devote all their energy to the revitalisation of the Congress.

In 1963, Kamaraj he suggested to Nehruji that senior Congress leaders should leave ministerial posts to take up organisational work. This suggestion came to be known as the 'Kamaraj Plan', which was designed primarily to dispel from the minds of Congressmen the lure for power, creating in its place a dedicated attachment to the objectives and policies of the organisation. Kamaraj was elected President, Indian National Congress, on October 9, 1963.

Well impressed by the achievements and success of Kamaraj, Prime Minister Jawaharlal Nehru felt that his services were needed more at the national level. In a swift move he brought Kamaraj to Delhi as the President of the Indian National Congress. Nehru realised that if he had wide learning and vision, Kamaraj possessed enormous common sense and pragmatism.

Wonders

K. Kamaraj reduced the ministry to 8 from 12. He included the supporters of Rajaji in his ministry. He also included C. Subramaniam who contested against him in his ministry. Bakthavathsalaam was also included one among the 8. The 6 Person who opposed Rajaji were not Included in the Ministry.

Kamaraj thought that it would be better to include Vannian Community who opposed Congress. He included Ramaswamy Padaiaachi in the ministry who was the leader of opposite party and opposed Congress in the assembly. Hence there was no opposition for Congress from out side. He formed such a ministry and avoided the opposition from in and out of Congress. He took charge as CM on 13th April of 1954, the Tamil new year day. He was not a member in assembly nor a member in Legislative Council.

He should become a member within six months from the date of taking charge in either of legislature.

It was easy to become a Member of Legislature Council but K. Kamaraj did not prefer it. He had a strong belief for a healthy government one should be elected through assembly election only. Also he thought that he could understand the opinion of the public only if contest for the assembly election.

Always Kamaraj was elected from the Virudhunagar constituency. Suppose if he wanted to be elected from there the elected member of that constituency should resign. As always he did not want to create problem ever.

At that time there was a vacancy in Gudiatham Constituency of North Arcot district. All wanted him to contest from there as the Chief Minister is common to the state and he contest from any constituency of the state. Finally he decided to contest from Gudiatham Constituency.

K. Kamaraj did not belong to North Arcot which consist Gudiatham constituency. Even then he contested from there, except Communist party all other parties supported Kamaraj. Since the Dravidian parties did like Rajaji to become the Chief Minister again they supported K. Kamaraj and made serious propaganda for his victory. The Congress volunteers of all parts of Madras state invaded Gudiatham since K. Kamaraj decided to contest from a new constituency which neither was his native nor a place he dwelled. The Dravidian parties and Muslim league openly supported Kamaraj and hunted for votes. Gudiatham was flooded by party people. Public worked for Kamaraj. K. Kamaraj visited all the villages and addressed the mass. He won in the election. He thanked the people of that constituency.

He didn't go for the post of minister. It came to him. The post which came to him in 1954 he resigned it 1963. He was the first Chief Minister who was in that post for such a long period.

Ministries changed in other states of the country because of Enmity, Plots, Jealous and for post but it was not in Madras state. There was no quarrel, enmity or jealous in the ministry of Kamaraj. After Kamaraj became Chief Minister the trend of Madras state was totally changed.

K. Kamaraj's period was called as Golden Period. When he became Chief Minister he said, "People who works people as Maharajas and Lords who are lazy and live on other labours. I have become the Chief Minister only to wipeout the troubles of poor, else I don't want this post at all."

From that day on wards all the poor had his portraits at their huts. When he was the Chief Minister of Madras state he went in the path of Gandhiji and followed the principles of Nehru. He did what was Right. People respected him as a "Model Man".

S. Balasundrammal, wife of Sathyamoorthy said as under about Kamaraj:

> "Kamaraj served for the nation for more than 20 years along with my husband. During that time he had the sense of sacrifice and public service. He was best companion to my husband and worked without rest to strengthen the Congress in Madras state. His Chief Ministership was the evidence to the dream of my husband". Thus, the disciple made the dream of his leader alive.

Jawaharlal Nehru appreciated the services of Kamaraj as under:

> "It is impossible to find a person overcoming Kamaraj in public service. As a friend for several years I had a chance to know him. The value I had on him increased on and on whenever I moved with him. He is the CM to a government which is a example for efficient and good governance."

Lord Eddianburro (husband of England Queen) congratulated Kamaraj and said that he should be the Chief Minister of Madras state during his next visit to India and Madras. Thus, Kamaraj ruled Madras State.

As per the judgement of news reporters his way of ruling was a lesson to others and his service was an example to the post he held.

Waning Power

Kamaraj's political influence began to descend in 1967 when he was defeated for a seat in Parliament, and the DMK, now respectable, captured control of the Madras government. An increasingly independent Indira Gandhi continued as Prime Minister, and a conflict ensued between the government and Kamaraj's group. The party formally split in 1969 with Kamaraj as part of the old guard that tried, unsuccessfully, to remove Gandhi from power. In the same year Kamaraj was elected to Parliament in a by-election and began to rebuild his Madras base.

Although Kamaraj was fluent only in the Tamil language, with English or Hindi being the power tongues of India, his political skills and the timing of crucial events combined to make him a respected national leader. His own low-caste birth helped him to bring others of comparable social order into the Congress fold. Kamaraj devoted himself to the affairs of his home state of Madras until his death there on Oct. 2, 1975.

Simplicity

Right from his young age Kamaraj never liked luxurious way of life. He adopted simplicity in anything. His food, dress and speech were very simple. But he was not a miser. When he was CM he used to spend most of his salary for the poor who came to him for help.

A coffee in the morning, lunch at 11.00 a.m. evening a cup of coffee and two Idlies and a cup of milk at supper were his daily food. His lunch was a simple vegetarian meal. Occasionally an egg would be added with his lunch. He never celebrated Hindu festivals. He used to get up from his bed at 7 a.m.

Kamaraj gave interview to all whoever came to meet him. He never sent anyone without seeing. He helped all as far as possible. He never helped anyone on the basis of cast or creed. For genuine reasons he never hesitated to help. He used to read books before sleep, some times up to 22 o'clock in the mid night. Sometimes he used to discuss serious political problem upto 5 a.m. in the next morning.

Kamaraj used to have a nap after everyday's lunch. Daily he received about 75 letters. But he never replied them. Just helped the needy ones. He never replied the letters from Virudhunagar. He never wounded anybody's feelings. He moved friendly with everyone without political enmity. He used to get angry at times.

Suppose if anyone confuses Kamaraj or tried to suppress the fact or telling the same matter repeated he gets annoyed. But that anger remains for a short period only. Later he forgets that and moved normally when he meets them next time.

Mr. Kamaraj has not grown rich; he is a bachelor and has no family ties. He has been and is a whole-time politician and has laboured to acquire personal knowledge of men and things all over the Tamil country and he knows all the leaders of his party from every part of India. He has also acquired facility in English and very considerable knowledge of world affairs. He is immensely popular for all these reasons and especially because he has no vices and leads a simple life. Above all he is the 'representative' Tamil as most Tamils imagine that figure. His ways of speaking, walking, eating and dress commend themselves to the many millions to whom these are familiar ways with nothing outlandish about them".

Memorial

In Rajya Sabha

At the entrance to the Outer Lobby of the Lok Sabha, we come across the statue of Kumaraswamy Kamaraj, a true son of the soil, a renowned freedom fighter, a staunch democrat and a committed socialist. As a member of the Madras Legislative Assembly, the Constituent Assembly and the Lok Sabha, he articulated the cause of the poor and the deprived. In his capacity as the Chief Minister of Madras, Kamaraj played a stellar role in laying the foundation of modern Tamil Nadu. He was also President of Indian National Congress for several years. Simple and unostentatious, he remained an unrivalled leader of the masses all his life.

The statue, sculpted by M. Mani Nagappa, was unveiled by the Prime Minister of India, Shri Atal Bihari Vajpayee on 15 July 1998.

The statue was donated by Thiru Vazhappadi K. Ramamurthy, President, Tamizhaga.

Memorial House

Kamaraj Memorial House is built in the memory of the former Chief Minister of Tamil Nadu, Shri Kamaraj. He was an ideal for all the Indians, as he rose out of poverty and became the Chief Minister thrice. The Memorial House was inaugurated in 1978 by the then Chief Minister, M. G. Ramchandaran. The memorial is spread on the two floors of the building. It showcases the personal photographs and effects of Shri Kamaraj, which provide an insight into his life.

The ground floor has a bedroom which was once the personal den of this venerated bachelor. The room is adorned with plain furniture that symbolises the plain and simple life Shri Kamaraj led. There is also a well stocked library in the house, occupied by the books like volumes of 'Lok Sabha Debates', '100 Modern Lives', 'Churchill' and 'Doctor Zhivago'. Shri Kamaraj had to discontinue his schooling, but it did not stop him from becoming a well read man. The Memorial House also exhibits a rare collection of his photographs.

The walls of the dinning hall are covered with black and white photographs of Kamaraj's life. The photographs provide a quick look at his childhood, youth upto his late life years. Some of the most intriguing pictures are those of his 1954 swearing-in as Chief Minister of Tamil Nadu, the first Kamaraj Ministry of 1954, the second of 1957 and the third of 1962. There are even pictures of him with eminent personalities, like Pt. Nehru, Sarojini Naidu, Rajendra Prashad, Lal Bahadur Shastri, Indira Gandhi, M. G. Ramachandran, Martin Luther King, Queen Elizabeth, etc.

The second floor of the House also displays a number of his belongings, like luxuriant Felicitation Shawls, his simple attire, his suitcases, timepiece, pens and utensils. One of the prized possessions of this exhibition is the prison coat, worn by him while serving term in prison in the year 1942. The displayed personal effects of Kamaraj include his spectacles, a spool tape player and even a Gillette shaving set. Apart from this, there are also pictures showing the leader in different moods.

Mani Mandapam

Kamaraj Memorial at Kanniyakumari: The Hon'ble Chief Minister of Tamil Nadu declared on 19-4-1998 that the Government would construct a Memorial to honour the services of Thiru K. Kamaraj, the former Chief Minister of Tamil Nadu. The memorial was constructed on the seashore, where the ashes of the Late Leader was immersed. A building at cost of Rs. 50 lakhs was completed in an aesthetic way with the permission of Government of India.

The Memorial spreads on extent of 6,300 sq m now contains the photographs narrating the life and services of the great leader. The Memorial was dedicated to the nation by the Hon'ble Chief Minister of Tamil Nadu on 2-10-2000. A library is also functioning here. The Memorial is open freely for the tourists and visitors.

The Photographs of Shri Kamaraj

The Black and White photographs that adorn the walls of the dining hall cover Kamaraj's life across all stages — Kamaraj at the age of five, in his youth, in middle age and in the final years. Notable among the collection are pictures of his 1954 swearing-in as Chief Minister of Tamil Nadu, the first Kamaraj Ministry of 1954, the second of 1957 and the third of 1962.

Photographs of Kamaraj's public life show him rubbing shoulders with stalwarts like Jawarharlal Nehru, Sarojini Naidu, Sathyamurthy, Dr. S. Radhakrishnan, Rajendra Prashad, Lal Bahadur Shastri, Indira Gandhi, Periyar, M. G. Ramachandran, Govind Vallabh Pant, Martin Luther King and Queen Elizabeth.

A Unique Collection

Several pictures showcase the leader in different moods: playing Cricket, hauling the rope in at a 'Tug of War' for the Legislator's Sports Meet, drenched under the Courtallam falls, supervising relief work for flood victims, chairing meetings, etc. Among the personal effects of Kamaraj that are on display are his spectacles, pens, a spool tape player and even a Gillette Shaving set used by him!

The second floor has displays of Kamaraj's several luxuriant Felicitation Shawls. In marked contrast are the displays of his own simple attire, his suitcases, timepiece, pens and utensils. Of special mention is the prison coat worn by him while serving term in prison in 1942.

Photographs on the second floor show several personalities paying homage to the dead leader. Among those pictured are Late

Prime Minister Mrs. Indira Gandhi and veteran actor Shivaji Ganeshan. Especially impressive is the bird's eye view of the multitude, on Mount Road (Anna Salai), who accompanied the body of their leader on his last journey.

Special Features

In the year 1923, he staged a Dharana before Toddy shop. All were arrested at the Congress office except Kamaraj since was not on the spot as he got out to supervise the Dharna. He very much felt for that.

During those days there it was a restricted to carry knife more than 6 inches blades. Kamaraj decided to disobey that order of the British and conducted a revolution. That spread to Madurai. To conduct the same at Madurai he prepared 5 Swords. People came from Madurai to Virudhunagar. When the procession was about to start some hesitated. Swords prepared for them was with Kamaraj. On seeing then he sang a son of Bharathi and started dancing. It shacked the entire town of Virdhunagar Swords gave clinging sound.

The then Law minister Sir C. P. Ramaswamy Iyer allowed to carry swords places except Malabar Region in order to stop the revolution in Tamil Nadu.

After the Non-cooperation Movement a big problem arise. Whether to go to Assembly or not. Desabandhu Chitranjandas, Motilal Nehru, S. Srinivasa Iyengar, Bulabai Desai and Sathya Moorthy joined together. Started Swaraj Party. They want to enter into Parliament. But Rajaji opposed it. Kamaraj obeyed the decision of Congress and did not work with Sathyamoorthy.

In 1926 election, Kamaraj went Sri Vaikundam, Nasereth and Arel along with the followers.

He came forward to conduct a revolution after the arrest of leaders like Saminatha Mudaliar, Somayajulu since trying to remove the statute of Gen. Neel who tortured the participants of Army Revolution in 1857.

In 1927, when Mahatma Gandhi came to Chennai Kamaraj consulted him about the revolution for removing the statute of

Gen. Neel. Gandhiji advised him to do it without any force just like pelting clay over the statute. But it was stopped due to boycotting Simon Commission.

Kamaraj conducted a conference under the name of 'Indian Democratic Congress' presided by Nehruji who came to Chennai in 1927 after finishing the tour of Europe.

On 1937 as one day the statute of Gen. Neel was removed and kept at Museum. When it was questioned at the Assembly Rajaji gave a Brick but answer the statute is of their own and could be kept anywhere. There came a full stop to the matter.

In 1928, a commission under the leadership of Sir John Simon came to India. All the political parties started Boycotting the same and flagged the Black flag. With an uproar asking the commission to return back. The Government handled the situation severely. Nehruji was assaulted. The 64 years old Lala Rajpathi Rai got wounded and died in the prison.

The commission came to Madurai. Nobles patterned the Government joined at Thirumalai Naicker Palace. Patriotic public of Madurai aroused.

Hundreds of people with black flag invaded the Mahal shouting the Simon to go back. They were stopped by the ruling powers. Kamaraj came there in a car in which a Tricolour flag was hoisted. Along with him there came the famous Congress leader George Joseph. They observed the situation and organised the volunteers. Kamaraj and George Jospeh led them. Police got stunned on seeing the crowd.

In 1929, the Conservative party lost the election and the Labour party came to rule. At that time Jatheenthranath went on fast opposing the way in which political prisoners were treated in Jail in India. He last his life in that fast. This provoked Kamaraj. He preferred independence when Gandhiji was alive.

Friendship

K. Kamaraj didn't have family responsibility. Since he was a bachelor he did not even have the responsibility of maintaining the property. He spent his whole time for the service of Congress day and night, he was thinking only about Congress.

So he could read the pulse of the public very well. He knew all the information about the Congressmen of every district. He was able to judge people and fore tell the election victory.

In 1934, Kamaraj got the friendship of Nagarajan who was attracted by his sincerity, courage and patriotism faced all the oppositions. He was with Kamaraj for 15 years. Like that Late Tuticorin Kandaswamy Pillai, Virudhunagar Muthuswamy, Dhanushkodi Nadar, Nellai Jebamani, Sathur Lakshmana Pillai, Madurai Chidambara Bharathi, D. Ramakrishnan Nithyanandam, Vengadathri Naidu, Trichy Arunachalam, Sanglia Pillai, Serkali Saminatha Chettiar, Salem Theerthagiri Mudaliar, Padruti Devanajaiah, Cuddalore Sundarsanam, Muthu Mutdaliar, Chidambaram Mariappan, North Arcot Upayadullah, Annamalai Pillai, Chennai Athi Kesavalu Naicker, Lakshmanaswamy Mudaliar, S. Venkatraman, Venkatachalam, Kumbakkonam Gopalakrishnan, T. R. V. Narayansamy, T. N. Ramachandra Naidu, Varadan and Thangavel Nadar all helped and cooperated with Kamaraj since Non-cooperation Movement.

The good relationship between Kamaraj and Sathyamoorthy stood as it was till the end of Sathyamoorthy. Sathyamoorthy was innocent, so Kamaraj had the responsibility of escorting him always. He never did anything without consulting Kamaraj.

In 1940, when Sathyamoorthy was offered Vice Chancellor's post in Madras University he consulted Kamaraj whether to accept. But Kamaraj advised him not to accept the same since Civil Disobedience Movement was about to come. If he accepts the post it may spoil his political carrier. Thus, Kamaraj saved him from many plots. He was a side supporter of Sathyamoorthy. Sathyamoorthy too felt Kamaraj as a sincere friend.

Sathyamoorthy was moving with high levels. Kamaraj made him to move in lower level volunteers too. Sathyamoorthy introduced the high level and their status to Kamaraj. Thus, they helped each other.

Sathyamoorthy loved only two, one was his daughter and other Kamaraj. Kamaraj too showed his extreme love towards Sathyamoorthy.

During Avadi Congress Conference, he named the place as Sathyamoorthy Nagar. When he became Chief Minister he went to Sathyamoorthy's residence and prayed before his portrait and obtained blessing's from his wife. These were the symbols of friendship.

The month of August 1942 was to be inscribed in golden letters in the history of Independence war. August revolution busted out only in that year.

The Asian light Nehruji informed only in this year that we were on the edge of sharp sword. We do not know what would happen. Anything may happen at any time, we should be prepared for it.

Mahatma Gandhi showed green signal for revolution only in this year.

World War began in 1934. Britain, America, Russia were on one side. German, Japan and Italy on the other.

In that very war without consulting India, Britain announced that India too would join in that war. Leaders including Gandhiji refused this. Gandhiji said when India was a slave how could it take part in the war for the interest of other countries. Suppose if freedom would be give to India at least at the end of war it may consider of supporting war arrangement.

But British PM Sir Winston Churchill arrogantly said that what a foolishness it was. He was not Prime Minister of British Empire to construct cemetery. He need not require guns to control beggar Gandhiji and his volunteer. Only lathis would do.

Then 'no support' said the National Congress Council. Sir Stafford Gribs was sent as a ambassador to discuss the problem regard freedom to India.

In 25th March 1942, Gandhiji and Abul Kalam Azad met Gribs. But that gentleman create difference of opinion between Hindu and Muslims and postponed the demand for freedom. Finally he was ready to give freedom at the end of the war with certain conditions.

Mahatama Gandhiji refused this as it was like a post-dated cheque. At this time Rajaji supported partition of India and

Pakistan. In result of that in 15th July 1942 Gandhiji himself, with the suggestion of Patel wrote a letter to Rajaji to quit Congress. Then there were a group of people who received salaries from British and supported them.

The Kamaraj Way

South India, once the stronghold of the Congress, had steadily slipped out of its hold since the demise of the veteran leader K. Kamaraj, because the INC leadership failed to realise the importance of the underprivileged caste factor in Tamil Nadu and other Southern states. Historically, even though the upper castes in the South produced quite a few brilliant leaders in political, economic and scientific fields, but their combined contribution could not match the massive popular appeal of the great leaders like K. Kamaraj, the famous son of the Nadar clan, who united all classes and creed in the South under the Congress banner. He was a political giant who represented "we, the people of India".

Old timers would recall the time when the Indian National Congress required rejuvenation and revival of its fading charisma among the masses, it was Kamaraj's initiative which gave birth to the famous "Kamaraj Plan" under which some of the tallest leaders of the party, in a spirit of service and sacrifice, came out of the senior ministerial positions to revamp and strength the party of the Nehru-Gandhi ideology. Even when the present leader of he Indian National Congress and the United Progressive Coalition in power at the Centre.

Sonia Gandhi, after her impressive victory at the polls, announced that she would not accept the prime ministerial office and instead supported Dr. Manmohan Singh to become the first Prime Minister of the country, technically representing a minority community but in reality representing the class dedicated to a new economic revolution for the benefit of the majority, the poor and the rural masses of the country. The world was reminded of the Kamaraj days when leaders held the party above the government and country above the party. That was the era of the Kamaraj Plan.

Despite knowing all the facts, the managers of Mrs. Sonia Gandhi would not bring to her notice the fact that, the present three ministers from Tamil Nadu belonged to upper castes microscopic community – Iyer, Chettiar, and Kannada-speaking Naidu.

Kamaraj also represented the epoch, when, under the inspiration of Mahatma Gandhi, the nation launched a powerful movement for the opening of the temples for those considered "untouchables" and sought the transformation of the depressed and deprived classes, christening them as "Harijans" or the family of god himself.

In the South, the Nadar clan, under the leadership of stalwarts like Kamaraj, played a very significant role in the battle for dignity and opportunity for the deprived sections of the society, who incidentally remained the most powerful life force for the Indian National Congress.

Jawaharlal Nehru wanted the elected representatives of the people to continue the movement for the uplift of the downtrodden majority of the country under a deferent name. It was then called the "Mass Context Movement" under Know Your Constituency Programme for MPs. The result of the "Know Your Constituency Programme" also brought the elected representatives closer to the masses and strengthened the Indian National Congress. Then where did the Congress magic in the South begin to fade?

Those who knew the caste factor influence in the Southern politics, especially in Tamil Nadu, felt that one factor was that Congress began to turn itself into a party of high classes rather than the masses. The Nadars, the Kamaraj clan, however stood by the party and were by and large responsible for Congress returning about ten members of Lok Sabha during the last poll which saw Congress slip the ladder in several states which were once considered the Congress fortresses, including Bihar, which had returned the first President of India in the distinguished personality of Dr. Rajendra Prashad. But somehow, the party had inadvertently forgotten to choose one of the Nadars in its UPA Cabinet, even though there was earlier a representative of the committed Congress force. Will the party include a member of this community in the future reshuffle, due soon? Even non-Congress allies like Karunanidhi of the DMK have already advocated in favour of inclusion of a Nadar man in the Cabinet openly in the press. They would have no objection to a Congress-member from the Nadar clan being given the responsibility and dignity of serving the party and the nation as a Union minister. In the present UPA coalition government, all major communities from Tamil Nadu got representation in the Cabinet except Nadar, which makes them feel worry and unhappy.

There were Congress MPs of the Nadar legacy who had the experience, having served earlier in ministerial position. The question was that in view of the future polls in the South, especially Tamil Nadu, it could be a wise step which would certainly be hailed by the devotees of K. Kamaraj and the traditional Congress supporting masses in the South.

There was no reason to suppose that a wise leader like Sonia Gandhi would not have already been seized of the situation. The Nadars and the masses of Tamil Nadu would be too happy if the legacy of Kamaraj was recognised and upheld by giving such a responsibility to one of the present generation of Kamarajists.

Agitation by Kamaraj

A volunteer was arrested on 9th December 1971 at 11.30 p.m. under Security act. He was kept in the IG's office throughout the night and sent to jail in the next morning.

He was arrested because of an editorial published in "Nava Shakti". Kamaraj sent Kakkan, the TNCC leader to know the situation. Secretary of TNCC P. Ramachandran went to the jail and saw him. Kamaraj sent Kakkan on the first day and Ramachandran on the next day. Kamaraj went twice to the house of lawyer Gopalswamy for his volunteer who was in the jail.

In 1972 all the farmers throughout the state conducted a protest against the government. It started in Coimbatore and spread over. More than 15 thousand farmers were arrested. Many died to oppression. Statue was laid for those who sacrificed their lives at Coimbatore. Kamaraj raised his voice for farmers pointing out the mistakes of the ruling party. He strongly condemned the government for what they had failed to do and what they had done wrongly in a hasty way. He conducted a big procession. He also warned the government. He also said suppose if the government continued its position he would have to preside the strike. He also gave a time limit to release the people arrested. The government released the arrested people.

National Festival at Madurai

Kamaraj who worried very much as the farmers were arrested in 1972 had cancelled his birthday celebration. In that year it was decided to celebrate the birth day of Kamaraj on October 1st and Gandhiji's birthday on October 2nd. To obtain his permission, leaders went to Madras. Kamaraj, who was sitting in a chair on the terrace got shocked once he came to know this. He gave on angry look at them. He refused for his birthday function as he could not be compared with Gandhiji. He was ready to participate only if Gandhiji's birthday was celebrated.

But Nedumaran said that people look him as the last heir of Gandhiji it could be celebrated. Even then he refused. However, they convinced him and got the permission.

National function was celebrated at Madurai. The function was in such a way it informed to the world that Kamaraj was after Gandhiji the whole Tamil Nadu gathered at Madurai.

Madurai Tremored

During the National Celebration Madurai Mayor Muthu challenged the procession of Bullock Carts. Kudanthai Ramakrishnan under the stewardship and guidance of Nedumaran worked hard and went to all the villages in and around Madurai, brought thousands of bullock carts for the procession and sent them back after the function. M/s Sunderajan Servai, Chonamuthu Servai, Muthukarupan Ambalam, Paramalai, Deyvanayagam, S. Balakrishnan, Jothilal, Azhagarsamy, Mrs. Poonammal and others were also worked hard. Nedumaran was in the green memory of Kamaraj after this function. He was honoured as "Maa Veeran" (Great Warrior) by Kamaraj.

Dharna

The meetings held on 2nd October 1973 at Kannapar Thidal and Sydapet Theradi Thidal was a turning point in the history of Congress. The sky was cloudy a cool breeze was their on that evening. Thousands of people gathered at both the places. There was no chance for the Congress to protest or strike on for Dharna after independence in Tamil Nadu since it was ruled by Kamaraj.

DMK came to power in 1967 defeating Congress. Kamaraj did not tell anything for a period of 6 months. Between the period of 1967 and 1971 the executives of Congress party in Tamil Nadu and the party people at the district level many times stressed for Dharna. In the interest of the public Kamaraj did not permit. He strictly said they should propaganda their views among the people. DMK government lifted the prohibition in Tamil Nadu. To the prolonged desire, to stage Dharna, of the Congress lot of supports came. Hike in prices, problems to farmer, implementing prohibition again, weaver's grievances caused for Dharna to Congress leader and they insist Kamaraj. Kamaraj gave his approval for a peaceful Dharna.

Congress working committee decided to stage dharna in front of the government office all over Tamil Nadu placing a 5 point demand. It decided to stage Dharna from 3rd to 12th of October 1973 for the following demands:

- To take steps to control the increasing prices.
- To eradicate unemployment
- To find a solution for the farmer's grievances.
- To wipeout the problems to the weavers.
- To implement complete prohibition.

Permission of Kamaraj to stage Dharna gave refreshment to the Congress volunteers. The two speeches at Saidapet and Kannapar Thidal were unforgettable. He said that the reasons for the problems was economic political situations. The plans were speedy but employment of shelter were not available. Because of the growing cheaters due to feverishness for money and power the country was deteriorated. "Let us stand on the path of Gandhism and stage Dharna. Gandhi would calls this a Sathyagraha. In that truth, justice and honesty were there No violence and force will be in the path of Gandhiji. Like that volunteers should stage Dharna". "Volunteers should bear the torture and should stage the dharna even if they are arrested by the police. You have come forward to face anything. I ask you only this. We do not know what will happen tomorrow. If you are arrested or not, if you like are don't like should not worry." "If you are arrested go to jail with courage. Truth will win. Be Bold." His speech encouraged the volunteers. More than 35 thousand people including leaders were arrested in the whole Tamil Nadu, there was no room in the jail. Jails were over crowded. Hence DMK government released all.

General election in Pondicherry was conducted in 1974. Both the Congress joined together and were in the field with new spirit. Kamaraj and Indira Gandhi spoke at two places (Karikkal and Pondicherry) in general meeting. At the end of the election though did not get majority to form ministry got more seats than other parties. A new party with a desire to form ministry came forward. Kamaraj gave way to it. Country appreciated his magnanimity. The new party joined with Communist party formed the ministry in a speed. With the same speed the government toppled down.

After the split in Congress Indira Gandhi criticised the Congress leaders. She blamed Sanjeeva Reddy, Nijalingappa, Pattil and Atulya Gosh. But she did not utter a word against Kamaraj. Kamaraj frequently visited to T. T. Krishnamachari who was sick. They discussed about the political problems. TTK met both Kamaraj and Indira Gandhi and made them to speak with each other regarding reunion of Congress. Kamaraj at the Tamil Nadu Congress working committee explained regarding the discussion with the PM Indira Gandhi.

A resolution was passed in a working committee meeting, the Congress should not be having any relationship with any party who had relationship with DMK or AIADMK. Following this the mouths of the people who looked Congress with doubts were shut. The loss of TTK shocked Kamaraj. In a period of 6 years Kamaraj felt the demises of Mr. Annadurai, Mr. Rajaji and Periyar E. V. R. as his own loss and consoled others.

On October 2nd 1975 Kamaraj got up from his bed at 6.30 a.m. Morning newspaper's were given to him. He read all the papers. After bath he took his breakfast.

He was given insulin injection by the doctor who usually checks up his health at 10 a.m.

Fifty law college students came to meet him at 11 a.m. They went into the reception room where he was seeing the number students. He come out with the help of his assistants as space was insufficient in that room. He was with their for about 3 minutes and then took leave.

He contacted the Congress secretaries at 12 a.m. Later he met news reporters and Joint secretary of Chidambaram Congress Mr. Thanigai Thambi. Lunch, which he used to take usually at 1 p.m., he took on that day at 1.30 p.m. He was sweating though the ceiling was in full speed. His assistants mopped his body. After lunch he went to bathroom and then to bed. He called his assistants at 2 p.m. and told to him to get the doctor as he was sweating through the air condition was on. As they could not Dr. Sourirajan over telephone they contacted Dr. Jeyaraman. Kamaraj himself talked to Dr. Jeyaraman and told him about his condition. Doctor asked him whether he was having breathing trouble and pain on the chest. Kamaraj said he was only having sweat. Then he lied down on the bed as his back.

Again he called his assistants to inform the doctor to bring a blood pressure apparatus when comes and asked his assistant to wake him up once the doctor comes.

At 3 p.m. Dr. Sourirajan came running went into the room where Kamaraj was sleeping by keeping his both hands under his head with folded legs. But his regular snore was not there. His mind trembled. He was shocked. He touched the shoulders of Kamaraj and tried to wake him up. To test the pulse he took his hand. It was cold. Immediately he cried saying that Kamaraj passed away. He threw down his stethoscope and pressure apparatus. He tried to poke an injection direct into his heart. But it was failed. Next second Dr. Annamalai came there. He announced the demise of Kamaraj. The time was 3.20 p.m. Last breath of Kamaraj went at his house at Thirumalai Pillai Road, T. Nagar, Madras.

Daily Life

Right from his young age Kamaraj never liked luxurious life. He adopted simplicity in anything. His food, dress and speech were very simple. But he was not a miser. When he was CM he used to spend most of his salary for the poor who came to him for help.

A cup of coffee in the morning, lunch at 11.00 a.m. evening a cup of coffee and 2 Idlies and a cup of milk at supper were his daily food. His lunch was a simple vegetarian meal. Occasionally an egg would be added with his lunch. He never celebrated Hindu festivals.

He used to get up from his bed at 7 a.m. He gave interview to all whoever came to meet him. He never sent anyone without seeing. He helped all as far as possible. He never helped anyone on the basis of cast or creed. For genuine reasons he never hesitated to help. He used to read books before sleep, some times up to 2 o'clock in the mid night. Sometimes he used to discuss serious political problem upto 5 a.m. in the next morning.

Kamaraj used to have a nap after lunch. Daily he received about 75 letters. But he never replied them. Just helped the needy ones. He never replied the letters from Virudhunagar. He never wounded anybody's feelings. He moved friendly with everyone without political enmity. He used to get angry at times. Suppose if anyone confuses him or tried to suppress the fact or telling the same matter repeated he gets annoyed. But that anger remains for a short period only. Later he forgets that and moved normally when he meets them next time.

Houses for Gipsy

He expects his time should not be wasted by anyone unnecessarily. He never noted his daily work. Only his assistants had to note down his appointments. He never took notes on any affair. He just kept them in his memory. He read, "Kamba Ramayanam" with interest. He used to discuss with his friends on that. He judged people by the impressions on their faces and their talks.

A veteran Congress man resided at Nungambakkam died suddenly. His wife and children were orphaned. The wife approached Kamaraj for help. He bought her a sewing machine for he livelihood and arranged for the education to the children.

Once a village Harijans of about 50 near Gudiatham met Kamaraj with a complaint that they were denied for water and electricity. Only the upper class people enjoyed the government facilities. Even their complaints with government officials were unanswered. Kamaraj immediately ordered to provide water and electricity to them.

Once 100 Gypsis of South Arcot district met Kamaraj with their families with a demand for construction of houses to them. Kamaraj fulfilled their demand.

Political and Social Boom

M. Bakthavathsalam, C. Subramaniam, A. P. Sheddy, M. A. Manickavel Naicker, Raja of Ramnad, Ramaswamy Padaiaachi and Parameswaran were in the ministry of Kamaraj.

Kamaraj made a social revolution in allotting the portfolios to the ministers. He gave Hindu Endowment to Harijan minister Parameswaran. Also prohibition was given to him. Whether he did it wantedly or not, this made trustees of the temples to reaper a Harijan, this made Kamaraj a morning star among Harijans.

Kamaraj and Files

Kamaraj proved himself as Chief of all the CMs in India. He was the first CM who was in the post for a long period of 9 years, i.e. from 1954 to 1963 unless he resigned the post voluntarily he would have continued to be the CM. He did his duty boldly and patiently without discourage. He listened the views of the opposite parties. He easily solved the political problems. He attracted every one to his side. He listened others without himself speaking. He never concentrated on his food or dress.

He honoured the news reporters,. He affectionately moved with photographers. He never angered with anyone. Replied letters immediately. Listened the grievances and solved them immediately. He gave more data. Understood the problems easily and keenly studied the files. He did not like luxury, flattering and advertisement. He was very simple. He never uttered harsh words. Because of these habits he ornamented the CM's post. It would not be an exaggeration that the post got honoured through him.

The words of W. R. S. Sathyanathan who was a high official were the evidence of the administration of Kamaraj. He served as Chief Secretary to the state under Kamaraj. He said that Kamaraj's efficiency made him to respect him. Kamaraj was fast and clean in finalising the things. He could judge people in a lightning speed who came to meet him.

He could solve even a sophisticated big problem within seconds. He approaches the problem directly.

Judgement would be very clean. He detected the problems in an astonishing way. He used to read the files kept for his advice completely, then only he used to decide. There was no village in our state which his feet never touched. Whatever the place whether Mountain area or river side he could explain with evidences about the climate of that region.

Let Me See

Kamaraj said, "I never said that I studied in any University. I know geography. I know almost all the places in Madras state. I know where the lakes are. I know how people are living by doing what business. Suppose if these are not called as geography and only the books that have straight and curved lines are called geography, I don't want to learn that at all.". He knew inch by inch the mind of the people and the day to day affair of the state.

Eastern shore at Ramnad was affected by heavy storm and rain in 1955. Kamaraj went to Paramakudi for rescue operation to save the public. He made lightning tour in the affected area. Because of this the relief work was in speed. He went places in poring rain. A bridge on a canal was washed away. He crossed the canal with a rope and went to Ramnad. Seeing the CM crossing the canal in chest deep water a revenue board member too tried to cross. But he had fever on the next day and was admitted in the hospital. But Kamaraj went out on the early morning to visit the affected area.

Whenever he returns from the tour he had new plans. All those were only for poor. He knew the mentality of people right from the district collector to the lowest grade government servant.

He increased the salary of elementary school teachers. He felicitated FREE education to their children. He gave concession to the children of government servants in school fees. Free education was given to the children of those who had an income of less than 100 rupees. An act was passed that no individual should have more than 30 acres of land. He brought Farmer's Act. The act insisted that the landowners should not change the farmers.

A state development committee was formed, all the ministers and secretaries of the government were in the committee. The meetings of this committee helped to improve the economic condition and to review the new schemes. Kamaraj oppose the formation of Dakshin Pradesh. The present New Tamil Nadu was formed in 1956. If a patriot like Kamaraj had not been the CM of Tamilnad today new Tamil Nadu would not have been formed. Kamaraj decided Tamil should be the language in government work.

He felicitated the old age pension for the orphaned elders without any political partialities in caste, religion, language he gave concession in education to the poor students. Only in his government Midday Meal Scheme was introduced to students.

He occupied the house bearing Door No. 8 at Thirumalai Pillai road, T. Nagar, Chennai. When he was the Chief Minister, though the police security was there to his house there was no strict procedures. Not less than 50 people met him daily. The number may go up to 100 to 200 at times.

Different type of people like Freedom fighters for help, Parents asking for recommendation for admission in Medical/Engineering College seats, complaints in local officials, asking seats for ensuing election, people asking him to preside meetings, to ask him to inaugurate the building, etc. met him daily. His regular answer to them was "Let Me See". Suppose if he felt that were impossible he never hesitated to say "No", even if they are his closest.

Beauty and Food

Once the Central government wrote a letter to the state Chief Minister regarding the expansion scheme of Madras Port. The Chief Minister replied to the central government regarding expanding the sea shore near Rayapuram, since the sea shore opposite to Fort if expanded may spoil the appearance. Again wrote to the State government the expansion at Rayapuram was impossible as it was rocky area. Whether the state government need food or beauty. Immediately Kamaraj wrote to central he wanted on bread not beauty. The result of that is the existing expanded port of today.

He took impartial decisions when problems arose. Even opposite party people cannot raise their finger towards him saying that he showed partiality to his party people.

Though he was the Chief Minister he never interfered in the affairs of other ministers. This trend earned a good name to his ministry. His rule was an example to other States. President Rajendra Prashad once said, under the govern of Kamaraj Madras state had developed in all the wings. He also said that other states should follow the governing principles of Madras State.

Pandit Jawaharlal Nehru said that there was no scam in daily routines and in implementation of schemes. The Central Planning Minister Mr. Naidu said that Madras State was the only state which fully utilised the subsidy of the central government.

Social Welfare Minister Mr. K. C. Day said that Madras State was ahead of all other States in elementary education and rural electricity. Central Deputy Minister Mr. Krishnappa said that Madras State was self-sufficient in food production.

When Kamaraj was the Chief Minister in 1954 he arranged to give Rs. 120 per month to his mother. This amount was not sufficient for her. Because she had so many visitors and she had to offer them some drinks. Hence she asked Kamaraj through a known person to both to arrange for a sum of Rs. 150 per month. For this Kamaraj refused saying that drinks to visitors need not be offered and further more if his mother had surplus money she would go on pilgrimage, which was not advisable in her old age. Marriage to his nephew Jawahar was fixed. Kamaraj's mother wanted a lavatory to be constructed at the house. This proposal was taken to Kamaraj. He refused for this also saying, if a land for construction was bought public may think that he bought a bungalow. Even it may appear in newspapers. Finally he accepted to buy land for construction of lavatory.

On 9th October of 1961 Nehruji unveiled the statue of Kamaraj. The mayor of Madras who presided the function said that Kamaraj was unselfish leader, a symbol of sacrifice and lighted the education in hearts of people. Nehruji who unveiled the statute said, "A Real Example for a true leader, hailed from the public, a leader who has a capability to complete the responsibility he has taken. I unveil the statute of the leader who forgets himself when he serves the public. I don't like to install statutes for the persons who are alive. I strongly believe to pay homage only after death. But, Kamaraj being a friend of mine and as he hailed from the public I accept to unveil his statute."

On 1927 when Nehruji came to Madras he resided at the residence of Sathyamoorthy. Due to tiredness he tried to sleep in the night but could not. A loud noise disturbed him. Nehruji who lost the patience tried to find out the cause for the noise. At last he found that the noise came from the Varanda of that house. He saw an youth was sleeping with heavy shore. He got angry. He asked Sathyamoorthy to drive the lad out of Madras or to shift his bed to the seashore. That youth who disturbed the sleep of Nehru with his heavy snoring was Kamaraj whose statute was unveiled by Nehru in latter days.

During British regime the education was only 7 per cent. But in Kamaraj's period it was 37 per cent. During Rajaji's period there were 12,000 schools in the state. Whereas it was 27,000 in the period of Kamaraj. Power supply in all the villages, industrial growth were in the period of Kamaraj. Tamils compared the education to our eyes. Hence Tamilians were considered as genius. Kamaraj who hailed from this group made a revolution in education. He removed the system of communal education started by Rajaji. He ordered to reopen the 6,000 elementary schools closed by Rajaji. Moreover he opened 14,000 new schools.

During first plan schools which were 21,500 in number had gone upto 26,750 during 2nd plan which crossed over 30,000 later. Likewise the admission of students also went up gradually from 25 lakhs to 33.8 and to 46.1 lakhs. During 3rd plan it was decided to admit 14 lakhs more students.

Wonderful Scheme

There was the situation that the construction of schools, serving midday meals, appointing teachers were the duties of the government. Kamaraj wanted to change this and started a great revolutionary plan. Because of that plan every individual realised to think the education was his responsibility. That was the plan for growth of schools. Conference were conducted and donations were collected from public. About four crores of rupees were donated by public. Poor students were given free books and slates. Lakhs of poor students were benefited.

A scheme for giving free uniform to poor children were organised and implemented. Kamaraj wanted to avoid the partiality between the poor and the rich students. Result was free uniform scheme. This stopped the inferiority complex among the students.

Kamaraj wanted to give free education to all the students. He decided to give free education up to eleventh standard to all the poor students in the year 1960. The annual income of the parents of those students who get the concession should be less than Rs. 1,200. He modified this order in 1962-63. Children of the parents whose income was Rs. 1,500 per annum could also get free education upto 11th Std., Apart from this order were issued that children of NGO's employees of Panchayat Unions may also get free education upto High School education.

To avoid illiteracy he formed compulsory primary education. He formed committee to make propaganda in villages about the importance of education.

Though compulsory and free education were there was no proper response. Kamaraj seriously thought the reasons, therefore he meet the villagers and discussed with them. Found out the reason. He arrived at an solution. How can a parent who is lean bodied due to poverty, powerless eyes, scattered hair without oil and who struggles for at least one time food send his ward to the school. He will send his children to schools at least if they get one time food. Immediately Kamaraj arranged for this. Free Midday Meal Scheme made lakhs of students to come to school. Countries all over the world praised this. Nehruji was much pleased.

The Midday Meal Scheme properly started in 1956. Over 14 lakhs students were benefited. This scheme got help from CARE

OF USA in 1961-62. Milk powder, corn flour and refined vegetable oils were sent free of costs to schools from CARE.

Kamaraj who was deeply worried about the growth of education decided to induce the interest of public. The government took responsibility to govern, fulfil the schemes for the growth of education. These were intensified during Kamaraj's period only. But public did not show their interest and direct involvement.

Right from 1956-57 free education was given to the children of elementary school teacher, police constables, head constables and the lower grade employees of government. It came to know in the next year that only 17 per cent of students were not getting free education. To compensate this a scheme for free education to all was announced in 1962.

The revolutionary schemes and the services of Kamaraj in educational side attracted the public. Because of that there are no villages in the state without elementary schools. A high school for every 5 miles distance with modern amenities was constructed.

Apart from increasing number of schools steps were taken to improve standard of education also. To improve the standard number of working day were increased from 180 to 200. Unnecessary holidays were reduced. Syllabus were prepared to give opportunity to various abilities.

Two session classes were started. 45 multipurpose schools were started. In the second plan 191 multipurpose schools came up. 286 double session schools were opened. Laborities with modern facilities and librarians were made available.

Salaries of the teachers were increased in order to improve there standard of teaching and to kindle their interest in teaching.

Kamaraj introduced a scheme providing pension, provident fund and compulsory insurance to teacher which were not their so far. Kamaraj had introduced this scheme for the first time in India. Along with this he introduced family pension scheme also to the teacher. Scheme was also introduced to provide quarters to the teacher of village schools. Rs. 25 lakhs were allotted to this scheme. Construction of 750 houses was planned.

He also arranged to give interest free loans to the poor students of medical college, engineering college and agricultural college. This has improved in admission of Engg. College and Medical College in every year. Facility to train nurses in hospitals were also increased. Number of Arts colleges were increased in the period of Kamaraj. 2 PT Colleges, 10 Teacher training colleges and 39 Teacher training schools were opened in his period. His government made arrangement to open one more university in his period.

More irrigation schemes were planned in Kamaraj's period. Lower Bhavani, Mani Muthuar, Cauvery Delta, Aarani River, Vaigai Dam, Amravati, Sathanur, Krishnagiri, Pullambadi, Parambikulam and Neyaru Dams were among them. The Lower Bhavani Dam in Coimbatore district was constructed with an expenditure of Rs. 10 crores. 2,07,000 acres of land are under cultivation. About 45,000 acres of land are benefited through Mettur canal of Salem. Another scheme was Krishnagiri in the same district. Vaigai, Sathanur facilitate to cultivate thousands of acres of lands in Madurai and North Arcot districts. Rs. 30 crores were planned to spend for Parambikulam River scheme in Kamaraj's period. This has helped for the development of Coimbatore district in agriculture field.

Small Irrigation Schemes

In 1957-61, about 1,628 Tanks were de-silted under Small Irrigation Scheme 2000 wells were digged with outlets. Long term loans with 25 per cent subsidy were given to farmers. Apart from formers who are having dry lands were given oil engines, electric pump sets on instalment basis. 150 lakhs of acres of lands were cultivated during K. Kamaraj's period. One third of this, i.e. 56 lakhs of acres of land get permanent watering facility.

Industrial Development

Industries with an investment in crores of money were started in his period. Neyveli Lignite Scheme, Raw photo film industry at Nilgiri, Surgical instruments factory at Guindy, Sugar factories, Bi-Carbonates factories, Cement factories, Railway coach factory at Avadi, Mettur paper industry, were started only in the period of Kamaraj. These are the backbone of the development of the nation.

Madras state stood first in India in providing electricity to rural areas.

Approx. 13,300 villages were give electricity during 1955-61. Using electric power for agriculture purpose Madras state stands first. Expense to improve electricity at Madras in 1959 was Rs. 2.71 crores. Hydro power station at Periyar was constructed at an expenditure of Rs. 9 crores. 1 lakh KW of electricity produced under this scheme.

Kunda Dam project was constructed at an investment of Rs. 3.5 crores. Nehruji inaugurated this project. It was completed in a very short period by over engineers which made foreigners to wonder. In 1958-59 the investment in electricity connection was 95 crores and the income increased to Rs 12 crores.

Avadi Congress Conference was held (20th January 1956). It was 6th Conference. Kamaraj constructed a city and named it as Sathyamoorthy nagar. Kamaraj told to Mr. S. S. Vasan who took the responsibility of decoration that it was not important one to say that he had not seen such a decoration there before, but it was important that one to say that he had not seen such a beautiful conference even after 25 years. Nehruji appreciated the decoration. Nehruji unveiled the statue of Sathyamoorthy.

The Avadi Congress had increased the prestige of Southern people in Northern part of India. People donated food grains for the meals. Kamaraj's mother came to Avadi Conference from Virudhunagar. Nehruji took photograph with his mother. In memory of Srinivasa Iyengar the AICC president his daughter Ambuja Ammal was nominated as the leader of reception committee. Newspapers wrote that Kamaraj was the main reason for the unforgettable Avadi Conference in the history of Congress. Maulana Azad proposed to form a society of equality in the action committee meeting. Kamaraj seconded the proposal. In the conference when all participated Nehru proposed this and Kamaraj seconded. Kamaraj said, "Only hard labour will save people. Wealth should not be massed with one group. No violence is necessary to form equality in society. It is also not desirable.

Gandhiji got the freedom in a peaceful way. Let us form this society in the same way. When Nehru came to Madras in 1936 Kamaraj joined with him in the tour. Since 1949, he attended the All India Congress Committee meeting. Avadi Congress conference was a turning point to K. Kamaraj.

The Salutation

Kamaraj was more than a leader, a perunthalaivar or a super-leader. Born in a lower middle class family one hundred and six years to this day, Kamaraj rose to the position of King-maker in Indian politics. That was no easy journey for a boy who dropped out of school when he was in the sixth grade.

The political career of Kumaraswamy Kamaraj spanning over fifty long years, from the colonial and post-independent phases of India's history, is indeed an enviable record.

In the early-60s, he suggested to Nehru that senior Congress leaders should resign from ministerial positions to take up organisational work. This Kamaraj Plan was designed primarily to rid the lure for power from the minds of Congress leaders and to create in them a dedicated attachment to the objectives and policies of the Congress Party.

Kamaraj was instrumental in solving the succession issue at the highest elected position of India twice. It was he who chose Lal Bahadur Shastri in 1964 (when Jawaharlal Nahru died,) and Indira Gandhi in 1966 (after the death of L. B. Shastri). He was affectionately known as the South Indian Gandhi. He is also known as Padikkaatha Medhai or uneducated genius.

His open opposition to the declaration of emergency by Indira Gandhi and to the arrest of great leaders brought out his dedication to the basic tenets of democracy.

Above all, he lived a simple austere life till he left this world. Though Kamaraj remained the Chief Minister of the State for three consecutive terms, he died a poor worker. He was a bachelor and had no family ties.

The great feature of the governance by Kamaraj was the universal and free schooling. It was he who introduced the free noon meal scheme.

A Freedom Fighter

A full time politician, Kamaraj did not have family responsibility. Since he was a bachelor he did not even have the responsibility of maintaining the property. He spent his whole time for the service of Congress day and night, he was thinking only about Congress. So he could read the pulse of the public. He knew all the information about the Congressmen of every district. He was able to judge people and fore tell the election victory.

In 1934, he got the friendship of Nagarajan who was attracted by Kamaraj's sincerity, courage and patriotism faced all the oppositions. He was with Kamaraj for 15 years. Like that Late Tuticorin Kandaswamy Pillai, Virudhunagar Muthuswamy, Dhanushkodi Nadar, Nellai Jebamani, Sathur Lakshmana Pillai, Madurai Chidambara Bharathi, D. Ramakrishnan Nithyanandam, Vengadathri Naidu, Trichy Arunachalam, Sanglia Pillai, Serkali Saminatha Chettiar, Salem Theerthagiri Mudaliar, Padruti Devanajaiah, Cuddalore Sundarsanam, Muthu Mutdaliar, Chidambaram Mariappan, North Arcot Upayadullah, Annamalai Pillai, Chennai Athi Kesavalu Naicker, Lakshmanaswamy Mudaliar, S. Venkatraman, Venkatachalam, Kumbakkonam Gopalakrishnan, T. R. V. Narayansamy, T. N. Ramachandra Naidu, Varadan and Thangavel Nadar all helped and cooperated with Kamaraj since Non-cooperation Movement.

The good relationship between Sathyamoorthy and Kamaraj stood as it was till the end of Sathyamoorthy. Sathyamoorthy was innocent, so Kamaraj had the responsibility of escorting him always. He never did anything without consulting Kamaraj.

In 1940 when Sathyamoorthy was offered Vice Chancellor's post in Madras University he consulted Kamaraj whether to accept. But Kamaraj advised him not to accept the same since Civil Disobedience Movement was about to come. If he accepts the post it may spoil his political carrier. Thus, Kamaraj saved him from many plots. He was a side supporter of Sathyamoorthy. Sathyamoorthy too felt Kamaraj as a sincere friend.

Sathyamoorthy was moving only with high levels. Kamaraj made him to move in lower level volunteers too. Sathyamoorthy introduced the high level and their status to Kamaraj. Thus, they helped each other.

Sathyamoorthy loved only two. One was his daughter and other Kamaraj. Kamaraj too showed his extreme love towards Sathyamoorthy. During Avadi Congress Conference he named the place as Sathyamoorthy Nagar. When he became Chief Minister he went to Sathyamoorthy's residence and prayed before his portrait and obtained blessing's from his wife. These were the symbols of friendship.

August 1942 was to be inscribed in golden letters in the history of Independence war. August revolution busted out only in that year. Asian light Nehruji informed only in this year that we were on the edge of sharp sword. We do not know what would happen. Anything may happen at any time, we should be prepared for it. Gandhiji showed green signal for revolution only in this year.

World war began in 1934. Britain, America, Russia were on one side. German, Japan and Italy on the other. In that war without consulting India Britain announced that India too would join in that war. Leaders including Gandhiji refused this. Gandhiji said when India was a slave how could it take part in the war for the interest of other countries. Suppose if freedom would be give to India at least at the end of war it may consider of supporting war arrangement. But British Prime Minister Sir Winston Churchill arrogantly said that what a foolishness it was. He was not Prime Minister of British Empire to construct cemetery. He need not require guns to control beggar Gandhiji and his volunteer. Only lathis would do. Then no support said the National Congress Council. Sir Stafford Gribs was sent as a ambassador to discuss the problem regard freedom to India.

In 25th March 1942, Gandhiji and Maulana Abul Kalam Azad met Gribs. But that gentleman create difference of opinion between Hindu and Muslims and postponed the demand for freedom. Finally he was ready to give freedom at the end of the war with certain conditions.

Gandhiji refused this as it was like a post-dated Cheque. At this time Rajaji supported partition of India and Pakistan. In result of that in 15th July 1942 Gandhiji himself, with the suggestion of

Patel wrote a letter to Rajaji to quit Congress. Then there were a group of people who received salaries from British and supported them.

Quit India Movement

Indian National Congress Conference was held in 8th July 1942 at Govalia Tank ground at Bombay City. To this history renowned conference. PCC Madras State President Kamaraj, leader Sathyamoorthy, Muthuranga Mudaliar, M. Bakthavathsalam, Kumbakkonam Gopalakrishnan, Varadan, T. N. Ramachandra Naidu and 30 others went to Bombay from Madras State.

Maulana Abul Kalam Azad presided the conference. As per Gandhiji's desire Nehru proposed the history famed Quit India Movement. Nehruji said at that time prestige of India can not be bargained. Struggle eternal struggle. It was his reply to British Empire.

Sardar Vallabhai Patel seconded the same. Maulana Abul Kalam Azad, Kavikuil Sarojini Devi, J. P. Kripalini, Pandit Bandh and Sathyamoorthy supported this.

Do or Die

Finally Gandhiji addressed. He spoke for 140 minutes. "Freedom should come immediately. If it is given tonight it should be given before dawn. From this moment you should think yourself as an independence man, you are not slaves. Essence of freedom is that I tell you a slogan. Don't forget this and keep this in your mind. Every breath of yours should be Do or Die We will free India. We ill die in that effort. We need not live being a slave". Then it was night 10'o clock.

Decision of the conference were as under:

- British rule should come to an end in India.
- Independent India will help to eradicate Nazism, Racism and Dictatorship.
- If Britain does not accept to go away a peaceful, war under the leadership of Gandhiji will be conducted.
- After eradication of foreign rule there will be communal harmony. Later a temporary Government will be formed by persons representing every community.

This decision was welcomed by all without any opposition. The British Government which could not tolerate this arrested at morning 5'o clock (9th August) Gandhiji, Kasthuri Bhai, Meera Ben Patel, Piyarelal, Mahadev Desai, Sarojini Devi, Vallabhai Patel, Nehruji, Maulana Abul Kalam Azad without leaking out that where they had been taken, sent Gandhiji and his group to Aagha Khan Palace, Pune. Nehruji and others to Ahamad nagar for jail.

Bombay became a Volcano at the dawn of August 9th when the public came to know that the beloved leaders were arrested and sent to unknown jails. Thus, came August revolution there was firing.

There was a proposal to hoist the Congress flag at 9'o clock morning at the conference. Since the leaders were arrested some doubted flag hoist. There came a lady in Khadi dress dashed towards flag mast and hoisted the flat at 9.00 a.m. as planned. British police rushed up to stop her. But before that lady gave lecture to conduct August revolution. She was Aruna Asif Ali.

On that day in that train bound for Madras from Bombay Kamaraj and representatives of Madras state returned. Leader of Andhra N. Sanjeeva Reddy came in that train. But he was arrested when the train entered Andhra Border.

Kamaraj was alert then itself. He understood they would be arrested once reaching Madras. He decided to get himself arrested only after the arrangement for August revolution in district wise. Police were on throughout the way. Armed policies were on each railway station.

They had orders to arrest the needed leaders. Then Kamaraj asked his Madras State representatives to depart immediately. Varadan was arrested before entering into Madras state border. Kumbakkonam Gopalakrishnan and T. R. V. Naryanaswamy come to Tanjore in disguise. Bombay express halted at Arakkonam station 35 miles before Madras. Kamaraj keep out of train and saw lot of police were deployed there. He decided to get down there as he expected to be arrested at Madras. He disguised himself as a village folk by having a turban on head and a bundle in head. That bundle contained the copies of the decisions taken at the Bombay conference.

He simply got down from train into the platform and walked away unnoticed by anybody. No police who came in front of him noticed. He came out of the station in deep thought.

He rushed to the bus stand and took a bus bound to Ranipet and sat in a corner without removing the turban. The bus flew but his mind was faster than the bus.

At mid night in the dark he got down at Ranipet and went to house of K. R. Kalyana Rama Iyer who was a committee member and close friend of Kamaraj. His house was locked when he knocked the door Kalyana Rama Iyer that it would be police to arrest him. But Kamaraj was a pleasant surprise to him at that night. He took him in, his aged mother gave some fruits and food to Kamaraj. She blessed Kamaraj and her son for their victory and prayed for the same.

3

The Kamaraj Era

Post-independence Period

In Madras State, in the last month of 1951 Praja Socialist Party went on strike. This created a sluggish and dissatisfied trend among the Congress Party men. All including Kamaraj had a doubt in capturing majority seats in 1925 general election. Kamaraj worked hard day and night to join all the Congress people in group before the intimation of election. To form unity Chockalingam arranged for a meeting. Ramakrishna Iyer, V. C. Palaniswamy Gounder, Chidambara Bharathi, Sudharsanam Naidu, Sanghu Pillai, Annamalai Pillai and Udaippa addressed the meeting. All insisted the unity.

There was a resolution at the end of the meeting. In that it was resolved to consult Kamaraj and Ramaswamy Reddiar to find way for unity. According to the resolution Chockalingam and others approached Kamaraj first. Kamaraj told them that he was ready to anything for unity. He was prepared to forego even 50 per cent seats in parliamentary committee. Then they met Ramaswamy Reddiar. He laid two conditions.

- Due to failure in monsoon people are poverty strikes. Government should arrange for their food.
- Land laze should be waived to the dried lands.

These two were to be carried out only by the Government. The then ministry of Kumaraswamy Raja failed to do this immediately. Hence Ramaswamy Reddiar did not cooperate.

In 1952 election Congress could not get majority. In 30th April 1952 election for PCC presidentship was conducted. Rajaji supported Kumaraswamy Raja and Kamaraj supported Dr. Subbarayan. As Kamaraj desired Dr. Subbarayan was elected as the president of PCC Though Dr. Subbarayan was elected as president Kamaraj did all the work for Congress with efforts.

Majority of members wanted to form the ministry with person won in the election independently. Kamaraj neither encouraged this nor supported.

Kumaraswamy Raja was defeated in this election. Who should be brought as the next Chief Minister? This was the general talk. Rajaji's name was proposed. Kamaraj too wished for it. Immediately he and Sanjeeva Reddy met Rajaji and asked him to be the Chief Minister for Congress party in assembly. The working committee meeting was held at Calcutta. In that it was resolved to form the ministry by Congress Party at Madras.

In March 29th of 1952 Congress Committee meeting of assembly was held. To invite Rajaji as leader of the assembly was resolved. A group members met Rajaji and informed the resolution. But Rajaji wanted them to consult Nehruji, so two of them met Nehruji.

But Nehru informed them it was the duty of the party to select its leader and he was ready to accept the same. But he also insisted that the leaders should be the member of the assembly. Suppose if a non-member is selected as leader he should contest in the election immediately and win.

On 31st March 1952 assembly meeting started. Kamaraj proposed the name of Rajaji as leader of the assembly. Sanjeeva Reddy, Sheddy and Kuttyammalu Ammal seconded the same. Selection of Rajaji as leader of the assembly was resolved. Meanwhile Rajaji was appointed as a legislative council member by the Governor based on the recommendation of Kumaraswamy Raja. Kamaraj did not know this before he proposed Rajaji's name.

Kamaraj felt for this. Later Rajaji formed the ministry after elected as the leader of Congress in assembly.

In 1952, 26th December election for PCC president was conducted. Rajaji wanted Bakthavathsalam to be elected.. But Kamaraj informed that he was going to contest. Rajaji did not come to the meeting. Kamaraj's name was proposed. Since no one contested Kamaraj was elected unanimously.

If You Have Courage, Shoot

In Madras state since 1940 Kamaraj grew up as a big power. Only after 1940 clash between Rajaji and Kamaraj was more even there was clash between them. Kamaraj never failed to meet and consult with Rajaji. He was even talking frankly with his group. He never got angry during that time.

There was a revolution in Madras state. Kamaraj was the total figure of that revolution. People those who wanted the changes expressed their desire through Kamaraj. The poor treated Kamaraj as one among them. They felt that they had close relationship with Kamaraj. Courage has born with him. The changes that happened since Kamaraj was elected as PCC president in 1940 and its repercussions made him as Chief Minister and a iron man who could decide the fate of India. Kamaraj could not speak in a riming language and never speaks always. But he attracted people with his speech and cover them to his side.

In 1949 when he was addressing a meeting at Friday there was a bustle in the meeting and the opposite threw tiny grade type crackers towards the stage. Then Kamaraj opened his shirt and showed his chest to them and challenged to shoot him if they have courage.

Also he said Gandhiji was shot by Gotche he became immortal. He also quoted Dasaratha from the epic of Ramayana as example. On seeing the boldness of Kamaraj the people alluded the meeting upto the end.

Gandhi in North - Kamaraj in South

The situation had come in Madras state as Kamaraj meant Congress and Congress meant Kamaraj since 1940. No political events without Kamaraj had happened after that. In 1920 Gandhiji conducted the meeting in Indian Civil Dress at North. People used to say Gandhi for North and Kamaraj for South. He never involved himself in arguments. But he was talented in rebutting the arguments. He used to suppress his feelings. He never showed them in his face. No one can understand anything from his facial expressions. He could judge people and their mentality well. This was the secret of his victory.

Rajaji did things suddenly without thinking. But Kamaraj never did like that. From 1931 onwards he involved himself in the affairs of AICC. He was a member in both AICC and PCC. In 1949 he was elected as a member in the working committee of AICC. He went to Ceylon in 1949 and in 1953 on the invitation of Ceylon Government. He toured Malaysia in February 1954. There was a warm welcome wherever he went.

After taking charge Rajaji made two announcements. One that the Congress should be dissolved since there was no necessity for it as we got independence, next to that free lands should not be given to freedom fighters. Those who got the free lands should return them to the government. Those two announcements made an uproar among the freedom fighters. The words of Brahmin and non-Brahmins created difference of opinion among the public. Rajaji introduced a new educational system called "Communal Educational System". He announced this without consulting the educational minister. This had lot criticism. He informed that he introduced this system to educate the traditional job of each community. All opposed this. Rajaji was questioned whether he was right to introduce such a system without consulting the education minister and the Congress party. He quoted Sankaran and Ramanujan for this.

Rajaji came to Madurai to open a building at TVS. C. P. Ramaswamy Iyer came to this function. In that function Rajaji commented that Brahmin was doing the motoring job which had to be done by a non-Brahmin. It vehemented Kamaraj. Rajaji also praised T. V. Sundaram Iyengar for handing over the trade to his sons.

Next Kamaraj rose to address. He quoted the speech of Rajaji in handing over the trade by T. V. Sundaram Iyengar to his sons.

He said that was also applicable in the case of politics. Thus, he expressed his views about Rajaji's ministry. It was appreciated by all. The scheme of Communal education created a heated argument in the assembly. Kamaraj accepted to postpone the issue without sending it for voting. His silence in this issue made the party men and public angry. People understood his political tactics.

When Andhra was bifurcated there was riot for new election for Madras State. Rajaji wanted to hold a party meeting in September 1953 to know whether to continue as a party leader. The next day he released a message stating that he wanted to organise the meeting under the impression that Kamaraj did not like his leadership. But after a talk with Kamaraj he came to know that Kamaraj was not having such a opinion hence the meeting would be cancelled. To form a bad impression and bad image upon Kamaraj, Rajaji cunningly behaved liked that.

There were 9 ministers after Andhra was bifurcated in Rajaji's ministry. He consulted Kamaraj in appointing new ministers. Kamaraj opposed this. But Rajaji increased the ministry by 12 from 9. Opposition party wanted to move a No-confidence Motion against Rajaji. They collected Signatures from the members. Rajaji too gathered for his supports. But majority was on the other side. On seeing the emergent situation the party high command invited both Rajaji and Kamaraj to Delhi. They had discussions with Rajaji and Kamaraj. Then Nehru announced that Rajaji to continue.

On seeing the Nehru's announcement T. G. Krishnamoorthy, Panchatcharam Chettiar and A. M. Sambandam went to Delhi and met Nehru. Explained him the actual situation in Madras state. On hearing this Nehru said that Tamils had rights to decide their Government . This put Rajaji again in a tight corner. Congress party assembled again in 6th May 1954. Rajaji was prepared to resign. But Kamaraj postponed the voting against "Communal Education Scheme".

Rajaji consulted Bakthavathsalam before his resignation. Bakthavathsalam said the only way to solve the problem was to have a talk with Kamaraj. Because Kamaraj never cares anyone's recommendations. He never went for obligations with any minister. He had no personal feelings on any ministry. He told only the facts. Anyone would accept his words. So meeting Kamaraj explains the matter and clearing his doubts was only the way.

Dr. Vardarajulu Naidu, V. K. Ramaswamy Mudaliar, Kochalram, T. G. Krishnamoorthy, Panchatcharam Chettiar, A. M. Sambandam were the members who opposed the Communal Education Scheme and the ministry of Rajaji. Rajaji threatened Vardarajulu Naidu by taking disciplinary action. Unpleasant incidents would have occurred if three member crew did not meet Nehru and explains him the situation. High command did not give its opinion on Rajaji tendering resignation. It ordered to conduct election.

Due to ill-health who did not attend the assembly on 25th March 1954 Rajaji suddenly came to assembly. He tendered his resignation showing his ill-health as a cause. Rajaji and Kamaraj met and had a talk in the assembly before a meeting was conducted.

Rajaji expressed his view of appointing one of the existing ministers for a period of 3 months till the budget session was over. Kamaraj accepted to this proposal. Kamaraj informed that Rajaji told select one among Bakthavathsalam, Sheddy and C. Subramaniam as Chief Minister for a period of 2 months.

Assembly session of Congress party started. Rajaji announce the name of Subramaniam as Chief Minister. But he did not specify the period as he told already to Kamaraj.

But Kamaraj rose and said that he accepts this arrangement for a period of two months till the budget session. Rajaji did not accept to this. Then there was a uproar. Members wanted to conducted election. Rajaji fixed 30th as date for election. But there was opposition to this, since time was too short. Rajaji insisted 30th as date of election.

Rajaji's group wanted C. Subramaniam to be the CM. There was also a proposal to elect Subbrayan. But Subbrayan did not come on 30th.

Group of Kamaraj wanted him to contest. Kamaraj finally accepted the proposal. The time was 3 p.m. Hearing this Rajaji's group shocked. They never expected Kamaraj to contest. The session began Subramaniam requested Kamaraj to postpone the meeting in order to have compromise talk. Subramaniam was pointed out about the instructions of high command in conducting the election. Kamaraj did not accept for the postponement.

Election began, Dr. Varadrajulu Naidu proposed the name of Kamaraj and N. Annamalai Pillai seconded the same. Kamaraj got 93 votes and C. Subramaniam got 41 votes. Kamaraj won and became Chief Minister.

Kamaraj went to Delhi and met the high command, asked them whether he can be a party leader in assembly and appoint another one as CM. But the high command insisted the leader of assembly to be the CM. After returning from Delhi he consulted his friend. They said if another election was conducted it may cause fresh problems. Hence asked Kamaraj to take charge of CM's post. Then he wanted them to promise that should not insist him to appoint ministers for their choice.

Man who did Wonders

Kamaraj reduced his ministry to 8 from 12. He included the supporters of Rajaji in his ministry. He also included C. Subramaniam who contested against him in his ministry. Bakthavathsalaam was also included one among the 8. The 6 person who opposed Rajaji were not included in the ministry. He thought that it would be better to include Vannian Community who opposed Congress. He included Ramaswamy Padaiaachi in the ministry who was the leader of opposite party and opposed Congress in the assembly. Hence there was no opposition for Congress from out side. He formed such a ministry and avoided the opposition from in and out of Congress. He took charge as CM on 13th April of 1954, the Tamil new year day. He was not a member in assembly nor a member in Legislative Council. He should become a member within six months from the date of taking charge in either of legislature.

It was easy to become a Member of Legislature Council. But Kamaraj did not prefer it. He had a strong belief for a healthy government one should be elected through assembly election only. Also he thought that he could understand the opinion of the public only if contest for the assembly election. Always he was elected from the Virudhunagar constituency. Suppose if he wanted to be elected from there the elected member of that constituency should resign. As always he did not want to create problem ever.

At that time, there was a vacancy in Gudiatham Constituency of North Arcot district. All wanted him to contest from there as the Chief Minister is common to the state and he contest from any constituency of the state. Finally he decided to contest from Gudiatham Constituency.

He did not belong to North Arcot which consist Gudiatham constituency. Even then he contested from there, except Communist party all other parties supported Kamaraj. Since the Dravidian parties did like Rajaji to become the Chief Minister again they supported Kamaraj and made serious propaganda for his victory. The Congress volunteers of all parts of Madras state invaded Gudiatham since Kamaraj decided to contest from a new constituency which neither was his native nor a place he dwelled. The Dravidian parties and Muslim league openly supported Kamaraj and hunted for votes. Gudiatham was flooded by party people. Public worked for Kamaraj. Kamaraj visited all the villages and addressed the mass. He won in the election. He thanked the people of that constituency.

Kamaraj did not go for the post of minister. It came to him. The post which came to him in 1954 he resigned it 1963. He was the first Chief Minister who was in that post for such a long period. Ministries changed in other states of India because of Enmity, Plots, Jealous and for post but it was not in Madras state. There was no quarrel, enmity or jealous in the ministry of Kamaraj. After Kamaraj became Chief Minister the trend of Madras state was totally changed. His period was called as Golden Period. When he became Chief Minister he said, "People who works people as Maharajas and Lords who are lazy and live on other labours. I have become the Chief Minister only to wipeout the troubles of poor, else I don't want this post at all." From that day on wards all the poor had his portraits at their huts. When he was the CM of Madras state he went in the path of Gandhiji and followed the principles of Nehru. He did what was Right. People respected him as a "Model Man".

S. Balasundrammal, wife of Sathyamoorthy said about Kamaraj: "Kamaraj served for the nation for more than 20 years along with my husband. During that time he had the sense of sacrifice and public service. He was best companion to my husband and worked without rest to strengthen the Congress in Madras state. His Chief Ministership was the evidence to the dream of my husband". Thus, the disciple made the dream of his leader alive. Nehruji appreciated the services of Kamaraj as under: "It is impossible to find a person overcoming Kamaraj in public service. As a friend for several years I had a chance to know him. The value I had on him increased on and on whenever I moved with him. He is the CM to a government which is a example for efficient and good governance." Lord Eddianburro, husband of England Queen congratulated Kamaraj and said that he should be the Chief Minister of Madras state during his next visit to India and Madras.

Thus, Kamaraj ruled Madras State. As per the judgement of news reporters his way of ruling was a lesson to others and his service was an example to the post he held.

Explanation of Nehruji

Kamaraj met Nehru at Hyderabad in July 1963. He informed his decision then. Nehruji welcomed his decision. He wanted to implement the decision of Kamaraj in a broad way and to created a welcoming change in Congress. The defeat in UP and Rajkot in the middle of 1963 echoed in Congress party. The stability was affected due tot he clashes between the ministry and party and mentality of groupism. Apart from this the desire for power and opportunitism had grown up. These were the reasons for Kamaraj's "K-PLAN".

When Nehru was worried seeing the undiscipline in the Congress Kamaraj explained his plan to him, when Nehru felt to take a sudden new action to establish the powers of working committee, Kamaraj told him his plan.

Kamaraj went to Delhi on the invitation of Nehru. His path was visible to him. No noise bored his ears.

Delhi city and the Parliament area were in tense. Congress working committee meeting was held in 9th August 1963. Kamaraj proposed his plan and resignation. The proposal asked that the experienced senior leaders in government service had to resign their posts. It was unanimously approved. It was decided in the working committee that the state CMs, Ministers should submit their resignation with Nehru and whose resignation were accepted by Nehru might return to party work.

Nehru's Resignation and Kamaraj's Opposition

Nehruji tendered his resignation and announced it in working committee. Immediately all including Kamaraj opposed it. Kamaraj told in working committee that Nehru should not resign, If he resigns the government would become unstable at that juncture and he was even ready to give up his plan if Nehru resigns. It was welcomed by the working committee members with claps.

In the national interest the working committee did not accept Nehru's resignation. But it helped to establish the powers of working committee. In the meeting conducted at the night of August 12th Nehruji said that he was very much wounded to accept the resignation of his good old friends when himself being in the post without resigning. But he had done it keeping in mind the problems that were to be faced by the Congress and the public of the nation and in order to see that the government could not be spoiled and also to see resolution of the working committee in victory.

In the list announced by Nehru the following CM's names found place. M/s Kamaraj, Patnaik, Bakshi Gulam Muhammad, C. P. Gupta, Binodananda, P. A. Mandloy. The ministers in the list from central were M/s Morarji Desai, Lal Bahadur Shastri, S. K. Patil, Jegajeevan Ram, B. Gopal Reddi, K. L. Mali. Nehruji said apart from the above many more central and state ministers would resign from their posts.

It was the first time in the world that the ministers resigned their posts voluntarily which made the world to wonder. Kamaraj was seen before their eyes. His plan was called as "K-PLAN". Kamaraj informed before his resignation that all the Congress men started rounding the Parliament for ministership and power. In order to divert their attention people like him had to resign from the posts under his plan. He resigned from his post on 2nd October the birth day of Gandhiji. Then mind thought the words of Gandhiji that "So long one in the post with power, socialism will leave him". Kamaraj thought that he was in the way of Gandhiji.

The man intention of his plan was to raise the feeling of national service and to strengthen the internal power. One of the important aims was to establish the powers of central high command and to establish unity and control in Congress. He fulfilled these two with his plan. The resignation under "K-PLAN"revealed one should act according to the orders of Congress high command whatever the high posts they held. On 3rd and 4th of November 1963 Jaipur Congress Conference was held under the presidency of T. Sanjeevaiah, the AICC president. In that conference the K-PLAN and its way of execution and effects were discussed for about 6 hours.

His plan gave good and wonderful results. It gave a new enthusiasm among public and Congress workers. There was no doubt that K-PLAN had created interest and speed in Congress party. Nehru said in that discussion as under: "K-PLAN has made a revolution turn in the history of the nation and Congress. Kamaraj is only the right person to be the president of AICC". It was appreciated by all. Earlier to this on 9th October Congress working committee meeting was held at Delhi to elect the party president. Names of Kamaraj, Alutya Gosh and Lal Bhagadhur Shastri were proposed. But Nehruji liked only Kamaraj to be the president of the party. It was unanimously accepted by the working committee.

When Kamaraj meet Nehru in July 1963 to explain about his "K-PLAN" Nehru informed his decision that Kamaraj should be the next president of AICC. But Kamaraj refused it saying that he resigned his Chief Ministership to work for Congress party, hence he did not want to be the president of AICC. Then Nehru did not insist him.

All India Congress President

Nehru's wish was fulfilled after 3 months. Kamaraj was elected as AICC president. He was the 3rd Tamilian to be the president of AICC after Salem Vijayaragavachary and S. Srinivas Iyengar. Many did not know that Congress Born in Madras state. When Diwan Bhadur Ragunatha Rao was the collector of Madras in

December 1884 at his residence under the advice of A. O. Hume, a foreigner, the preliminary meeting was held. A. O. Hume was the main person for the establishment of Indian National Congress.

In the preliminary meeting Dr. Sir Subramanya Iyer, Panapakkam Rangacharlu, Egmore Rangaiah Naidu, Surendranath Banerji, Manmohan Gosh, Dadabai Narouji, Vaman Ramayan Mandlik, Kasinath Triambak Tilong and other participated. It was resolved that every one who likes to serve of the nation truly should introduce them selves to each other and to discuss the efforts to be done in that year for the development of the nation. It was also resolved in that meeting to meet at Pune in 1885 and to invite all to that meeting.

The first Congress meeting was held at Gokuldas Tejpal Sanskrit College, Bombay on 28th December 1885 at 12:15 noon. 72 representatives from all over India and 50 newspapers reporters attended the meeting. From Madras state famous leaders and representatives of "Sudesa Mitran" and "Hindu" attended the meeting. Dadabai Nouroji invited all and gave welcome address. W. C. Banerji presided over this fist meeting. Bengal Christian and Barrister A. O. Hume proposed. Dr. Sir Mani Iyer seconded. Banerji was the first Congress president.

Aim of Congress was those who work for the development of nation should behave friendly, without differentiation in caste, religion, creed and state should work for the nation, should discuss all the problems and record the seniors views in national interest and decide the work of patriots after the meeting of the Congress. Founder of "Sudesa Mitran", Tamil daily, Mr. G. Subramaniya Iyer had the opportunity of proposing this in the meeting.

This Congress got the freedom to India after sending out the British.

W. C. Banerji was the president of the Congress. His successors were George Yule, Anathachari, Dadabai Nouroji, William Wilterban, Vier, Badruddin Dayabji, P. S. Mehta, Lal Mohan Gosh, Sankara Nayar, Chandra, Anantha Mohan, Wacha, Gopala Krishna Gokale, Ras Bihari Gosh, Mahalkan, S. P. Sinha, Madan Mohan Malavya, Syed Muhammad Majumdar, B. N. Dhan Basu, Dr. Anni Besant, Hasan Imam, Lala Lajpat Rai, Abul Kalam Azad,

Vijayaragavachari, Deshbandhu C. R. Das, Gandhiji, Sarojini Naidu, Nehruji, Nelli Sen Gupta, Srinivasa Iyengar, Sardar Vallabai Patel, Rajendra Prashad, M. A. Ansari, Sait Rangalal, Subash Chandra Bose, Kripalani, Purushottam Das, Tandon, Pattabi Seetharamiah, U. N. Tebar, Sanjeeva Reddi and Sanjeevaiah. After all these people Kamaraj become the president of AICC. By facing oppression and bullets it got freedom to India.

After the election of Kamaraj as AICC president the 68th conference of Congress made a history. Kamaraj went to this meeting in a special train. All the representatives of Madras state went along with him. "Buvaneshwar Special" train departed from Madras Central Railway station at night 2 o'clock on January 3rd of 1964 and reached Capital Orissa on 5th evening at 3 p.m. Throughout the distance of 900 miles people gathered at the in between stations showed their affections raised slogans pro Kamaraj. At Nellore Station the district president Shankar Reddy and hundreds of Congress volunteers garlanded Kamaraj and took him tot he near by stage in the platform. There they welcomed Kamaraj and conveyed their regards. Baskets full of flowers were showered on Kamaraj.

Kamaraj plunged in the ocean of flowers and affection of the public. His speech was very short but contained lot of sense. His speech in Tamil was translated in Telugu by someone. Madras State Chief Minister Mr. Bakthavathsalam also spoke for a minute. A poor labour with soiled cloths and scattered hair came running with a garland in his hand. On seeing him Kamaraj stood there till he come and garlanded him.

After the meeting was over coffee was served to all the 700 volunteers by the party people of Andhra. At Bitrakunda station breakfast was served to all the 700 volunteers by the public of that area. Ongole was not in reception list. But the train was stopped, by the public fruits like orange, banana, were given. Lunch was served at Tenali. Reception was held before the CM of Andhra Sanjeeva Reddy. A minister took the responsibility of the reception and feast. Telugu people raised slogans pro-Kamaraj and Tamils pro-Sanjeeva Reddy.

At Vijayawada the reception was very grand. Kamaraj spoke in Tamil and Sanjeeva Reddy translated it in Telugu. 17 years had passed after getting independence under the stewardship of Gandhiji. Gandhiji told on that day, that only after independence people could live without parity. But even after 3 five year plans and after spending crores of Rupees poor did not get any benefits. Lot of people were suffering without food, shelter and clothes.

Where had the earned wealth and results of the plans gone? Had they mixed in the sea like Krishna River? or evaporated and reached the Sky? NO. It was amassed by some group that is dangerous.

That should be distributed to all equally. The aim of Congress was to give shelter, clothes, education and equal chance to all. It was discussed at Jaipur. That was the democratic socialistic discussion to gather the support of the public to drive a plan and to implement this that Bhuvaneswar trip. This was the 5 minutes speech of Kamaraj at Vijayawada. After the meeting Kamaraj was taken in a procession in a jeep to the railway station.

At Eluru a girl garlanded Kamaraj cashew nuts were given in large quantity. After Tiffin train went to Niditavole. Later the train did not stop at Pasuvatanam, Kovoor and Godavari. But people gathered *en route* came running behind the train. At Rajmundry Kamaraj and Bakthavathsalam spoke in the meeting. It was presided by Andhra State Congress Committee president Pottipattu Brahmaiah. There a welcome address was read in Tamil. Train stopped at Thuvarakudi for supper. Veg and non-veg items were served to all the 700 volunteers. 17 thousand people attended the meeting organised by the panchayat union. Speech of Kamaraj and Bakthavathsalam were translated in Telugu by Sanjeeva Reddy. On the 5th morning the train reached Srikakulam, hot water for bath and break fast were ready for all.

After Palasa's meeting the train stopped at Berhampur of Orissa. Lunch was served at 11 a.m.. Later, the train without stopping anywhere reached Bhuvaneshwar at 3 p.m. The former CM of Orissa and the reception committee chairman Mr. Patnaik, Orissa's CM Prem Mitra, Orissa's Congress president Bejanpani and Lal Bhagadhur Shastri received Kamaraj. To denote the 68th meeting rifles were shot for 68 times. Lakhs of people gathered at the ground before the railway station to see Kamaraj. Leaders

Kamaraj, Patnaik and Prem Mitra were taken in procession in a open car. 1,500 volunteers marched behind the car. 2 lakhs people went behind them. The procession of INC leader started. Before the procession went, the Orchestra, the Orissa's famous traditional dance march. The procession reached Gobandh Nagar at 5.30 p.m. after crossing a distance of 3 miles. Kamaraj garlanded Thyagi Late Uthkalmani Gobandh's statue and paid homage to him. Later the procession reached the conference stage.

Two lakhs people shouted slogans of pro-Kamaraj. There was no such huge gathering to any other Congress committee the president after independence. Because of Kamaraj the Tamils had raised their heads on that day. Kamaraj conducted the conference of 78 year old Congress committee by sitting in its seat.

He delivered his speech on 9th January at 5 p.m. amidst lakhs of volunteers to eradicate the poverty of 45 crores of Indians,. It was the place where Emperor Ashoka fought with his warriors against Kalinga's empire's lakhs of soldiers 2,500 years ago to establish Magada Empire. It was the place where Emperor Ashoka decided not to fight and preach peace. Two lakhs people heard his speech.

His speech at the conference was as under:

> "You have given me the responsibility to administer the INC by electing me to this highest post unanimously you have exposed your affection towards me. I expect your full cooperation and enthusiastic support to execute my duty to the entire satisfaction of you all".

His speech had explained in a way about the steps to be taken to fight against economical conditions after paying homage to the departed freedom fighters and the soldiers who lost their lives in Indo-China war. "There are certain items in our economical conditions which worries us. I point out at first that massing of wealth with certain people. So there is monopoly in some trade. Tax evasion, black marketing of scare products. No honesty in trade, no regularity in trade. It is essential to take proper steps in this matter". He also explained the procedures to be followed, "Since our aim is socialism we have to stop amassing of wealth with certain people and its hereditary continuance. If we allow this it will be hurdle for our development. At the end the rich will be more rich. We have to see now whether the present laws and administration will fulfil our socialistic aims. INC should examine the developments in each state. Government should take action to stop monopoly and also they are to be examined. We have to develop new areas and start new industries. Districts should give free education upto secondary school education gradually."

To Form New India

"When Congress has come to a decision it is the sacred duty of every Congress worker to abide himself and act accordingly. After a policy decision different types of laths and blaming each other confuses the public. So we have to join together and work with control in the national development scheme."

"We had the opportunity to work under Mahatma Gandhi earlier. Since we are the followers of Gandhiji, we, Congress people have to adopt the principles of our aim with control. People expect best activity only from Congress than other parties. So I humbly request you all to follow the path of Gandhi in our day to day life. In the best characters of Gandhi only two are most important. They are simplicity and service to human. Let us form our NEW INDIA, which is our dream, with these two simple tools."

Thus, he conducted his speech. G. Rajagopalan was his assistant. When Kamaraj was the AICC president. After 6th Nehru did not participate in the conference as he was ill. The conference was held from 5th to 7 p.m. of 10th. Later only the ground was thin. The volunteers spread over the country to fight against poverty.

Speciality of Bhuvaneshwar

The decision taken at the Bhuvaneshwar Congress was the turning point in the history of Indian Country, Congress conference and Socialism. Though the Congress accepted socialistic society it strongly decided that the democratic socialism was its aim and it added this first and in its basic principles. Apart from this following were the important points:

- After a long time a Tamilian became the Congress president.
- The speech in Tamil at his first conference which was never before in the history of Congress.
- The man who was whole heartidly accepted by all as the president of Congress after Nehru.
- Though Nehru was not there about 400 members attended the conference and participated in discussion with attention and responsibility.

After becoming the president of AICC he went on tour throughout the country. He was called as KALA GANDHI (BLACK GANDHI) by the public. He went to Punjab, Nepal Border, Orissa, UP, Andhra and Mysore under tight schedule. He went on tour in Madras state for 18 days in may 1956. It was called as SAMADHARMA YATHRA by the people of Madras state.

At that tour he gave an announcement which he had not before. He said that it was final struggle to for a socialistic pattern of society and he was ready to struggle for it. And for this he wanted the full support of the public and he asked for it. Lakhs of people were ready to cooperate with him. He covered 300 places in 18 days. Went over 2,000 miles and met 1 crore people. He at 5 large meetings and 15 small meeting sat 20 to 30 places in a day. In all the meetings he explained about the principles of socialism in general. Then he explained about the enemies for it and how to face them, etc.

Facts of his explanations were:

> "Some are shouting to fulfil the Nehru's promise in language problem. Likewise if a poor asks to fulfil the Nehru's promise on socialism have to support him or not? Why these people are opposing it? They want eh promise of Nehru only in language problem and not for other". In total he explained about "SAMADHARMA" in Tamil to the public in his tour of 18 days.

Election of Shastri as Prime Minister

June 2nd . It was the day which made a turning point in the Indian history. It was the day which answered to the question of "who is after Nehru" Kamaraj created another history that day. Generally Congress party meeting never held in the central hall of the Parliament. Kamaraj conducted the meeting there. Exactly at 9'o clock Congress party members gathered at the Central hall of the Parliament. State CMs , Leaders and Foreign Ambassadors were in the Visitor's gallery.

In his presidential speech Kamaraj said that it was not possible for them to fill up the place of the departed leader Nehru. So to do the duty which was before them they require a joint leadership, joint responsibility and unique view. He also gave them warning. He said, "We were under the umbrella named Nehruji. Whatever we did we had the courage as he was there. He excused us for our mistakes. Now that situation is not there. So, in future we should act with utmost care."

Mr. Nanda who was the interim PM for a period of 6 days proposed the name of Lal Bhagadhur Shastri as the party leader of the Parliament. Morarji Desai seconded the proposal. Shastri was elected unanimously. Immediately all the members stood and welcomed the new leader with applauses. Lal Bhagadhur Shastri became the PM Morarji Desai, S. K. Patil, Jegajeevan Ram and Krishna Menon whole heartily appreciated Shastri. India's First PM (Nehru) was nominated by Gandhiji. India's Second PM was given to us by the Southern Gandhi, Leader Kamaraj. Yes, our state gave the Second PM of India.

True nature could be seen only at the time of troubles. In such occasions Kamaraj developed his intelligence, courage and sacrifice. His political growth was an astonishment. In whichever post he was he had more talent than required to it. There was no place above to his talent.

The shock due to the demise of Nehru and the shock to Kairon's affairs worried India's position. Kamaraj beautifully managed the situation. Public had a feeling that they need not worry as long as Kamaraj was there.

Affection towards Children

In 1964 he opened a Girl's high school at North Madras. N. D. Sundara Vadivelu presided. Rajeswari, a 9th Standard Student, in her welcome address praised Kamaraj and his government for having given free education upto SSLC. She further said that the broad minded rich people helped for the uniforms, books and midday meals to the poor students like her. Even then Kamaraj should make arrangements to provide all these permanently by the government. In reply to that Kamaraj said that NO parents should suffer to provide food, clothes and education to their children. Government must take the responsibility of bringing up the children upto 15 years and he stressed that the government would take. People realised, Kamaraj who had no children had the high regard about the children.

At Guntur

In 1964 AICC meeting was held at Guntur. At that time, health of G. Rajagopalan, party secretary and the right hand of Kamaraj, was very serious. He died there. His body was brought to Delhi. PM Shastri came to Madras and paid his homage. On seeing the body his wife cried. Kamaraj's eyes shed tears. After this he never shed tears in his political life till the end. Even at the death of his mother Kamaraj did not tears.

Kamaraj's house in Delhi was at Jantar Mantar Road. His house was always neat and tidy. Even Indira Gandhi praised this. All wondered as how a bachelor could keep his house so clean. All the politicians throughout India visited his house. News reporters never failed to attend. In 1965 Indira Gandhi went to his house to greet him for the Tamil New Year's day. Then his assistant Ambi offered Indira Gandhi a cup of 'Payasam'.

At the gate of his Delhi house there was a small name board with his name as 'Kamaraj', the house of the 'King-maker' was always open. Sri. Sankaracharya Swamigal once praised Kamaraj as a 'Great man of India'. He blessed Kamaraj as the man who without caring his personal inconveniences had the mind to serve for the nation. He knew the morals well.

Had the Congress did not get his leadership it would be the end of it. The 69th conference was held at Durgapur on 9th January 1965. He explained about the danger of China's atomic bombs and the relationship of Pakistan. He also pointed out that they were trying to created a new era to wipe out poverty, unemployment, and ignorance in a short period. So they had to give priority to the plans which would fruitful result to in a short period.

Amidst the Soldiers

When the war started between India and Pakistan in 1965 he air dashed to the war front and met the soldiers and encouraged them. He was one among them. They heard his emotional speeches with interest. A soldier said 'VANAKKAM' in Tamil. Immediately he enquired about his native place. When he replied as 'Vellore' he started to enquire about his address and the people living there. After getting the answer Kamaraj assured the soldier to meet his relatives at Vellore. This made them happy.

War Fund at Madras

Lal Bhagadhur Shastri came to Madras in 1965. Leader of Madras state gathered to give him their donation for the war fund. Congress workers meeting was held at Abutsbury Palace as a final programme. The speech of Shastri was a melting one. Whenever he uttered 'Kamaraju' 'Kamaraju' the public applaused. He said, "Our soldiers are forwarding in the war field. If it is due to the efforts of the government only Kamaraj's advices helped for it. Kamaraj is my brother who did not born with me. He is a guide to me, through him I rule the nation. His advices to end the war helped a lot. The encouragement he gave me helped the battalion to march forward in the war."

The meeting of Congress working committee was going on in 1965 December 24. It was 1 p.m. Then Dhanushkote drowned in the sea due to storm. The causality could not be ascertained. The message came to Madras. Immediately the meeting came to an end.

Leader Kamaraj and CM Bakthavathsalam discussed urgently about the rescue operations. They went by flight from Madras.

When the flight was halfway through, one of the engines of the aero plane failed. Passengers cried. With the ability of the pilot the efforts were taken to land the flight when then the flight was 10 feet above the ground level the other engine also failed. The flight fell down. Luckily no one was injured. All the passengers run shelter to save their life. But Kamaraj without any tension got out of the flight and asked for things to do next.

Wireless message was sent to Bangalore. In few hours military plane came. Both Bakthavathsalam and Kamaraj went to Ramanad in that. Then they took the helicopter which was ready there. From the helicopter they saw Dhanushkote and Rameshwaram islands which were seriously affected by the violence of the nature. Curd Rice, Bread and Food stuff were dropped from the plane. It helped for the survival to those who lived between the dead.

Rescue operations were fastened on hearing the arrival of Kamaraj. Naval ships Sarada and Hamidia were on the roaring sea to rescue the people who were drowning. Kamaraj consoled the public who were affected by famine, diseases, torrentional rain, storm.

The year 1965 it was a problematic year in the Indian political and economic affairs with foreign countries.

The food problem was there throughout the country, linguistic problem rose in south. Crops dried due to monsoon failure. Natural calamities like flood and famine were the stone on the track of economic development. Above all Indo-Pakistan war increased the problems and troubles.

The world appreciated Lal Bhagadhur Shastri of his courage, the way he acted during the war with Pakistan. Relationship with Russia and Czechoslovakia were improved.

Shastri went to Tashkent on the invitation of international leaders on 4th December 1965. He had a compromise talk with Ayyub Khan the premier of Pakistan. The talk continued till 10th. Finally he made Ayyub Khan to sign in the agreement to seize war. He died on the same night. Shastri, Who went to Tashkent to find a way for peace agreement between India and Pakistan passed away there itself.

Students of school's said, "Shastri is short but his work is big". His body was brought in a plane by Russian Premier Kosigin and Pakistan Premier Ayyub Khan. At the airport they brought the body on their shoulders. They were there till the cremation and consoled the relatives.

On 11th all the newspapers in the world flashed the news about Tashkent agreement and demise of Shastri. With 2 years after the death of Nehru India was forced to elect another PM. Again a big responsibility chased Kamaraj who solved the question of "Who after Nehru" Congress men and the public looked at Kamaraj with a belief that India would be safe in his hands and he would solve the problem of "Who is after Shastri". The world also turned towards Kamaraj.

There were 6 people with full qualifications for the post of PM. They were not ready to withdraw themselves from the contest. The working committee meeting was conducted on 14th January 1965. Under the presidency of Kamaraj, it was discussed to elect the PM. In the meeting it was resolved that Kamaraj should elect the PM after knowing the opinions of the members. Kamaraj invited the MPs and state CMs. This time his approach was different. He drew the members to his side who had difference of opinion. His talent was appreciated by the MPs throughout the day. Atulya Gosh gave a suggestion. He suggested Kamaraj as PM. For this he gathered the supports of the MPs and CMs

Kamaraj refused it immediately. When Kamaraj refused the Prime Minister ship MPs and public called him as "Maharishi Kamaraj" (Saint Kamaraj). Kamaraj was prepared to face the situation suppose if the contest was unavoidable. He predicted that only Morarji Desai would contest against Indira Gandhi. Nanda and Chavan were not having enough support, hence they would involve themselves.

The good reasons to elect Indira Gandhi were, she was the president of AICC then, So the country knew her well. More than 50 per cent of the population was ladies and they would prefer a lady to be the PM. Also international leaders knew Indira Gandhi well. State Chief Ministers openly supported Indira Gandhi. On 16th January of 1966. 14 out of 16 state Chief Ministers openly announced that they were supporting Indira Gandhi. At that time Morarji Desai and his followers were seeking the support of MPs.

Indira Becoming PM

News reporters interviewed Kamaraj at this house. He gave wireless interview. When a reporter said to Kamaraj that it was said the CMs were not having votes hence they had no rights to decide. Kamaraj got angry and said not to ask foolish questions. He also said that when they were trying to solve a tough problem every one should think about the interest of the nation and should not drag in many directions. Another reporter asked whether there were two contestants. His immediate reply was he did not know.

Morarji Desai wrote a letter to the Parliament as his final attempt. On 18th January Kamaraj meet Morarji Desai at his residence and informed that Indira Gandhi had the support of majority of the members and it was for Morarji to give way to Indira Gandhi to become the PM by avoiding the contest. But Morarji replied that the ballot box would speak on the next day. Kamaraj took leave of him.

All the members assembled at the Parliament house on 19th January 1966 to elect their new leader. Kamaraj presided. 26 members did not attend. But they sent their ballots denoting their choice. After independence it was the first contest for the Prime Ministership Nanda proposed the name of Indira Gandhi and Sanjeeva Reddy seconded the same. Morarji Desai's name was proposed by K. Hanumanthaiah and seconded by T. R. Palivel. Secret pooling took two hours. Ballots were counted. The ballot box spoke. Indira Gandhi won by getting 355 votes and Morarji got only 169 and was defeated. This election proved that Kamaraj's power was in his good behaviour and sharp political knowledge.

In the felicitation function Kamaraj said that India had to face serious problems and all the members should cooperate with Indira Gandhi to solve them. Then he invited Morarji Desai to speak. Morarji said that he was ready to offer his full cooperation. Then Indira Gandhi spoke in Hindi first and later in English. She said that, she would go in the same track of his predecessors and she requested the cooperation of the members.

4

A Rustic Statesman

The story began at Virudupatti, called Virudhunagar now, which had a census of 16,000 people. A tank is important to that city. Sulochana Nadar street is on the Western side of the tank. The house of 'Nattanmakara' Sulochana Nadar is in that street. Kamaraj who saved the prestige of our country by controlling the famine, etc. born only in that house in the year 1903, July 15th.

The Way the Name Has Come

During those days the people of Nadar group at Virdhupatti had many branches. 'Naattanmaikarar' branch and 'Megavarnam' branch are the most important one in that group.

A marriage between Chinnappa Nadar of Megavarnam group and Parvathi Ammal, sister of Sulochana Nadar - Naattanmaikarar group took place. As they had no children they (Chinnappa Nadar and Parvathy) adopted Kumaraswamy, who belonged to Megavarnam group.

Kumaraswamy married Sivakami the daughter of Sulochana Nadar (Parvathy Ammal brother's daughter). Kumaraswamy-Sivakami Ammal gave birth to a male child on 15th July of 1903. The child was first named as Kamatchi by its grand mother

Parvathy Ammal. Since she worshipped Goddess Meenakshi she named the child as Kamatchi. Though all called the child as Kamatchi with love and affection Sivakami Ammal used to call the child as Raja. Then all became to call the child as Raja. Kumaraswamy, who thought that the name of the god should also be in the name of his son mingled both the names (Kamatchi + Raja) and named him as KAMARAJA. Four years after the birth of Kamaraj his sister Nagammal was born.

Kamaraj — A Lesson

The school which educated Kamaraj, he took the school as a lesson and became a lesson to the nation. According tot the custom of those days Kamaraj was admitted in the school at his 5th year, the next day of "Saraswathy Pooja", dressed in coat and dhoti. As per the custom of those days, the whole family members joined together and took Kamaraj in the school. The first teacher for Kamaraj was Velayutham. He was knows as "Lame Teacher" in the public because of his lamed fingers of the leg.

The 'Lame Teacher School' is nothing but a Varandah School (Thinnai Pallikudam) Velayutham equally treated the rich and poor. Basics of mathematics and other lessons were thought to Kamaraj here.

After some period he was admitted in Yenadhi Narayana Vidhya Salai. A teacher by name Murugaiah conducted this school. Here only Kamaraj learned to read and write Tamil. Next year Kamaraj was admitted in Virudupatti High School — Chatria Vidhya Salai from Kasukadi street school. Chatria Vidhya Salai is the only high school in Virdhupatti which has the classes upto School final

It was called as "Fist Rice School" (Pidi Arici Pallikudam) by all. Free Education was given here since 1888. Each and every family in the Virdhupatti had donated a fist full of Rice to this school every day hence the name of "Fist Rice School".

The school was run by 'Magamai' a sort of donation. Hence free education was given since 1888. Kamaraj, when he became the Chief Minister has brought Free Education System in all high schools throughout the State and gave free education to the students. Chatira Vidhya Salai, the school in which Kamaraj studied was the forefoot for Free Education. Took the school in which studied as a lesson and brought his dreams to true gave free education and became a lesson to nation and thus became a Leader who gave the eye of education.

Growth of the Plant can be Know from Its Embryo

One afternoon — in the sixth year of Kamaraj when he joined in Chatriya Vidhya Salai his father Kumaraswamy lied down in the bed due to unbearable headache. The next day he expired. The sudden demise of the person who led the family by wholesale dealings in coconuts had given a severe shock and pain to Sivakami Ammal. Kamaraj did not attain the age to recover her mother from her sorrowful mood. He also could not understand irreparable loss happened to the family.

Short while ago his grand father Chinnappa Nadar expired. Continued death of Kamaraj's father, the family knew not what to do.

Kamaraj was only the star of hope to the family. Karuppiah Nadar maternal uncle of Kamaraj, was running a cloth store at Virdhupatti. It because his duty to help Kamaraj's family.

Ganesh Chathurthi was celebrated at Chatria Vidhya Salai, where Kamaraj studied. During that period holy poojas were performed. Students used to join joyfully. Students were given Prasadams. Money was collected from every student for this pooja. In that day's pooja one-and-a-half anas were given by the student.

Kamaraj also gave his share. He went to pooja and prayed the God too. At the end Prasadams was given with a severe instruction they should get prasadam only in Q. But students were pushing each other to get the prasadam and went home in a joyfull mood.

Kamaraj did not entangle himself in the rush, he stood in a corner. He stood in that corner with hope of getting the prasadam for his share of money. He was noticed by the person who distributed prasadams when the crowd was thin. Kamaraj got only a little quantity and even in that some items were missing.

He went home with what he got. His grand mother saw the little quantity and questioned him where others got a large amount.

Kamaraj asked her back why should they given him a little quantity where he has given a equal share of money and has he to fight for it like others. His grand mother said however he should have got it first like others. Kamaraj questioned back to his Grand mother that he too gave money like others and was it the duty of the teacher to him his part of the share properly and why he did not do it.

Grandmother shut her mouth on hearing the rebutting questions. It was a new experience to the old lady. It was also quite new to her the nature of Kamaraj that differed from others of his age group. Perhaps she knew not that Kamaraj laid a foundation for his future to fight against the big shots who thronged for power and status and spread the equality.

Predicaments and Achievements

The leader Kamaraj had managed the crisis and predicaments cleverly. In ordinary days and in peaceful time any one can be the leader. But when there are crisis, problems and strikes, leading with big responsibilities is a difficult to any body. Kamaraj did that achievements many times. It is not an exaggeration that his experience he had at the streets of Virudhunagar seeded and exampled to this. One day the Temple elephant weir off the control of its trainer and a calamity was about to happen. Kamaraj saw this. Public was running shelter. Kamaraj saw that there was no chain in the trunk of the elephant. He ran to the temple and brought the chain and threw it towards the elephant. All these happened in lighting speed. The elephant cooled down and Kamaraj led that to the temple.

Due to the friendship of the Mahout Marriappan Thevar Kamaraj used to give fruits tot his elephant. This friendship was helpful to control the elephant whenever it went out of control, i.e. on seeing Kamaraj it became soft and lame.

Political Call

He stopped his education at his 12th year when he was studying sixth standard. He was at Trivandrum and Bodinayakanur in shops for few years. His attention was not in business and he started concentrating in freedom fighters speech. So he came to Virudhunagar.

He used to read newspapers and shared the news with his friends. Then K. S. Muthuswamy was his intimate friend.

It was the period when congress committee was going towards freedom fight. There were two groups in congress. One was optimisers and the other one extremist.

Dr. Vardarajulu Naidu, V. Kalyana Sundara Mudaliar and George Joseph conducted meetings at Virdhupatti and delivered speeches in which Kamaraj participated.

It was the end of first world war. He read the newspapers daily and saw the invitation of Gandhiji for Dharna against Roulette Act on 6th April of 1919. It was the period when VOC navigated own ship, due to Home Rule Movement the British duped the people by dual Government and caused Punjab Massacre - Kamaraj became a full time worker of Congress.

Turning Point

Punjab Massacre made a turning point in Kamaraj's life and his aim was to put an end to British rule.

The family members sent Kamaraj to his uncle at Trivandrum with a fear that he may involve himself in the political uproar. There too he joined Vaikam revolution but was not arrested. On seeing this he was brought back to Virudhunagar by his uncle Karuppaiah Nadar.

Kamaraj entered again in Law Disobedience in 1920 when Non-cooperative Movement led by Gandhiji.

Teacher's View

Mr. Sargunam the teacher of Kamaraj knew that Kamaraj will be having a bright future in politics.

He said that in 40 years experience of teaching profession where 3 generation learned. Only Mr. Kamaraj earned a prestige to Mother, Native place, and teacher and his is the only Model student "I used to advise that little boy who ran to me on my call, born in a simple family not having interest in studies to study well. But he was interested only in Dharna, Gandhiji, etc. and used to propaganda the same between students. On seeing this I came to a conclusion in one day he will take a big post in politics in future."

As to his expectation Kamaraj stopped his education and entered in politics seriously. In due course his student became a respectable SIR KAMARAJ. He found no change in Kamaraj's simplicity, affection and obedience.

When Kamaraj visited along with high Government officials, few Ministers and Big-shots saw the teacher amid the crowd enquired his welfare and introduced him to the surrounded. There was no change in his manners.

The Teacher's mind was overwhelmed when thinking that a person who born in an ordinary family came up by hard work and in notable position in the nation was his student.

Political Services

Only on reading the speeches in Newspapers about self-Government Patriotism sprang the mind of Kamaraj. He participated in General Meeting conducted in the Town. Some days he organised general meetings. He was attracted in political strikes. He became a member in Tamil Nadu Congress. He gathered public for Congress propaganda. He collected money from public at the Railway station, public places, market, etc. He organised meetings and promoted patriotism.

During those days he explained politics to his friends. Though there were incidents of stone throwing at his meetings he never retreated. Rather his interest grew more. According to some people Virdhunagar was known as "Fort of Justice Party". This imagination got demolished. He send friends to the meetings of Justice party and never failed to rebut at his meetings.

Since he developed patriotism in the public against Justice party he was in the vision of police. It was induced by some of Justice party. He also conducted meetings in the near by villages and towns. He used to go by in the evening and returned at mid-night. Sometimes he spent the night only with a cup of water. He used to go to Madurai often which is 27 miles form Virdhunagar. He engaged himself in selling Khadi. His national work had become a challenge to Justice party.

Proposal

Kamaraj participated in the Non-cooperation Movement in 1920. Gandhiji stopped it all in a sudden. But not in Tamil Nadu. Followers of Congress staged Dharna before "Arcak" Shop. His severe participation made his mother to afraid as he was the only son. Hence she and his maternal uncle Karuppaiah Nadar proposed to get him married. They arranged everything including the Bride and the date of marriage. Kamaraj returned from out station and saw the arrangement. His patriotic sense made him wild. For the time-being the proposals was stopped but not for ever. Again it came up. But Kamaraj was against of everything and he stood as a bachelor till the end of his life and served for the nation. He was selected as a state committee member one among the five in 1922.

Patriotism and Broken Friendship

Hurdles and plots gave him interest and strength. He got wounded by belie stones but never discouraged. He took it as his daily routines. He was insulted by his enemies. Even he was called as a Black sheep. But they came to him at a latter stage after independence for their benefits. He never went down as expected by his enemies.

He faced so many hurdles, troubles caused by his enemies but never lost himself. Once, a friend who helped Kamaraj on many occasions was addicted to 'Arrack'. When Kamaraj came to know this he avoided his friendship.

A Soldier

In 1923 he staged a Dharana before Toddy shop. All were arrested at the Congress office except him since was not on the spot as he got out to supervise the Dharna. He very much felt for that.

During those days there was a ban to carry knife more than 6" blades. Kamaraj decided to disobey to that order of British and conducted a revolution. That spread to Madurai. To conduct the same at Madurai he prepared 5 Swords. People came from Madurai to Virudhunagar. When the procession was about to start some hesitated. Swords prepared for them was with Kamaraj. On seeing then he sang a son of Bharathi and started dancing. It shacked the entire town of Virdhunagar Swords gave clinging sound.

The then Law minister Sir. C. P. Ramaswamy Iyer allowed to carry swords places except Malabar Region in order to stop the revolution in Tamil Nadu.

After the Non-cooperation Movement a problem arise. Whether to go to Assembly or not. Desabandhu Chitranjandas, Motilal Nehru, S. Srinivasa Iyengar, Bulabai Desai and Sathya Moorthy joined together. Started Swaraj Party. They want to enter into Parliament. But Rajaji opposed it. Kamaraj obeyed the decision of Congress and did not work with Sathyamoorthy.

In 1926 election he went Sri Vaikundam, Nasereth and Arel along with the followers.

Kamaraj came forward to conduct a revolution after the arrest of leaders like Saminatha- Mudaliar, Somayajulu since trying to remove the statute of Gen. Neel who tortured the participants of Army Revolution in 1857.

In 1927, when Gandhiji came to Chennai Kamaraj consulted him about the revolution for removing the statute of Gen. Neel. Gandhiji advised him to do it without any force just like pelting clay over the statute. But it was stopped due to boycotting Simon Commission.

Kamaraj conducted a conference under the name of "Indian Democratic Congress" presided by Nehruji who came to Chennai in 1927 after finishing the tour of Europe.

On 1937 as one day the statute of General Neel was removed and kept at Museum. When it was questioned at the Assembly Rajaji gave a Brick but answer the statute is of their own and could be kept anywhere. There came a full stop to the matter.

In 1928, a commission under the leadership of Sir John Simon came to India. All the political parties started Boycotting the same and flagged the Black flag. With an uproar asking the commission to return back. The Government handled the situation severely. Nehruji was assaulted. The 64 years old Lala Rajpathi Rai got wounded and died in the prison.

The commission came to Madurai and nobles patterned the Government joined at Thirumalai Naicker Palace. Patriotic public of Madurai aroused.

Many people with black flag in hands invaded the Mahal shouting the Simon to go back. They were stopped by the ruling powers. Kamaraj came there in a car in which a Tricolour flag was hoisted. Along with him there came the famous Congress leader George Joseph. They observed the situation and organised the volunteers. Kamaraj and George Jospeh led them. Police got stunned on seeing the crowd.

In 1929, the Conservative party lost the election and the Labour party came to in rule. At that time Jatheenthranath went on fast opposing the way in which political prisoners were treated in Jail in India. He last his life in that fast. This provoked Kamaraj. He preferred independence when Gandhiji was alive.

Marriage of a Friend

In 1930 K. S. Muthuswamy, a friend of Kamaraj had been to Kaitharu on the requisition of his uncle and happened to marry his daughter under unavoidable circumstances for which he invited Kamaraj. Kamaraj too went to the marriage Police shadowed him. It was usual on those days a police tail was kept behind him wherever he goes.

In March 1930 Gandhiji started Civil Disobedience Movement to break Salt Laws. People marched to Dandi under the leadership of Gandhiji in North and Vedharanyam in South under the leadership of Rajaji. The whole country joined together and shouted to abolish tax on salt. Government took stringer action. Newspapers censored. Leaders were arrested. Power of Gandhiji was known to the world. Public were lathi charged. Western countries hated the arrogant behaviour of British government. Even the British people condemned the act of the Government.

Kamaraj took part in Salt Sathyagraha. He was arrested by the police. He was imprisoned for 2 years. It was his first arrest. He was kept in Alipuram jail. The prisoners at Alipuram jail were release 1 hour a day. There was a tree in with a hole in that garden. Kamaraj wrote a slip for his needs and kept in the hole. Kumbakkonam Goplakrishnan used to go there take out the paper and acted according to the instructions. It went on for several months.

The jail authorities were in surprise they did not know how Kamaraj could able to get his needs. But they came to know about the hole in that tree and tried trap Gopalakrishnan. But Gopalakrishnan escaped from there and came back to Kumbakkonam, where he was arrested for the first time. On hearing the arrest of Kamaraj his Grand mother took ill. She was bedridden. Volunteers of Virudhunagar Congress were thirsty for his release.

Duraiswamy Nadar other went to Alipuram jail informing about the health condition of his grandmother and asked him to come on parole. But he refused. He was released in 1931 under Gandhiji-Irwin pact. He came to Virudhunagar. Public took him in a procession from railway station to his house which a mile away. Such a huge procession was never seen at Virudhunagar there before. He was asked to address a few words to the public. He accepted. In his address he thanked the public for the felicitation and asked them to pray god that he should not get proud. It was his first speech. His first stage speech was at Elinga Naaiackan patti which was 5 miles away from Virudhunagar.

Habit of Having Folded Towel on Shoulder

Health condition of Parvathy Ammal became worse. The desire to see the grandson had made her to hold her life. Few days after the release of Kamaraj his grand mother expired. Kamaraj performed the cremation. There was a change in him after that. A week after the death of his grand mother he used to have a folded towel on his shoulder.

Work in Congress

Tug of War with Rajaji

Kamaraj was called as a king-maker by foreigners 35 years ago. Since as he was having the capacity of doing anything in the party he had this title. He did this achievement in 1931 itself. Congress committee conference was held at Madurai in 1931. There were two parties in Congress then. One was headed by Sathyamoorthy and the other by Rajaji. Poor were on the side of Sathyamoorthy. Hence others neglected this group. Kamaraj got wild of this. He supported Sathyamoorthy. As Sathyamoorthy was the leader of the Conference he was taken in a procession in which the group of Rajaji did not participated. After the meeting the election for Tamil Nadu Congress Party presidentship was conducted.

Dr. Varadarajulu Naidu, Thiru. V. Kaliyana Sundara Mudaliar, E. V. R. Periyar and Srinivasa Iyengar left Congress. At the end of the conference there was a proposal to elect Rajaji as President of PCC and Sathya moorthy as Vice-President. Accordingly Rajaji was elected as President. But in the case of Vice-President Sathyamoorthy was elected as Vice-President only after some tussle as Rajaji's group betrayed the proposal. Sathyamoorthy's group captured the working committee.

The working committee was completely taken over by the group of Sathyamoorthy and Rajaji had to act only as a President without any power in that year since Sathyamoorthy's group had the full control of working committee. This had happened only because of the sincere and severe work of Kamaraj. This task was not a big affair to Kamaraj who was able to control a wild elephant at his boyhood. The working committee had the power to decide the fate of the party.

Cases Filed

In 1931 Round Table Conference was held at London. Gandhiji participated in that. But the result was nil. Again Britishers handled oppressed in India. Many leaders were arrested. Case was filed against Kamaraj. He refused to pay the penalty. He was imprisoned for an year. Kamaraj was in the jail at Trichy. Later he was transferred to Vellore Jail. There he meet Jaidev Kapur and Kamalnath Divari who were friends of Bagath Singh, who were imprisoned in case of Bagath Singh.

Since Kamaraj met the prisoners who were arrested in the case for plot a case for plot was filed against him in 1933.

Police tried to include the name of Kamaraj in the case of Composite State Plot under the name of Chennai Plot. Police pleaded that Kamaraj, Arunachalam and others tried to shoot Sir John Anderson, Governor of Bengal who was staying at Ooty, and for that Kamaraj gave 2 revolvers to Arunachalam. Since this case failed they filed another case of Plot against him. It was Bomb blast at Srivilliputhur-Virudhunagar Police station.

In this case K. S. Muthuswamy was accused, Kamaraj the second and Reporter Marriappan as third accused. Narayanaswamy as fourth accused. Venkatachalam turned as approver.

At Virudhunagar Bombay show was conducted. Muthuswamy was in that show upto night 2 o'clock along with the Sub-Inspector of Police Mr. Anantha Ramakrishnan. Only on that night Bomb throw case was fabricated.

A CID Inspector by name Thothari Iyengar came from Madras to fabricate this false case The Sub-Inspector Anantha Ramakrishnan was instructed to five false witness. But he refused. Hence he was transferred to some other place. DSP, Sivakasi , Parthasarathy Iyengar (Later he was the IG of Madras State) took active part in fabricating the case.

Police obtained a statement from approver Venkatachalam by torture and submitted the same in the court. But Venkatachalam explained the same before the judge. Leader George Joseph, brother of the famous Newspaper Editor Pothan Jospeh argued for Kamaraj and Muthuswamy and won the case. The magistrate J. P. S. Manro who presided acquitted Kamaraj and others from this case stating that the evidences filed by the police were not satisfactory. At that time Gandhiji was touring Tamil Nadu and stayed at Rajapalayam in the house of Kumaraswamy Raja and asked Dr. T. S. S. Rajan to conduct the case vigorously.

Rajan too helped very much for the victory of the case When the case was filed police went to the house of Kamaraj for search. Kamaraj was not there. His mother did not allow the police to enter into the house. When there no male member. Only after a male relative was called in she allowed them. Police could not get anything.

The trial went on few months. Had the judgement was on the other side. Nation would have lost the last heir of Gandhiji.

Golden Jubilee of Congress was celebrated on 28th December of 1935. A book of "History of Indian National Congress" written by Pattabi Seetharamaiah was released on that day. Even at Virudhunagar it was celebrated under the direct supervision of Kamaraj.

Murder Attempt

In 1936 the life of Kamaraj had been a turning point of Tamil Nadu. At the Congress committee election held at Karaikudi Sathyamoorthy was elected as President and Kamaraj as Secretary. All activities were done with the help and suggestion of Kamaraj. In 1936 Pandit Nehru toured Tamil Nadu. Sathayamoorthy and Kamaraj went along with him. British Government conducted the first election with a hope that the Justice Party would defeat Congress and that may result loosing of Victory throughout India. But they did not know that this election would intricate the youth for Independence and the control over party by Sathyamoorthy wood give many in formations. Also they did not know that this would seed the youth Kamaraj would fight for Independence.

Acid Throw against Kamaraj

In 1937 Assembly election held Kamaraj contested from Sathur. Virudhunagar came under Sathur constituency. There were two constituencies in Sathur. One is reserve and the other is general. Kamaraj in Congress and Ramaswamy in Justice Party contested in General constituency.

In reserve constituency Manickam of Congress party contested against Meenambal Sivaraj. Ramaswamy withdrew his nomination against Kamaraj before election. Kamaraj was only the candidate. Even then election was conducted. In those days each party was given a colour. Congress was given Yellow colour ballot box. Election propaganda were on. 3 candidates for 2 constituencies . Kamaraj and Manickam won.

Kamaraj was taken on procession in a Chariot around the tank. When the chariot went on the Southern bank of the tank nitric acid bulbs were hurled against Kamaraj. But they did not fall on Kamaraj. Villagers got wild. Procession reached Desabandhu maidaan.

Rajaji's Plot and Kamaraj's Disappointment

Kamaraj expected Sathyamoorthy to win in the assembly election and form ministry. As Rajaji entered in the last stage it did not happen. Sathyamoorthy wanted to contest in the graduates constituency. But friends like Hindu Srinivasan and others asked

Sathyamoorthy to give up that constituency for Rajaji and Sathyamoorthy magnanimously gave it to Rajaji. In Central ministry opposition member struggled of Sathyamoorthy's talents and speech. So he was asked to be a member there itself. But an assurance was given to him to include him in Chennai Ministry if formed.

Sathyamoorthy left to Delhi before formation of Ministry. Before leaving he meet Rajaji. Rajaji asked him not to contest for assembly since he would be included in the ministry through council.

On the way to Delhi Sathyamoorthy met Sardar Patel. Patel informed him that the ministry at Madras headed by Rajaji was formed without Sathyamoorthy. T. S. S. Rajan was nominated for council and appointed as a minister. Sathyamoorthy informed Patel about Rajaji's assurance and how he cheated him. It was a great disappointment to Kamaraj. He thought they revenged his Political teacher.

Bharat Ratna Kamaraj

"Every person who has any intelligence, initiative or enterprise will be encouraged to engage himself in productive enterprise for the benefit of the nation", said K. Kamaraj in his presidential address at the 68th Session of Indian National Congress at Bhubaneshwar in 1964. These epoch-making words are amazingly relevant today in the backdrop of globalisation and encouragement for private initiative.

Born in a poor family at a small place called Virudhunagar in the southern part of Tamil Nadu on July 15, 1903, Kumaraswamy Kamaraj is one of those selfless, dedicated and visionary freedom fighters whose sacrifice and service not only won us freedom but also led the nation into the path of self-reliance and all-round development.

Bharat Ratna, Kamaraj was first jailed in March 1930 when he participated in the Salt Satyagraha at Vedaranyam and was sentenced to a two-year imprisonment at Alipore jail. Then onwards, British jails literally became another home for Kamaraj who spent over 3,000 days there for taking part in freedom struggle.

Prison life helped him develop contacts with various leaders and freedom fighters from different parts of the country and he utilised his time in self-education through books. In 1940, when Kamaraj was in Vellore jail, he was unanimously elected as Chairman of Virudhunagar Municipal Council. On his release after nine months, Kamaraj went straight to the Municipal office and tendered his resignation stating, "One should not accept any position to which one could not do full justice".

Trained by the great parliamentarian and freedom fighter, S. Sathyamurthi, who found in him "an efficient, loyal, indefatigable worker and a skilful organiser", Kamaraj was elected as the President of the Tamil Nadu Congress Committee in 1940 and continued in that position till 1954. He was member of the Congress Working Committee from 1947 to 1969.

Kamaraj was elected to the Constituent Assembly of India in 1946 and to the Lok Sabha in 1952. He became member of the Madras Legislative Assembly in 1937 and 1946 and was sworn-in as the Chief Minister of Madras on April 13, 1954.

As the Chief Minister of Madras State for nine successive years, Kamaraj laboured hard to transform the State into a model State of the country. His no-nonsense approach towards administration and issues concerning the common people and his sterling perception of the complexity of the rural India helped Tamil Nadu attain a massive socio-economic transformation in full conformity with the Nehruvian vision. Kamaraj's approach towards development was statesman-like and was astonishingly identical to that of Rajiv Gandhi who said, "In the final analysis, the development is not just about factories, dams and roads. Development is basically about people. The goal is people's material, cultural and spiritual fulfilment".

Kamaraj's rule, rightly acclaimed as the Golden Era of Tamil Nadu, led to massive industrialisation, rural electrification and unprecedented government investment in education. It may appear unbelievable, but it is true that during Kamaraj rule in Tamil Nadu, over 20 per cent of the total government revenue was spent towards education, as he was aware that investment in education is investment in future. He introduced free education up to high school level and provided free school uniform to poor students. In fact, he pioneered a free Midday Meal Scheme for primary school children, aided by the American voluntary organisation, CARE, in 1957, which has now become a national mission.

A visionary with his feet firmly on the ground Kamaraj had solutions for any difficult situation. When Pt. Nehru found that the post-Independence Congress was losing its mass appeal, he turned to Kamaraj who came out with the "Kamaraj Plan" under which senior Congress leaders in the Central and State governments resigned and took up party work. They included Lal Bahadur Shastri, Morarji Desai, Jagjivan Ram and S. K. Patil.

In 1964, Kamaraj was elected as the President of the All India Congress Committee and successfully navigated the nation through the stormy years following the sudden demise of Jawaharlal Nehru and his successor, Lal Bahadur Shastri. In recognition of his contribution to the nation during the freedom struggle and thereafter, the country's highest award Bharat Ratna was conferred on him in 1976.

Kamaraj was a shining example of simple living and high thinking. All through the years, he led a simple life, in fact, he was the only Chief Minister who stayed in a rented house in place of occupying a government bungalow. When he passed away on October 2, 1975, all Kamaraj left behind were ten sets of khadi dhotis and shirts and one hundred rupees under his pillow.

Global Relations and Up-Downs

There was a heavy crowd at the airport of Moscow on 22nd July of 1966 at 1.45 p.m. The President of "Supreme Soviet" Sprikinove, Vice-President John Thieve, External affairs Minister Brubin and other important officials, officials of Embassy and the public of Russia were waiting for the arrival of Kamaraj. The place in which Kamaraj went landed at Sharmythiyova Airport at Moscow. Kamaraj stepped at the land of Russia with smile. He answered in short to the welcome address of Russian Premier, Russians were surprised to see Kamaraj without any woollen clothes on him against the winter.

In Russia

He first visited the Russian Premier at his residence in a formal way. He had long discussion with Mayor of Moscow city which had a population of 65 lakhs.

23rd July was a busy day to Kamaraj. He visited the Kremlin Palace constructed during the period of King Jaar.

Lenin's Library

He wrote in the visitor's book as under:

> "I am happy to see the place where Lenin lived. I am delighted to see the place where that leader lived a life with simplicity."

He laid a wreath at the place where Lenin's body was preserved with oils. He felt very much with R. Venkatraman who stood near to him for not having preserved the body of Gandhiji like that of Lenin.

Meeting with Kosign

He next met the P. M. Kosign. Kosign's first question was whether he was not feeling the winter. Kamaraj's reply was, he was there as he was in Delhi. Then those two leaders discussed about the international problems for about 11/2 hours. Later he visited the Inton Thushanpe Park.

On 25th July he met Mr. Rasalove, the secretary of Tajic Communist Party. He also met the workers of that party office. Kamaraj was surprised to learn that members of the Communist party should donate a part of their income to the party and accordingly Mr. Rasalove too gave it to the party.

26th July he went to Valgagrade City where Russians fought against Hitler. He was invited by the Mayor of the city and was taken to a park and a war memorial place.

He said to the Mayor that when he saw the city he could understood that the people of that city were not only a brave warriors but also a hard workers.

Then he visited the historical famous Lenigrade. He took part in the feast given by the Mayor of that city. In his speech at the feast he praised the Russian leader Lenin and the Russian revolution. Also he sang a song in Tamil written by Tamil poet Bharathi. About the King Jaar. He also said that India would cooperate with Russia to save the world from the evil of war.

Again he left for Moscow. On 30th July he met Mr. Kapinove, the secretary of Soviet Communist Party at Moscow. He learned from him the Party's principles and activities and its power.

The last person he met at Russia was Mr. Brishnove, the Chief Secretary of the Communist party, which was the very very important post in Russia.

Brishnove was on leave then. He was about to return to Moscow only on 1st of August but returned on 29th July itself. Brishnove was to met Mr. Uthand, the UNO Secretary from 11.00-12.00 noon and to met Kamaraj after 12 noon. He went that office which was protected by armed forces at 12 noon. Kamaraj was given a royal salute and taken to the room of Brishnove. He received Kamaraj with smile and talked to him. Since his Russian tour was almost over, the Supreme Soviet Leader Sprithinove, who was with Kamaraj all along the tour gave an official dinner to Kamaraj.

On Sunday the 31st July he was to leave from Russia. In the morning, before his departure, he delivered a speech in the radio of Moscow praising the hospitality of the Russians and the good relationship they had with Indians. At 2 p.m. he completed his 10 days Russian tour and left for East Germany. Mr. Sprithinove gave him a send off at the airport. Kamaraj landed at "Shon Belt" airport at Berlin the Capital city of East Germany on 31st July. Dr. Erry Sams, the national leader of East Germany, Mr. Stiby, the Deputy Minister for External affairs, The Trade Union Representative of East Germany for India Mr. Sherbert Fisher, invited Kamaraj at the air port. There was a heavy down pour when he landed. The reception programmes went on ignoring the rain.

Dr. Herbert Fisher was with Kamaraj throughout the tour.

On 1st August Kamaraj met Albert Morttan, Herman Medorn, the key personnel of the United Socialist Front at their office. He also met a student at East Germany who was studying Tamil. He thanked the leaders and the public of East Germany and left for Czechoslovakia.

In Czechoslovakia

On 2nd of August when he landed at Praha City he was received by the Socialist Party Leader, Law and Legal Department Minister Mr. Alias Newman and other government officials and the Indian Ambassador Mr. Gokak. He met Mr. Cadar, the secretary of Communist Party Central Committee of that country, Minister for External affairs, Interim PM and the Vice-President of the Parliament. He learned about the standard of living of the people of that country through so many questions with them. On 5th August Indian Ambassador gave a feast to the leader. Students who studied Tamil there, Ministers came to the dinner. Then he left for Hungary.

In Hungary

He landed at Budapest the Capital of Hungary on 4th August. He agreed for a tour of 3 days due to continued compulsions of those people. On the fist day he visited the Budapest city and its surrounding places. Next day morning he met the Hungarian PM at the Parliament palace. Mrs. Banoj Bahova, the assistant general secretary of people's front joined in the meeting. Official dinner was given after the meeting. Kamaraj next went to Bulgaria.

In Bulgaria

At 2 p.m. on August 7th he landed at Sophiya the Capital of Bulgaria. All the Bulgarian leaders received Kamaraj and took him to the guest house. He paid homage with wreath to the body of George Tito, Father of Bulgaria which was preserved with oils. Next day he met Mr. Stryhop, the leader of the ruling party "Country Front of Father." A dinner was given to him on that night and he left for Yugoslavia.

In Yugoslavia

When Kamaraj landed at Belgrade the capital of Yugoslavia on 8th August he was given a grand reception by the leader of Socialist Alliance and the President of Macedonia. Mr. Golia Sebaski and his assistants. He met Golia Sebaski and the planning commission members at the head office of the Yugoslavia central committee. Indian Ambassador gave a feast to Kamaraj. He left in a special flight on August 10th to met Marshal Tito who lived in an island called Bryony. He rested for a while in Neptune hotel at Bryony sea shore, later left to meet Marshal Tito. No news reporters were allowed. Only Kamaraj, R. Venkataraman and the Indian Ambassador went to Tito's Bungalow. With Marshal Tito, Golia Sebaski and a Deputy minister were there.

Meeting with Tito

On seeing Kamaraj Tito eagerly gave his hands to him. Tito remembered his at Avadi Conference and the crowd and Traffic blocks. Later they discussed the world problem. After one hour's discussion Tito said that he would met him at Delhi at the meeting of the Non-alliance Countries.

Kamaraj completed his 20 days tour on 12th August. Many leaders came to the airport and gave him the send off. Kamaraj said that tour gave him a chance of knowing many important matters and was very useful.

He left in a Yugoslavian plane which flew via Rome *en route* to Delhi.

Indian flight took off since the Yugoslavian flight was late. This caused Kamaraj to stay at Rome for 2 days. Because of this delay he could reach India only on 15th August at the 21st Independence day instead of 13th as scheduled before.

Madras Tremored

Though the arrival of the flight was only at 1.30 p.m. people of Madras crowded the air port right from the morning. Crowds were throughout the way to the air port. Once he landed from the flight, a plane showered the flowers on him from the sky. People were running to garland him. He was taken in procession in an open car. 120 soldiers of Cavalry marched before the car. His car was followed by number of cars and thousands of cycles. Madras had never seen such a procession so far.

Mr. K. R. Nayar who worked in PTI once asked Lal Bhagadhur Shastri about Indo-Ceylon Agreement. He questioned whether the next government would honour the agreement entered between Indian and Ceylon by Shastri and Sri Mao Bandranayake.

Shastri hesitated to answer. But Kamaraj immediately answered to the reporter which gave him a surprise. Because it was in clear English, which is given below:

> "Don't go and print any such suggestions in the paper. This is an agreement signed by two Democratic governments, just as any Democratic government India would honour this agreement. We expect any successor government in Ceylon to honour this agreement."

Shastri said with joy, "I agree with Kamaraj". It was a proof of his political knowledge about the international affairs.

There was a Congress conference in February 1966. His foresight was very clean.

He pointed out his talk at the conference of Bhuvaneshwar about to start new industries to produce essential commodities to the poor to control price hike. In his presidential speech he also said that it would be essential to take steps by the central and state government to stabilise the economic conditions and to minimise the expenditure. He also requested for the cooperation of the public.

Attack at Delhi House

On 7th November 1966 a procession came towards Kamaraj's house at Delhi. They are the opposers of Cow slaughting. Some people in the procession engaged in violence. Kamaraj was in the house then. This gang robed the house of Central minister Raguramaiah. They set fire to the house of Kamaraj. This had happened within 15 minutes.

First the gang damaged the compound gate and entered. A lone constable who was there could not stop the gang. They pelted stones on the windows since the door was locked. They set fire to the rooms through the windows. Kamaraj was in centre of the hall without any fear. His bed room was damaged due to fire. By god's grace he escaped. On hearing this news MPs came running to Kamaraj and took him with them to their place. He stayed there for few days and then came back to his house.

The incident of Nov. 7th was seriously discussed at the working committee meeting. They blamed Nanda the Home Minister. Following this Nanda resigned. PM Indira Gandhi accepted his resignation immediately. Defence minister Chavan took the portfolio of Nanda. Indira Gandhi gave complete freedom to Kamaraj to shuffle the ministry.

Kamaraj felt that the number of ministers to be reduced as the general election was fast approaching.

Including the incident of Nov. 7th all the events of 1966 made the future as a question mark. Kamaraj felt very much for this. He thought that the Congress should take immediate decisions to some serious problems. He felt that food condition, internal security and peace should immediately be taken care. In December he informed this to his colleagues. During this time Kamaraj observed the in disciple in the party. The clashes between the various state Chief Ministers worried him. 12 Ministers resigned at Orissa having difference of opinions with the CM Kamaraj returned their resignation an saved the discipline of the party. Kamaraj met the challenge when Rival Congress started in West Bengal, Orissa and Madhya Pradesh. He thought that the public would not believe the promise of the opposite parties though there were shortages in food and other commodities.

He involved himself in election propaganda and toured the entire nation in 1967 election. A gang of news reporters went along with him. He explained the economic condition of the country in every state. Seeing his common sense the newspapers praised him in their editorials. Ashok Mehta joined in Congress only when Kamaraj was the AICC president. Kamaraj was the only reason for his joining in Congress.

He contested at Virudhunagar constituency for assembly in 1967 general election. He toured the other constituencies in Tamil Nadu without working in his constituency.

He met with an accident when he was going towards Tirunelveli. News came as he got serious injuries. Immediately M. S. P. Raja, Iya Swamy Nadan and other went in a car to Tirunelveli. Kamaraj was at the Travellers Bungalow of Palayamkottai. He had severe injuries on his leg and lips. His face was swelled. When these people saw him with tears on their eyes he enquired them about election work. He explained them the way they have to work. Also he said that he would come a week before the election and do the work in person. But he could not come. From Tirunelveli he went straight away to Madras.

Shortage in Rice in Madras State caused defeat to Congress. The elephant slipped. Kamaraj lost by a difference of 500 votes. This election result shook India. The entire nation shocked to see his first and last defeat. But Kamaraj never shattered. Not only in Madras state Congress was defeated but in many parts of India. Congress could get only the majority to form the government.

Kamaraj who used to say to worship the work only and not the money, took his defeat lightly and left to Delhi. He could not walk. He had walking stick in his hands. He walked slowly with his stick at Delhi air port. His face did not indicate the sign of defeat. He said that he accepts the defeat of Congress and respects the judgement given by the public and he would work hard to win the confidence of the public. He made Indira Gandhi as PM for the second time. He seated Morarji Desai as Deputy PM C. N. Annadurai, who formed the DMK ministry said that the leader like Kamaraj should not get defeated. He went with his colleagues to the residence of Kamaraj for his blessings. Kamaraj had the capacity to attract even the opposite party members. He ordered to his party people not to open their mouth for a period of 6 months about DMK government as the public gave them a chance to rule.

Newspapers wrote that his magnanimity was an example to the affection towards democracy. Papers wrote that he fixed a golden letter in the history of the world.

Independence day was celebrated in 15th August 1967. It was first independence day after freedom that Congress celebrated and by sitting in opposition at the assembly.

Election of Nijalingappa

Kamaraj was AICC president twice from 1964 to 1967 continuously. During this 4 years period he did his service strongly. He never entangled himself in the policy matters. He exposed the difference of opinion in the policy matters if any, only at the party meetings. Even in that he never entered in lame arguments.

He acted according to the views raised in the meeting. He never created any problems. His position was simple. He approached the problems only with a view whether the public could get any benefit out of it. His presidential speeches and achievements were the evident.

He did not like to be AICC president for the third time. For the post of president there would be a severe contest between S. K. Patil and Alulya Gosh.

Kamaraj informed that whoever might be elected by they should be elected unanimously. That only would safeguard the interest of the party. Pattil, Mohan Dharia, Hanumanthaiah had failed their nomination for the post of AICC president. PM Indira Gandhi and Kamaraj meet and discussed about the election for President. They talked about Sukadia, Nanda, Sanjeevaiah, U. M. Thevar for the election of AICC president. At last Kamaraj sent a message to Mysore. Nijalingappa went to Delhi and met Kamaraj. It was nigh hours. Kamaraj said that Nijalingappa would be the next AICC president and asked him to meet him on the next morning.

Finally Nijalingappa took charge as AICC president. The interim poll came at Nagarkoil in January 1969 due to the death of Marshal Nesamani. To find out the situations of the constituency Nedumaran and Sironmani toured the entire constituency. Kamaraj carefully heard what those two lads told him. They wanted Kamaraj should definitely contest there. Others also insisted Kamaraj. Kamaraj accepted the request of the younger generation. In the interest of the party he was ready to enter into an experiment. He addressed in a general meeting at KARUNGAL on 30th November 1968. At that time he conveyed his acceptance to contest for MPs election.

Interim poll was conducted on 8th January 1969. People of CapeCamrion worked for his victory. The entire Tamil Nadu was there. Kamaraj pinned the badge on his body. Ladies received Kamaraj with enthusiasm. Kamaraj won in the election with a margin of 1,28,201 votes.

Mother's ill-health

Kamaraj received a message about the bad health condition of his mother. He went by flight to Madurai and by car to Virudhunagar. He was informed that his mother was in death bed. He never got tensioned, he was talking to Nedumaran as usual. He sat near his mother who was in a swooned condition. His arrival was informed to her by his sister. She opened her eyes and saw Kamaraj with tearful eyes. He enquired about her diet and medicines with his sisters. His mother wanted to tell something, but could not. Kamaraj told her that he would be leaving. His mother wanted him to have food and go. He said that he would have it at Madurai. His mother wept again. Kamaraj saw this and asked his sisters to set the meal. His mother wanted him to sit and eat at the kitchen. As he did not want to discard the request of his mother who was in the death bed went to kitchen and took the meal. He back a good-bye to his mother and left. On the way Nedumaran asked Kamaraj since how long after he took meat at his house. His reply was after 25 to 30 years.

In the Prison

Cases were filed on Congress volunteers in 1969. His victory was celebrated at Nagarkoil. There was procession. Friends of Madurai who participated in the procession were assaulted. One Mr. Pandurangam was stabbed. Nedumaran opposed this. Immediately police filed a case against him. Nedumaran met Kamaraj at Madurai air port and explained him the situation. He listened carefully and advised to oppose the injustice boldly.

Bad Time for Congress

There was problem for Congress in August 1969. Sanjeeva Reddy was the speaker. It was decided to nominate him for the election of President. Indira Gandhi made him to resign. She nominated him for the election and signed in the nomination form. But she herself supported V. V. Giri. Finally V. V. Giri became the President. Sanjeeva Reddy was defeated. Kamaraj and other senior leaders felt very much. For Kamaraj discipline was his breath. Congress working committee wanted to take action on those who did not obey to the party's discipline. When there was 2 months to the 84th Anniversary for AICC in 1969 Congress splitted into two. Though the Congress splitted into two Congress party men in Tamil Nadu were on the side of Kamaraj.

During freedom fight money was necessary to take part once in the strike. Kamaraj did not have the money. He decided to stage a Drama and collect money. He arranged for the Drama of Viswananthadas. 144 was imposed by the police and ordered not to stage the drama. In the drama a song of Viswanathadas used to humiliate the public. The ban order was imposed particularly for this song. Immediately Kamaraj sent Thirumangalam Puli Iyer to Sivakasi Sub-Collector for getting permission to stage the drama with an assurance of not signing that particular song in the drama,. According Puli Iyer got the permission.

Drama was staged at Rajapalayam. The situation became riots. Kamaraj sent his men wherever the riot took place and embedded them. In 1979 when Kamaraj expressed the grievances the ruling party challenged them. He met the challenges. He took action according to the pulse of the party men. He questioned the ruling party about their promise of giving 3 measures of Rice per Rupee and whether they could give it. He also blamed that they did not know what to do and did not know to tell what they could do. They had given cheap promises and the ministers said that they would work without salary, reduce the tax and increase the facilities. But what happened, increased tax.

In 1971 Congress met another great defeat. When he was asked about the election fund he said that there was money for the election work and they should have worked still harder. There was no people got victories like him, he never jumped high when he won and never lost himself when he was defeated. For the benefit of the poor he again started his tour throughout Tamil Nadu.

5

Character and Personality

A true follower of Mahatma Gandhi, Kumaraswamy Kamaraj was an ordinary man with extraordinary qualities of head and heart. From humble beginnings, he rose to the highest position of helping make two Prime Ministers of India, first Lal Bahadur Shastri and then Indira Gandhi. The demise of Nehru was expected to create a political void leading to instability of sorts, but Kamaraj as Congress president played the man of destiny, settling the succession issue amicably through a democratic consensus. It was perhaps the crowning glory of his life.

When he enlisted himself as a soldier in the freedom movement, he was totally under the spell of Mahatma Gandhi and to the very end he remained Gandhian by conviction and practice. There were occasions when he had his differences with Gandhi in running party affairs in Tamil Nadu but his loyalty to the Mahatma remained unwavering. For him Congress was the creed. All through his life, he was guided by native commonsense and that made him a real leader of the masses. He spoke to them in a language they understood. His speeches were embellished with ideas and not with grandiose eloquence. He was a man of simple habits and permitted himself the sole luxury of smoking a cigarette of relatively costly brand. Even this luxury he enjoyed in privacy and rarely in the company of his intimate friends.

Kamaraj was a multi-faceted political personality, and power and position sat lightly on him. He was Chief Minister of Tamil Nadu for nine years and that period was considered a "Golden Age". For him, power was only a means to serve the people and he served them well. He was a down-to-earth planner and visualised and executed an infrastructure that was essential to satisfy the needs of ordinary folk. He made education free up to the high school level and provided midday meals for school-going children to prevent dropouts on account of poverty. Only during his Chief Ministership did every village of a thousand people get a school. He laid roads connecting rural areas to urban centres, creating easy access for village produce to reach town and city markets.

He paid special attention to the energy sector and electricity reached almost all villages in Tamil Nadu. The power generation helped many industrial estates to come up and grow. The industrialisation of Tamil Nadu started in right earnest. He ruthlessly cut the red tape of bureaucratic inertia and his watchword was action and result. He appointed efficient officers as Heads of Department where dynamism and quick decision were essential. He had talented and hard-working men in a compact Cabinet of eight to assist him and mention should be made of C. Subramaniam, M. Bhaktava-tsalam and R. Venkataraman. Not personal loyalty but commitment to serving the people was the criterion he employed to select his Cabinet colleagues. The Tamil Nadu administration became a model for other States and no less a person than Prime Minister Jawaharlal Nehru openly acknowledged it.

Kamaraj was not only a great administrator. He was a strong organisation man as well. He rose from the grass-root level and, in his political life spanning more than half a century, there was no place in Tamil Nadu where he had not set foot. Under the tutelage of a great orator and parliamentarian, S. Satyamurti, he blossomed into full-fledged leadership. When he was elected president of the Tamil Nadu Congress Committee, he knew every region as he would know the palm of his hand. He had a retentive memory and knew every important party member by name. During the evening years of Nehru, the Congress started losing its vitality and the Prime Minister in declining health was a worried man. He was impatient to rejuvenate the Congress and consulted Kamaraj who came up with a plan, which was christened the K-Plan. The plan reflected the sacrificial attitude of Kamaraj to public life. Senior leaders holding offices of power were asked to quit and take up organisational work. Kamaraj set an example by giving up his Chief Ministership.

Kamaraj's elevation to the presidentship of the Congress at the instance of Nehru was a historical recognition of the man's national stature and capacity to steer the ship of the party in critical times. The choice was historical in more senses than one. After Nehru, he not only saved the Congress from immediate disintegration brought on by leadership squabbles but proved to the world the vibrancy of Indian democracy. His later confrontation with Prime Minister Indira Gandhi was a consequence of the inevitable power struggle between the organisation and the parliamentary wing of the party. It was also a reflection of the contradictory perceptions of the old guard and the new generation of leaders.

Kamaraj lost the battle to Indira Gandhi. The leaders who rallied around Kamaraj were a spent force; they wanted to continue their hegemony even after it had been played out. Kamaraj, a progressive, unfortunately aligned himself with the reactionaries, losing his colour and clout and getting politically marginalised. What is more, the Dravidian current in Tamil Nadu was so strong that it swept him off his feet in the 1967 elections. From then on he could not gather enough strength to meet the challenge. The political alignments and devices he tried desperately in Tamil Nadu did not work in his favour.

Kamaraj's life was one of total dedication and selfless service to the people. As a freedom fighter, he played a self-effacing role, shunning the limelight and taking upon himself risky and arduous jobs. Yet he was one of the noted targets of British repression. Though unschooled, he learned a lot in the treadmill of experience. His understanding of men and matters was impressive and his incisive brain always went into the root of the matter. Even for elusive problems, he found easy and practical solutions. As an administrator he sometimes waived rules and regulations when it was a question of granting immediate relief to suffering people.

He was easy to approach and even the lowliest felt at home in his presence. His hefty figure exuded humility and he carried a benign smile that disarmed his opponents and soothed the ruffled feelings of his detractors and critics. Basically, he was a consensus man, ever ready for reasonable compromises. There were occasions when he exhibited dictatorial streaks and stifled dissent; perhaps he felt they were needed to make mischief-mongers and trouble-makers fall in line.

Kamaraj showed little taste for the fine arts but saw to it that the state recognised and encouraged outstanding artists. He was frugal and lived a Spartan life. Wealth he desired for the nation, not for himself. For his aged mother at Virudhunagar, he sent a pittance of a hundred rupees every month. He visited her only when he happened to tour the area where she lived. He would stay with her for a few minutes, enquire after her health and take leave of her. He always stood by his political loyalists and evinced keen personal interest in the welfare of freedom fighters.

All through his political life, he had an excellent rapport with the press. He often invited eminent journalists to his house for a discussion on current matters. He used to say many things off the record and would listen patiently to the views of visiting journalists. He would not mind adverse criticism of his stand or policies by well-meaning journalists and he would ask probing questions to understand their point of view better. He was also aware of the power of the press and in spite of heavy odds, he was instrumental in running a Congress Tamil daily, Navashakti, for several years. There were some eminent editors who targeted him in their writings. He would tell his friends that the editors had no personal grouse against him but were trying to present their point of view in the larger public interest. He was convinced a free Fourth Estate was essential for the healthy functioning of democracy. During the time of Emergency, he was greatly annoyed with censorship of the Press.

Some critics accused Kamaraj of keeping a coterie around him all the time and listening to their advice. No doubt he had some personal friends who were non-political and naturally he might have looked to them for non-partisan views on certain issues.

Kamaraj had a mind of his own and it was rather difficult for anyone to pressurise him with their pet or slanted views.

He kept himself abreast of the latest developments, especially in the international arena. He was quite aware of his limitations in certain fields and was not shy about learning from others. As Chief Minister, he was credited with giving a patient hearing to the views of department officials to understand the nitty-gritty of administration. On some critical occasions, he would register his dissent by the eloquence of his silence.

Kamaraj had an uncanny talent for assessing men after a short acquaintance. In carrying his colleagues with him, he believed in consensus. In implementing programmes and schemes, he was ruthless to a fault. He was unsparing in extracting work from bureaucrats but at the same time treated them with respect. He had supreme self-confidence and could do business with any diplomat of international repute on equal terms. He was not conversant either with Hindi or English, but that did not stand in the way of his interacting with leaders at the national level. His grasp of the problems of the masses was extraordinary and that endeared him to the millions who looked up to him for alleviating their misery. His life was an illustration of how greatness and simplicity can go hand in hand.

As a leader and man, he had his own failings. He was wary of assertive intellectuals and tended to keep them at bay lest they should encroach on his political domain. He was also a master of manipulative politics and to ensure his political dominance, he would place powerful men in powerless places and vice-versa. He practised his own type of groupism and that worked to his advantage, until an assertive leader with an all-India image, Indira Gandhi, challenged it effectively. In Tamil Nadu politics, a younger generation of leaders emerged in the Dravidian movement who cleverly exploited all the mass media to strengthen their mass base. Kamaraj's decline began when he failed to strike a working equation with Indira Gandhi, who outsmarted him in his own game.

Nevertheless, Kamaraj's contribution to the freedom movement and the building of the nation was enormous. He left deep footprints in the political domain.

The Personality

Kamaraj is believed to have led a spartan life unlike most Indian politicians for whom politics is just an easy way to feather their nest.

Writing in The New York Times, the late Pulitzer Prize winning journalist J. Anthony Lukas described Kamaraj thus:

> "Kamaraj's real achievement, then, has not been in remaking the party but in manipulating the diverse and disputatious elements within it. His genius lies in dealing with men as they are, not in changing them, and this ability is based on a realistic assessment of human nature."

Books he Liked

Gandhiji's "Self Experiment", "Nehru's political life by Michale Britotsul", "Laski's political grammar", "Kamba Ramayanam" were the books he liked. An editor of a Tamil Daily met Kamaraj at Delhi. Kamaraj while invited him opened his suitcase and removed all the clothes inside. He saw the books like "Inside Africa", "Ends and Means" and C. V. Kandekar's "Treasure of Thoughts" and Magazines like "Time" and "News Week".

Kamaraj's mentality was the reason for his elevation in his life. We have seen so many leaders who were elevated to the top level in public life. The direct reasons for them would be different. Born in a high society, born in a rich family or due to high educational qualification might be the reasons for their coming up to a top level. But without any of there aforesaid reasons Kamaraj was the only leader who came to a top level only by his hard work.

Kamaraj was not only a renowned national leader but also he was internationally famed. His main aim of the plan was that every Congressman in power was to abide to the order of the working committee. They should be ready resign any post at anytime or to do anything the working committee wanted them to do.

The goal and the public service trend to Congressmen gone down when the Congress party came to power when compared as it was under the eminent leadership of Gandhiji. Kamaraj felt that they wanted to be ministers and powermongus. Kamaraj thought that they should resign their posts if they were to be service oriented.

He wanted to show it practically that there are so many other ways to serve public, Kamaraj desired that however only a few can be the ministers and should not envy it and they should serve for the nation in some other way. He decided to resign his Chief Ministership as a mark of his clean heart.

Change in History

The State Congress meeting was held at Batlagundu. For Muthurang Mudaliar's victory Kamaraj took special interest.

Municipal election was conducted at Virudhunagar Congress contested in 24 wards and won in 22 wards. Kamaraj won from the 7th ward. All the 21 councillors compelled Kamaraj to be the Chairman but he refused. Sankarapandia Nadar became Chairman.

In 1940 election for TNCP President Sathyamoorthy nominated Kamaraj. Rajaji nominated Kovai C. P. Subbiah.

Kamaraj got 103 votes and won by 3 votes. Those 3 votes changed the history of Tamil Nadu. A man who started his political life as a volunteer in 1919 became a President to the same party in 21 years. Once he was elected as a President public were interested in knowing his life history. They were attracted in his simplicity and sacrifice.

To help Kamaraj Sathyamoorthy took the post of Secretary.

During 2nd World War Aurther Hope, the Governor of Madras collected war fund from public. Kamaraj toured all over the state asking the public not to give war fund to foreigner. Hence war fund collection was disturbed. So Kamaraj was arrested under Security Act and sent to Vellore Jail. This was his 3rd Arrest.

People who come for Sathyagraha should have got the approval of Gandhiji. When Kamaraj went to Gandhiji with one such list for Gandhiji's approval he was arrested in the train at Gudur railway station.

According to the individual Satyagraha started by Gandhiji all municipal chairman should go to jail by breaking the law. Accordingly Sankarapanida Nadar Chairman of Virudhunagar went to jail.

Political Career

The political career of Kumaraswamy Kamaraj (1903-75) spanning about 50 years, cutting across the colonial and post-independent phases, of Indian history, is indeed an enviable record. Representing a novel political culture neither bordering on Gandhian thought and action nor possessing the anglicised sophistication and cosmopolitanism of the Nehruvian vision, Kamaraj, rose from an underprivileged background, stood forth as a sober and robust figure winning the confidence and respect of the common people.

He showed a rare political acumen and the uncanny ability to grasp social and political realities from the grass roots level upwards. A hard core political realist, his political life was never governed by any high theories or fancy jargon. Accredited with the capacity to be at ease with cliques, groups, factions and castes, Kamaraj applied his energies in favour of common people. Endowed with an extraordinary memory, his minimal formal schooling was never a serious impediment. In fact rarely could a man from such a humble origin possess such knowledge about Tamil Nadu, be it geography or ethnography, which is beyond most intellectuals and academicians.

Kamaraj rose from the lowest Congress ranks during the freedom struggle to become the president of the Tamil Nadu Congress Party for over 20 years (1940-63) interspersed by short intervals, the chief minister of Madras (1954-63) for nine years; and, as the president of the Indian National Congress (1964-67), he assumed the crucial role of 'king-maker'. Kamaraj's ascendancy is all the more significant because he belonged to the low caste Nadar community, which had a long history of struggle against social oppression and economic deprivation.

The Nadars, originally known as Shanars, were found principally in the two southern districts of Tirunelveli and

Kanyakumari. Palmyra climbing and toddy tapping were their traditional occupations. In the Hindu caste hierarchy the Nadars were ranked very low just above the untouchables and were forbidden entry into temples because of their association with alcohol. Mercantilism and Christianity played crucial roles in facilitating their upward mobility. Within a span of two centuries, they rose from near untouchability to a position of social and economic power. Though Kamaraj typified the Nadar success story he never was a leader of his community and transcended the bounds of Nadar caste identity dropping the caste title early in his political career.

Hailing from Virudhupatti (now Virudhunagar), one of the early settlements of migrant Nadars, Kamaraj, born in 1903 into an ordinary small scale Nadar business family, was a school dropout at the age of 11 and for a number of years never had steady and proper employment. Kumaraswamy Kamaraj evinced interest in politics at the age of 15 when the news of the Jallianwala Bagh massacre reached his ears. Responding to the call of Gandhiji's Non-cooperation Movement, Kamaraj entered the freedom struggle as a Congress volunteer organising meetings, processions and demonstrations. He soon found an abiding place for himself in the Congress ranks as a gritty grass roots level, full-time worker and mass leader of the Congress; and he was imprisoned a number of times for actively participating in the freedom struggle. He spent a total of eight years in British Indian jails during six spells of imprisonment.

When the Brahmin dominance in the Tamil Nadu Congress leadership was firmly entrenched and the rivalry between the two key Brahmin leaders, C Rajagopalachari and S Satyamurthi, was brewing, Kamaraj wove his way into the top echelons of the Tamil Nadu Congress organisation as the representative of the non-Brahmin enclave. The 'Brahmin image' of the Congress found its affirmation at the hands of Rajaji when he introduced compulsory Hindi in schools in 1938 when he was the chief minister.

This move was met with resentment and brought about an open confrontation between him and E. V. Ramaswamy in 1938. A massive anti-Hindi agitation was launched by E. V. Ramaswamy unleashing a vehement onslaught on the nexus between Rajaji, the Brahmin and Hindi, the 'Aryan language of oppression'. The statewide anti-Hindi campaign involved picketing schools, picketing in front of Rajaji's residence and hunger strikes. E. V. Ramaswamy was arrested in December 1938 and imprisoned for a year.

This confrontation sharpened the conflict between the non-Brahmins and Brahmins within the Congress organisation. The agitation was continued till Rajaji had to opt for making Hindi an optional subject in schools in February 1940. At this crucial moment, Rajaji's candidate, C. P. Subbiah, was defeated by K. Kamaraj with the support of the Brahmin leader, Satyamurthi. Kamaraj was elected as the president of the Tamil Nadu Congress in 1940, the post which he held till he became the chief minister of Tamil Nadu in 1954.

The advent of Kamaraj as the party boss from a low caste non-Brahmin background made a "powerful appeal to the vast non-Brahmin majority" and attracted the non-Brahmin elites and the political-minded elements "who had long resented the power and privileges" of the Brahmins, and broadened the social base of the Congress. The non-Brahmin presence in the Congress gained ground, rallying around Kamaraj, a 'rustic' leader who transformed the Congress into a people's party championing the causes of the lower castes. Kamaraj grew steadily from strength to strength displaying his organising skills to control men and matters. During these years his contact with the people and the respect he commanded made his position unassailable. The untimely death of Satyamurti in 1943 improved his position and gave him a further lease of power. With the Congress machinery under his control, he overshadowed his party men and effectively reduced the Brahmin dominance in the party.

As the party chief, Kamaraj commenced his active role in the successive elections of the Congress legislative party of Madras and was the prime author of installing three chief ministers between 1946 and 1952: T. Prakasam, Omandur Ramaswamy Reddiar and Kumaraswamy Raja. The next successor Rajaji was certainly not Kamaraj's choice but was appointed by the Congress high command. The re-entry of Rajaji as chief minister without even an election could have derailed Kamaraj's emerging equations with non-Brahmins. The die was cast when Rajaji, flaunting his authority, introduced a vocational educational scheme based on hereditary calling, which met with stiff opposition not only from the Dravidar Kazhagam and Dravida Munnetra Kazhagam, but also from a large number of non-Brahmins in the Congress quarters. This educational pattern, aimed at imparting to school children the traditional caste occupation of their parents, came to be condemned by E. V. Ramaswamy as kula kalvi thittam, devised to perpetuate varnashrama dharma. Rajaji also took the drastic step of closing down nearly 6,000 schools, citing financial constraints.

E. V. Ramaswamy campaigned against the new educational policy much to the chagrin of Rajaji. The Dravida Munnetra Kazhagam (DMK), formed in 1949 by breaking away from the Dravidar Kazhagam, also joined the crusade against Rajaji's scheme. E. V. Ramaswamy did not rest on his oars till the scheme was dropped. This second confrontation between them proved too costly for Rajaji. Rajaji, the statesman of Brahmin hagiography, had to bow out ingloriously tendering his resignation in 1954. Rajaji's political vagaries in 1938 and 1953 meant the passing of Brahmins as the controllers of Tamil Nadu's political destiny till the next four decades. With the resignation of Rajaji, Kamaraj was perhaps the natural and logical choice. At the meeting of the Congress legislature party on March 31, 1954, with Rajaji presiding, his arch rival and the target of his ridicule Kamaraj was elected as the leader, securing 93 votes as against 41 received by C. Subramaniam who was propped up by Rajaji.

Kamaraj as Chief Minister

Kamaraj was 'reluctant to accept' the chief ministership but the circumstance prevailed upon him as there was no 'alternative to the king-maker himself ascending the throne.' Kamaraj took the mantle from Rajaji, and formed his first Cabinet, which did not contain a single Brahmin contrary to Rajaji's first ministry in 1937, 'dominated by Brahmins'. The elevation of Kamaraj as the chief minister on the wave of opposition to the Rajaji scheme of education, led to the development of closer ties between Kamaraj and E. V. Ramasamy. The Congress gained the support of E. V.

Ramaswamy and Kamaraj's equation with the non-Brahmins was kept intact. E. V. Ramaswamy was all set to endorse his solidarity with Kamaraj on the grounds that in all these years he was the first and only non-Brahmin with Tamil as his mother tongue to become the chief minister; and for the first time a full-fledged ministry had been formed without a single Brahmin headed by Kamaraj.

According to E. V. Ramaswamy all credit should go to Kamaraj for dropping Rajaji's educational scheme despite opposition from upper castes led by C Subramaniam and Bakthavatchalam who were in favour of it. Extolling Kamaraj as the pacchai Tamilan he urged his followers to extend every support to sustain the Kamaraj rule and prevent it from being ousted, as the interests of Tamils were safe in his hands. However, Kamaraj did not follow the exclusion of Brahmins as a deliberate policy. In fact, Brahmins were incorporated into his ministry at a later stage, one of the prominent gainers being R. Venkataraman.

For Kamaraj, E. V. Ramaswamy's open proclamation of support was a great source of strength, arriving precisely at the right moment when he himself was under pressure since doubts were being echoed in certain circles whether Kamaraj, a low caste man without formal education, would be able to cope with the administrative exigencies of the office of chief minister. For Kamaraj, seasoned for the occasion, E. V. Ramaswamy's endorsement was an unmistakable political gain and he saw its usefulness in countering his critics. Soon Kamaraj proved his capabilities as one of best chief ministers silencing the critics and sceptics. Kamaraj silently used the non-Brahmin movement in his favour though he did not 'share Periyar's anti-Brahmanism'. E. V. Ramaswamy's crusade against Brahmanism, religion and the threat of imposition of Hindi from Delhi would continue unabated under Kamaraj's rule only so long as it did not weaken Kamaraj's ministerial governance. Kamaraj distanced himself from Ramaswamy and his followers when the mode of agitation culminated in a call for burning the national flag (August 1, 1955), maps of India and copies of the Constitution.

One of the first political acts of Kamaraj during his tenure as chief minister was to widen representation of the rising non-

Brahmins in the Cabinet. Ministerial berths were given to the non-Brahmin caste-based parties, Tamil Nadu Toilers Party and Commonweal Party. Both the parties were subsequently 'subsumed' by the Congress. In a move to counter Tamil cultural politics espoused by the DMK, Kamaraj made conscious attempts to partake in the linguistic cultural matters. In order to placate Tamil aspirations, Kamaraj effected some measures. The efforts towards introducing Tamil language as a medium of instruction in schools and colleges was accompanied by the publication of textbooks on 'scientific and technical subjects' in Tamil. In 1960, the state education minister took steps to introduce Tamil in government arts colleges as a medium of instruction.

The introduction of the Tamil typewriter in government offices was another effort to change the language of administration gradually. Similarly the usage of Tamil in the courts received encouragement. To affirm his role in the linguistic politics of the state, Kamaraj did introduce a bill in February 1962 in the legislative assembly for changing the name of Madras to 'Tamilnad' for 'intra-state communication', the bill also proposing Madurai as the capital. But no decision was taken on it. However, these moves were on a low key and inadequate to woo the masses. The DMK made capital out of this, routing Congress in the 1967 elections four years after Kamaraj relinquished his office as chief minister in accordance with the Kamaraj Plan to concentrate on Congress organisational work.

Committed to his version of 'socialism' meaning that "those who are backward should progress", Kamaraj remained truthful to the simple dictum of his 'socialism', providing 'what is essential for man's living' such as 'dwelling, job, food and education'. The great feature of Kamaraj rule was the ending of the retrogressive educational policies and setting the stage for universal and free schooling. Six thousand schools closed down by Rajagopalachari were revived and 12,000 schools added. The percentage of school going children in the age group between 6 and 11 increased from 45 per cent to 75 per cent within a span of seven years after he became the chief minister.

Almost every village within a radius of one mile with a population of 300 and above inhabitants was provided with a school. With a view to encouraging and attracting the rural poor children to the schools Kamaraj pioneered a scheme of free midday meals for primary school children in panchayat and government institutions. This scheme, aided by the American voluntary organisation CARE, was launched in 1957. In addition the government came forward to supply school uniforms to poor students. To make the education easily accessible to children from various backgrounds, full exemption from school fees was introduced. Public enthusiasm and participation in raising funds and procuring equipment for the schools were entertained through different schemes making education a social responsibility. Such measures made education affordable for many who were denied basic educational opportunities for centuries.

Kamaraj's other major feat was his role in facilitating developmental programmes chiefly electrification and industrial development. Thousands of villages were electrified. Rural electrification led to the large-scale use of pumpsets for irrigational purposes and agriculture-received impetus. Large and small-scale industries were flagged off generating employment opportunities. Kamaraj made the best use of the funds available through the Five-Year Plans and guided Tamil Nadu in deriving the maximum benefit.

His efforts in these directions not only enhanced the profile of Tamil Nadu as one of the best-administered states in the post-independent era, but it also raised it high in social and economic rankings compared to other states. As chief minister for nine years Kamaraj headed a stable administration and managed two elections successfully and his reputation soared high as 'shrewd and competent' and 'one of the most effective chief ministers in India'. He proved himself more than equal to the task and his detractors retracted the statements made about this 'village-green trundler' and his capacity to govern the state when he took the mantle from Rajaji.

His competent ministerial colleagues and the excellent set of senior state officials saw in Kamaraj 'a man with a mission' who could set aside any stricture in order to serve the common people. He was able to invoke cooperation, dedication and willingness ungrudgingly. Importantly his approach to governance and party control was never tainted with religious overtones and a secular commitment was natural and integral to his mission in life. Among his cherished political mentors, Kamaraj held George Joseph, a Kerala Christian nationalist who chose Madurai as his base for practising law and for his political activities, in high esteem.

Kamaraj's association with George Joseph began early and grew in strength from the days when Kamaraj frequented political meetings addressed by George Joseph in Virudhunagar. It continued through the period of his involvement in the Vaikom Satyagraha then led by George Joseph, to the organising of demonstrations against the Simon Commission along with Joseph. It was George Joseph who defended Kamaraj and got him released when he was accused of making bombs and implicated in the Virudhunagar Conspiracy case. Profoundly fond of George Joseph and his family, Kamaraj continued to pay visits to the Joseph family especially his wife Susannah, even with his busy itinerary as chief minister.

His lifestyle never changed; power and position failed to dislocate his simplicity. His illustrious career as the chief minister of Tamil Nadu ended in 1963 and he commenced his political life in Delhi as the president of the All India Congress Party. Explicating Kamaraj's long stint and stature in Tamil Nadu politics, reputed political scientist, R. Bhaskaran, observed:

> "Mr. Kamaraj was not rich and has not grown rich; he is a bachelor and has no family ties. He has been and is a whole-time politician and has laboured to acquire personal knowledge of men and things all over the Tamil country and he knows all the leaders of his party from every part of India. He has also acquired facility in English and very considerable knowledge of world affairs. He is immensely popular for all these reasons and especially because he has no vices and leads a simple life. Above all he is the 'representative' Tamil as most Tamils imagine that figure. His ways of speaking, walking, eating and dress commend themselves to the many millions to whom these are familiar ways with nothing outlandish about them."

Bhaskaran's judgement is indeed right. That is certainly the reason why the beleagured Congress in Tamil Nadu is wooing the Tamils today with the promise of 'Kamaraj Rule.'

Most know why it cannot promise a 'Rajaji Rule'.

Last Pillar of Gandhism

The birth day of Gandhiji is October 2nd Kamaraj passed away on the same day.

Demise of Gandhiji shocked the public. Rain came extinguish the forest fire. But the demise of the leader Kamaraj even in the heavy down pour spreaded like a forest fire.

In a short period people rushed towards the house of their great leader. The man who got freedom, who served for the poor was sleeping, where usually sleeps, for ever. There was a silent smile in the face. The great leader mixed with glory in a simple look. The CM Karunanidhi with his tearful eyes saw the duty oriented leader who was beyond the party feelings. Sorrow surrounded the place of the man who toiled himself to wipe out the sorrows of the poor.

Stream of tears plunged the house and the down pour plunged the state. What was next? Duty challenged the tears. Police could not control the crowd. The house having the door No. 8 at Thirumalai Pillai Road, was crowded by the public. Sons who lost their father, weeping brothers and sisters who lost their mother, volunteers who lost their leader, devotees who lost their go, the sound cry in all directions. Car came to take his body to Rajaji Hall.

In an arranged special car the body of Kamaraj was brought to Rajaji Hall at 5.30 p.m. on October 2nd. On hearing the news the flags were half hoisted in all over the country. Shops were closed, cinemas were cancelled. Gandhi Jayanti programmes were cancelled in order to pay homage to Kamaraj. Friday, the next day, was declared as Govt., holiday. Tamil Nadu Government announced a 7 days mourning. The portrait of Kamaraj was garlanded and candles lighted before it in all the streets of villages and cities of Tamil Nadu. Police could not control the flooding crowd. His body was covered with Tricolour Flag. It was placed in front portion of Rajaji Hall. Tamil Nadu Governor Sha, CM Karunanidhi, Pondicherry Governor Sethilal, Ministers of Tamil Nadu, All India New Congress Committee General Secretary Narasimha Rao, Tamil Nadu Congress President P. Ramachandran, New Congress President K. S. Ramasamy, Sivaji Ganesan place wreath at the feet of Kamaraj. Few swooned. Two died due to

Cardiac arrest. Additional coaches were attached in all the trains bound for Madras from South. More than 20 died due to accidents in traffic. The crowd was increasing second by second. People were in queue of 2 to 3 rows upto a distance of 2 miles to pay their last homage to their departed leader. Chief Minister Mr. Karunanidhi and Congress Secretary Thindivanam Ramamoorthy were searching a place in rainy night to construct a memorial building for the leader.

It was decided to construct in an area of 2 acres of land near the building of the father of the nation Gandhiji. Our station people gathered during night. People tried to enter through all the gates of Rajaji Hall. Police suffered to control the public. The queue disordered. Aged around 95 years, youths, ladies, poor, hut dwellers, children were in the queue to see the face of their leader last time. Kakkan was brought by 3 people. He was consoled by other leaders. Thyagis, Central and State Ministers, Officials, Artists, Ambassadors of various countries, leaders of political parties paid their homage.

British government sent their condolence message to PM Indira Gandhi. In the message it was said, "Royal Britain Government conveys its heart felt Condolences to the demised Kamaraj who was a senior and respectable leader. It all also keeps in its memory the remarkable development Tamil Nadu had when Kamaraj was its Chief Minister."

Wife of Tirupur Kumaran paid homage by placing a wreath. Tears were streaming down from her eyes.

His sister Nagammal cried like anything. The government printed a special gazette with black border in memory of the demise leader Kamaraj. PM Indira Gandhi arrived at the afternoon. She came to Rajaji Hall straight from the air port. Exactly she enter at 3.10 p.m., through the Eastern gate. Along with her Governor Sha, CM Karunanidhi, Central Ministers came.

Indira Gandhi observed 2 minutes silence after placing a wreath. She saw the sorrowful public. Tears rolled down from her eyes. The she left through the eastern gate.

Kamaraj's sister's son, Jawahar performed the rituals. His body was bathed. Dots of Holy ash, sandal and saffron powder were placed no his forehead. He was dressed with a new Khadi dress.

His body was at Rajaji Hall for 21 hours. 20 lakhs people paid their homage.

The body of the leader was handed of to Military. Soldiers of all the 3 forces, Army, Navy and Air force stood with bowed heads and downed rifles in their hands.

M. S. Subbulakshmi sung a melody. On the other side the sound of people's cry.

Soldiers kept his body in Canon Truck, Guns were fired as a mark of respect. His sister Nagammal got swooned. The military respects were usually given only to existing President, Ex-President, Existing PM, Chief Ministers. But, leader Kamaraj though he was not in any position at the time of his death the military respect was given.

His last procession started 3.30 p.m. from Rajaji Hall. Flowers showered on the Canon Truck. In the next Truck Tamil Nadu Congress President P. Ramachandran, Central Minister C. Subramaniam, Rajaram Naidu, Sivaji Ganesan, Nedumaran, Kumari Ananthan, Kudanthai Ramakrishnan, Dhandauthapany and some other were standing.

There was a rain. People were standing in the rain. Throughout Mount Road, in the multi-storeyed buildings at the bus stop shelters, at the top of hoardings, telephone posts only human heads were seen.

The procession which started from Rajaji Hall crossed 10 km took 3 hours to reach Gandhi Mandapam. On a special platform sandal woods were kept. Soldiers of the 3 forces carried his body and kept on the sandal wood. Ministers and leaders placed wreath. Rituals were performed. It only 15 minutes. People were shouting slogans Pro-Kamaraj, the last heir of Gandhi and their unforgettable leader from a distance of 1 km. Canon was shot for 3 times before setting fire to the body. Kanagavel, the grandson of Kamaraj's sister set fire to the body. The fire went up. Indira Gandhi, who was made as Prime Minister by Kamaraj, could not her control herself and cried. The light of our life was put off. Affectionate and respectable great leader is no more. Every thing is finished. Kamaraj mixed with Gandhiji.

Kamaraj was the MP of Nagarkoil at the time of his death. He was as a MP for a period of 6 years, 8 months and 24 days from January 1969 to till his death. Before Gandhi died he called "Hey Ram", Nehruji said, "I have seen all the files" before his death Kamaraj said, "Put off the light". On 26th January 1975 he delivered a speech on the eve of Republic day. In that he said, "We all should take an oath on this Republic day and do things that we will bow for love but not for power. We will not be afraid of force."

It was his last on Republic day. He travelled till June 1975. He collected election funds for Congress. He was affected by influenza fever then. Later he avoided the public functions.

He replied to PM for her letter. He wrote in that, "I am getting well. Thanks for enquiring about my health." It was his last letter.

He did not attend the 2 days working committee meeting held on July 2nd and 3rd of 1975. This was the first working committee meeting in which he did not take part.

It was resolved in that meeting to consult Kamaraj according to the situation. Emergency should be withdrawn. Arrested should be released. Kamaraj met Actor Sivaji Ganesan at his residence on 1st October 1975 and conveyed his birthday greetings. This was the last function he attended.

Gandhiji's birth day celebration was about to be celebrated on October 2nd 1975 at Gandhi Mandapam. Governor had sent and an invitation to Kamaraj to participate in the function. He replied to Governor thanking him for the invitation. He informed in that letter that he would participate in the function. But passed away and merged with Gandhiji. He had planned to tour throughout Tamil Nadu from November 1975. For that a special van consisting stage and mike, etc. was presented by Madurai T.V.S. to Kamaraj.

His feet did not touch the van. Before that the god of Death took his life. His last message to public was delivered on the eve of Gandhiji's birthday. In that he said, "October 2nd is the Gandhi's birth day. On that day we should remember Gandhi and his high principles and philosophies. Let us follow the way Gandhiji showed us and eradicate envy and parities."

After the death of Mr. Kamaraj, as per his last wish Mr. Nedumaran arranged for the merger of the party with Congress (I) at Marina, Madras. All the true followers of Kamaraj joined with Indira Congress. Bharat Ratna Posthumously awarded to Perunthalaivar Kamaraj in the year 1976.

Great Leader to Serve the Poor and Deprived

But when Kamaraj left Tamil politics to become president of the Congress Party in 1963, the Congress lost its base in society. After Kamaraj, the Congress did not win a state election again in Tamil Nadu. Kamaraj and the Congress Party was let down in 1967 elections by his own Congress Folk who worked against him as Kamaraj was believed to have denied opportunity to K. T. Kosalram for Chief Ministership and favoured Bhakthavatchalam in 1963.

Dravidar Kazhagam in its offshoot form, that went on, in muted form after his ejection, to displace the Congress as the government of Tamil Nadu in 1967.

One can observe the plain speaking Kamaraj as a political stone mason, tapping away at a piece of rock, listening and feeling for ways that it will slice or split. No one can ever equal the charisma of Kamaraj among the poor masses.

Shri Kumaraswamy Kamaraj who rejected the idea of entering into family to serve the people through political system of India in pre- and post-independence era remained a high integrity personality in his lifetime without counting a penny. When the family elders put pressure on him to enter into matrimonial ties, he not only vowed to remain a Brahmachari till the country is free of foreign rule and other economical shortcomings, he also made few more of his friends in his home town to swear to similar promises for the welfare of the nation.

When people have ambitions of accumulating wealth, he refused to even allow his partymen to purchase the residence at Chennai where he we residing, as he feared any property in his name would lead to dispute among his relatives in the future.

While he hails from a depressed community that gives a high importance to lavish food with varieties of curry, Kamaraj preferred a simple diet without salt and spices and ensure he did not succumb to the taste of food to rule him. For this simple reason, he never invited anyone to dine with him at his residence where his food was prepared by his assistance.

In the history of political world, no world leader can match to this noble statesmanship of Kamaraj. The Tamil community cannot dream of one more political leader to the selfless stature of Kamaraj arising from the state in the near future.

He lead a simple personal life based on Gandhian values and upheld the Gandhian values while his ruling in Tamil Nadu and later when he was heading the Congress in New Delhi. Later even when Kamaraj had to lose his political power in Tamil Nadu and sit in the opposition, he still remained a respected national figure both among his colleagues and opponents. Kamaraj died of a massive heart attack on October 02, 1975. But the one that came from Justice Krishna Iyer said it all: A common man with an uncommon common sense.

The saga of beneficiaries post-Kamaraj period in Tamil Nadu continue to be limited to privileged and high profiled personalities connected to business and film industries who can manipulate million to billions and trillions and were essentially the offshoot of Self-respect Movement and the earlier Justice Party in the various new political formats which he coolly kept under control in his influential days.

No son-of-the-soil leader from Tamil country of subsequent generation, has the capacity and capability to mobilise the poor masses in the right mass need based economical and socio-political direction for the betterment of this state and the country. The people of Tamil Nadu plan to build social schemes in every villages in memory of this great leader to serve the poor and deprived. The society to which he belong realise to celebrate the World Nadars Day annually on birthday of Kumaraswamy Kamaraj.

Will We Ever See Another Kamaraj?

"Public figures cannot afford private life", Nehruji is reported to have lamented once. But there was one figure in Indian politics in the recent past who willingly merged his private life into his public life. The former Chief Minister of Tamil Nadu and All-India Congress President, K. Kamaraj was one such personality. July 15, 2003 marks his birth centenary. A life-long bachelor, this freedom fighter had only aspired for his motherland's freedom from foreign rule and to serve its people afterwards.

K. Kamaraj's life story had been stranger than fiction for its unbelievable incidents and turn of events. Almost an illiterate with no formal education and born in a poor family in a remote village, he rose to great heights of eminence in the political arena.

K. Kamaraj was born on 15th July, 1903 to the couple Kumaraswamy and Sivakami in Virudhunagar, Tamil Nadu, in the southern-most part of India. His father Kumaraswamy had a small coconut shop to support his family. While Kamaraj was studying in the primary school, the family was struck with a misfortune. His father, the only breadwinner of the family, succumbed to a massive heart attack. This put an end to the education of Kamaraj. He had to take up all kinds of odd jobs including that of a street vendor to support his widowed mother and sister.

The independence struggle was in full swing in the country at that time. Kamaraj was eager to contribute his mite to the freedom movement pioneered by Mahatma Gandhi. Inspired by the patriotic leader Satyamurthi's fiery oratory against British atrocities, Kamaraj plunged headlong into the movement. From then on there was no looking back for him. He became an able organiser in mobilising people for public meetings addressed by patriots. Appreciating his skill, Satyamurthi took him under his fold. In due course, Kamaraj, by his selfless devotion, rose in stature. Starting as Satyamurthi's personal assistant he ultimately rose to become the President of the INC.

A pre-independence party like the Congress which had nothing to offer to its cadres except suffering and imprisonment under the British rule, became the home for Kamaraj. With terrific energy and dedicated service Kamaraj converted the Congress into a formidable organisation in Tamil Nadu. Himself a grass-root level worker, he became very popular among his party rank and file. He was imprisoned for the first time when he took part in the Salt

Satyagraha undertaken by Mahatma Gandhi. Later, participating in almost all the agitations he courted arrest and underwent long periods of imprisonment. His association with stalwarts in prison helped him broaden his outlook. He grew fond of books and through interactions with intellectuals in prison Kamaraj developed his leadership skills that proved a valuable asset to him as an administrator in later years of his life.

Kamaraj succeeded C. Rajgopalachari, another great stalwart, as the Chief Minister of Tamil Nadu on April 13, 1957. Undoubtedly, this was a great achievement for him as he was the unanimous choice for the high office. He was honest and selfless to the core. Almost half a century has passed since he administered Tamil Nadu. But his pivotal role in the State's all-round development is still remembered. Keeping pace with Nehru's visionary efforts at the national level, Kamaraj was instrumental in building many irrigation dams, linking the villages by all-weather roads and constructing hospitals in remote places.

Today he is talked about for making primary education completely free. Perhaps he might have felt that the asset of education which he was deprived of due to poverty should not befall similarly placed children. In fact, he felt that a major part of his life's mission was fulfilled by this one act.

Kamaraj had also introduced the Midday Meal Scheme for the poor students at school. It helped arrest dropouts. It is now being replicated at the national level. Even the Supreme Court in one of its recent judgements has asked every State to implement the scheme besides instructing the Central Government to release foodgrains from its godowns for this purpose. The President, Dr. A. P. J. Abdul Kalam, while inaugurating a similar scheme under 'Akshaya Patra' at a function in Bangalore recently, acknowledged the pioneering work done in this field by Kamaraj.

The result of Kamaraj's work was there for all to see. There was an all-round development with village as the nucleus. By inducting colleagues like Shri R. Venkataraman and C. Subramaniam in his Ministry he paved the way for the growth of industrial, agricultural and educational sectors. Tamil Nadu set itself as an example for other States to emulate.

Well impressed by the achievements and acumen of Kamaraj, Prime Minister Jawaharlal Nehru felt that his services were needed more at the national level. In a swift move he brought Kamaraj to Delhi as the President of the Indian National Congress. That Nehru should have lent his ears to a little-educated leader like Kamaraj on party and national issues amazed everyone.

Nehru realised that if he had wide learning and vision, Kamaraj possessed enormous common sense and pragmatism. This was amply proved when Kamaraj suggested to Nehru to seek the resignation of some of his senior Cabinet colleagues to draft them for party work. Kamaraj had realised that the Congress party was losing ground among the people due to the absence of dedicated leaders. Nehru promptly accepted his suggestion and some of his Cabinet ministers resigned.

Kamaraj's political maturity came in full view when Nehru died in 1964. How he settled the succession issue for the Prime Ministership was amply proved by his choice of Lal Bahadur Shastri and Indira Gandhi in succession.

Though later in life Kamaraj had to lose his political power and sit in the opposition, he still remained a respected national figure both among his colleagues and opponents. He had no enemies in politics and remained endeared to the masses as before. This was evident when a multitude surged to bid the final farewell to Kamaraj on October 02,1975 after he died of a massive heart attack. Countless condolences came in from various parts of the country. But the one that came from Justice Krishna Iyer said it all: "A common man's man with an uncommon common sense".

Facing the Challenges

Though he faced so many problems in Congress he never thought to quit Congress. It was the reason for his victory. Sincerity, hard work, analysing the problems thoroughly and proper approach were causes for Kamaraj's victory.

India was ruled by the British over 200 years. A decision was taken in 1929 at the conference held at Lahore under the presidency of Nehru for complete independent rule. Gandhiji proposed this. Peoples suffered lot they died due to shooting and death sentences.

At last at the midnight of 14th August 1947, i.e. the early morning of 15th August a complete independence was given. This was celebrated at Delhi. Kamaraj overwhelmed with joy.

15th August is a golden day in Indian history. On that day the Union flag of British in all the government buildings were down hoisted and the TRICOLOUR Indian flag was hoisted. Nehruji released a message to public of the nation on that day "Today our thoughts are going to the Father of the Nation who is the architect of freedom. He drove away the darkness surrounded us with the light of independence".

That day was celebrated throughout the nation. Nation got independence. Kamaraj explained the reason there for as under:

> "Gandhiji sacrificed and devoted his life for the service of the public. He got independence through Ahimsa. He conducted the freedom fight in the path of truth. His life itself is a Test of Truth"
>
> "He gathered all the Indians. Prior to Gandhiji's entry in the politics people were poor, innocent and were afraid to express their views and thought, and simply walking like a corpse. Gandhiji realised this, he echoed their feelings. People identified their guide. They marched in his path, that is why nation got independence".
>
> "We got lot of advantages from him. He made us brave, he insisted self-confidence in public and private life. He not only advised this to public but also adopted in his life. He was role model"
>
> "His ambition of independence attained during his life itself".
>
> "Crores of people of this nation have lively hood, no food, cloth, shelter, education, job and money. This has got to be changed. These poverty stickers should live like others. All should live with unity. There should not be difference in cast and creed. These were his aims".
>
> "All should be equal not only in life status but also in social status. Only for this Gandhiji wanted independence".

Kamaraj lived up to his last breath for Gandhism. He lived as his last heir. He worked for downtrodden. Every year 15th August is celebrated as independence day. In 1950 26th January India was declared as a Democratic Republic Country. Kamaraj engaged himself vigorously in the service of nation and fight for freedom upto the end. But Rajaji left at last stage. Equal rights were given to freedom fighters and those served for British. Any one can come to power. No special rights were given to Congress people who to jail in freedom fight. The right given for freedom fighters are equally given to those opposed freedom. Kamaraj who fought for freedom had a vote. The traitor too got the same vote. This is our Democracy.

In 1948 election for AICC presidentship was conducted. Strong contest was there. Pattabi Seetharamiah and Tandan contested for the post of president. Tandan used to criticised the ministry of Nehru and its policies. Tandan openly criticised the policies of the ministry headed by Nehru.

The contest of Tandan in the election created fear in the minds of many. If Tandan was elected as a president Nehru may resign from the post of Prime Minister. So Kamaraj wished to support Pattabi Seetharamiah. Tandan was supported by many in Andhra. As Madras Congress gave a vast support, Pattabi Seetharamiah won in the election. Kamaraj was the reason for this. But Patel supported Tandan.

At a later date when Patel met Kamaraj they were talking about affairs of the nation. It turned towards the election of Congress presidentship. As Patel supported Tandan at that time he asked Kamaraj whether he had any difference of opinion. Kamaraj said he had none since 1946 after Rajaji's affairs. He could do nothing when Madras PCC liked to elect Seetharamiah. But Patel knew well that Pattabi Seetharamaiah won only because of Kamaraj. In 1948 Tamil State Conference was held at Coimbatore. Kamaraj presided the conference. The Conference was held in every district too. Kamaraj presided everywhere.

Election for PCC President was held on June 13th of the same year. Kamaraj was elected unanimously. January 30th of 1948 a Friday, the time was evening 5.00. Since Patel was addressing the gathering Gandhiji was late by 10 minutes to the prayer meeting. Gandhiji went along with his grand daughters Aba Gandhi and Manu Gandhi.

All got up and gave way to Gandhiji. All on a sudden one man jumped towards Gandhiji and pushed him. The book and the 'Jaba Mala' fell down from Gandhiji's hands. Immediately he shot down Gandhiji with a pistol. 3 bullets parsed Gandhiji's chest and straight away in the heart. Due to severe bleeding Gandhiji died on the spot. Before dying he said, "Hay Ram" twice, the time was 5.17 p.m.

Nehru came in running. He sat down near Gandhiji. He cried, the whole nation cried. Kamaraj got a severe shock. The nation became an orphan. When Kamaraj opened a park at Arcot for children, this news of assassination of Gandhiji came. Kamaraj was weeping. He refused his food. Tears flooded from his eyes. All were stashing Kamaraj.

Kamaraj immediately asked the people not to create religious violence and to work for the welfare of the society with strong will-power. Kamaraj shed tears for the first time in his life. Election to elect the party leader for assembly conducted in 1949. Groups of Rajaji and Prakasam joined together. They proposed Dr. Subbarayan. The relationship between Kamaraj and Ramaswamy Reddiar was not good at that time. Most of Kamaraj's group did not like Ramaswamy Reddiar. They felt Ramaswamy Reddiar may loose if contested. They wanted to propose Bakthavathsalam. Information was given to Ramaswamy Reddiar.

Kumaraswamy Raja, T. S. Chockalingam and C. Subramanian went to Ramaswamy Raja as representatives of Kamaraj informed the proposal about Bakthavathsalam. Ramaswamy Reddiar did not accept it next day he laid a condition. If Kumaraswamy Raja was proposed instead of Bakthavathsalam he was ready to withdraw. This information was given to Kamaraj by Chockalingam. M/s Chockalingam and C. Subramanian were sent to Kumaraswamy Raja who was admitted in a hospital for treatment.

Kumaraswamy Raja was conveyed the latest development. He never expected. He saw duty oriented Kamaraj before his eyes. At last he accepted to the desire of Kamaraj.

The opposite group of Rajaji and Prakasam never expected this turning point. Kumaraswamy Raja easily won in the election as the groups of Ramaswamy Reddiar and Kamaraj joined together keeping aside their ill feelings and worked for the victory of Kumaraswamy Raja.

The Foresight

Kamaraj used to go to Delhi now and then and met Rajaji at Delhi whenever he went. In 1950 he went to Delhi. As usual he met Rajaji. Talk regarding. During the course of talk Kamaraj informed that 29th August was fixed as date of election for PCC President.

Rajaji wanted C. P. Subbiah to be elected. Kamaraj said he had no objection. Rajaji informed the same to C. P. Subbiah. C. P. Subbiah involved himself in the election work. He canvassed for himself and requested the cooperation of all. This was informed to Kamaraj by his group. Kamaraj said nothing. But his people wanted him to be elected. In the last minute Kamaraj accepted to contest. Kamaraj won this election with 155 votes. C. P. Subbiah lost it by only getting 99 votes. Kamaraj was elected again as PCC President.

In 1950 Congress conference was held at Nasik. Election for AICC President conducted. It was a Triangular contest. Purushotham Das Tandon, Acharya Kripalani and Sankararao Dev contested. It was a severe contest.

Poll began, Tandon won by a margin of 214 votes. Tandon criticised the ministry of Nehruji. He never cooperated with Nehru. Tandon formed a working committee which Nehru did not like. He asked Tandon to reform it. Tandon refused then Nehru resigned from the working committee.

All could understand only then why Kamaraj did not support Tandon 1948 election and supported Pattabi Seetharamiah. They appreciated his foresight. A power fight started between Nehru and Tandon. Working committee meeting was held in 8th September 1951. Kamaraj supported Nehru who was called as the heir of Gandhiji by Gandhiji himself. He personally worked in the field. He started collecting supports for Nehru in Madras State. Then he collected supports in Kerala and Andhra.

It made an uproar and shocked Tandon.

He thought Kamaraj could get the things done. He thought Kamaraj reduced his power in Congress and increased Nehru's. Hence he resigned his post before the conference.

In his resignation he said that Nehru wanted a change in the working committee. Informed the reasons therefore. But the reasons did not have any evidence.

Tandon's resignation was accepted by AICC in its conference held in September 8th. Nehru was elected as the President of AICC. The support of Kamaraj helped in general election too.

Counsellor of Sathyamoorthy

In 1935 the Congress conference held in Lakshmanapuri, Nehruji presided the conference. During that period Kamaraj was the Secretary in PCC and Sathyamoorthy as President. Kamaraj felt that he was not fit to be the Secretary. When he informed the same to Sathymoothy. Sathyamoorthy said if Kamaraj was not fit enough to be the Secretary he too could not continue as president, since he was also not fit for that post.

Kamaraj did not go to the conference of Congress. Even when he was invited by the friends. He never used to go saying that he had a lot of work to be done at the state level and it was his duty.

Central Cabinet meeting was held at Delhi. When Sathyamoorthy was there Kamaraj went to Delhi. His arrival made Sathyamoorthy happy. He introduced Kamaraj to his colleagues. He told them Kamaraj was an outstanding Congress worker in Madras state. He was not only a colleague of him but also a counsellor.

Kamaraj in Crisis

On 27th May 1964, Kamaraj received an express telegram when he was on tour. It stated that Nehru's health condition was very bad. Immediately Kamaraj left to Delhi. Alulya Gosh was at Bangalore *en route* to Ooty. He and Nijalingappa boarded in the same flight with Kamaraj. When they were flying to Delhi they received another shocking news of Nehru's demise around 2 p.m. All the three cried in the flight itself. No one talked to each other. Kamaraj shed tears for the second time in his political life.

G. Krishnamoorthy came to Delhi Palam airport. G. Krishnamoorthy said that Nanda was to take charge as interim PM.

Kamaraj, Nijalingappa and Alulya Gosh went straight to Nehru's residence. Lakhs of people gathered there with tears in their eyes to pay their last homage to their departed national leader. People's eye of the world turned towards India.

Ambassadors of foreign courtiers, state Chief ministers and MPs left to Delhi on the next day.

An era came to an end. The body of Nehru, who was the first man for about 17 years administered 45 crores of people and got a primary place to India in the world was cremated. He became immortal.

His demise shocked not only India but the entire world. Indians were not strong enough to absorb the shock. They had to get it step by step. As a first step Gulzari Lal Nanda became the interim Prime Minister.

The second step to find out the answer for 'Who after Nehru?'. We had to note a point before finding out the answer. The political gamblers of the foreign countries spread a rumour under political prediction that in India there would be military rule because the confusion between Congress leaders due to quarrel for leadership which would shutter the democracy. Even some senior politicians in India expected the same. But their expectation did not happen Congress people behaved in a gentle manner as expected by the Indians and the people of the world. Congress leaders found a solution within 6 days after Nehru's death. They showed to the world that after Gandhi and Nehru they could elect a suitable person to take the people in a right way and this save the prestige of the party. This was done by the son of our State Sri. Kamaraj who had a special place in the history of India.

He diverted the leaders who had a slight idea to contest and met 540 Congress MPs, 15 state CMs and some important Congress leaders and understood their views and conveyed his and the public opinion to them and finally gathered all together and elected next PM which was not an easy task of Kamaraj. As S. K. Patil and Nanda said it was history famed giant task.

After cremation of Nehruji, Kamaraj met President Radhakrishnan. President informed Kamaraj that the senior minister, Mr. Nanda took charge as interim Prime Minister and the leader to Congress for Parliament was to be elected.

From that time onwards the eyes of the world which were on India had turned towards Kamaraj. The people who asked "Who was after Nehru" now eagerly looking at Kamaraj as what he was going to do. From that day onwards Kamaraj did not even wink his eyes. The name "KAMARAJ" appeared in bold letters in the newspapers of the world.

For the first time he invited Malavya and Morarji and had a talk with them. He convinced them to obey the orders of Congress working committee, there were opposition to elect the leader of the party to Parliament (PM) according to the instructions of the working committee Kamaraj did not care that. He pointed out the election of President and Vice-President by the working committee.

A meeting of AIC working committee was organised on 30th May to elect a new leader to Parliament. 13 CMs of the state where Congress was in rule and V. R. Krishna Menon were participated in the meeting as special invites. Kamaraj presided over the meeting and wanted them to save cooperation. He also said that they were there to fill up the vacancy caused by the death of Nehru hence they should act with cooperation and elect the leader of the party to Parliament unanimously. Finally the working committee gave the power to advice in the election of Prime Minister to Kamaraj. It was his second victory. He took the responsibility of deciding the fate of the country again.

In the next 3 days he invited the Congress members of the Parliament and the Chief Ministers and talked to them. Kamaraj who crossed all the political storms faced this challenge too. Newspapers flashed that whether Lal Bhagadhur Shastri or Morarji Desai. Who was the next PM. Countries of the world were looking upon this.

Kamaraj was keen in electing the PM unanimously.

Majority supported Lal Bhagadhur Shastri. It was the wish of Kamaraj too.

On 1st of June (Monday) night Kamaraj met Morarji Desai and informed him about the interest of the majority members in electing Shastri as PM. Then Morarji Desai gave an interview to Newspapers reporters about the decision of the Parliament members in electing Shastri as PM. They appreciated his act of obedience to the party's high command.

6

Kamaraj's Life at a Glance

July 15, 1903: K. Kamaraj was born to the couple Kumaraswamy and Sivakami in Virudhunagar, Tamil Nadu, in the southern-most part of India. His father Kumaraswamy had a small coconut shop to support his family. While Kamaraj was studying in the primary school, the family was struck with a misfortune. His father, the only breadwinner of the family, succumbed to a massive heart attack. This put an end to the education of Kamaraj.

1923: One of the pioneers of the scheme was the Madras Presidency that started providing cooked meals to children in corporation schools in the Madras city. The programme was introduced in a large scale in 1960s under the Chief Ministership of K. Kamaraj.

1925: With a view to unseat C. Rajagoplachari from power and bring in K. Kamaraj, a non-Brahmin leader Periyar relaxed the intensity of the anti-Congress crusade he began. By getting K. Kamaraj elected in a bye-election.

June 9, 1930: At Virdhunagar, a posse of police constables headed by the Circle Inspector, surrounded the house of a Congress worker Muthuswamy and placed him under arrest. K. Kamaraj was also arrested. The local people greatly resented it. To discourage *khadi* production the Divisional Superintendent of Railway issued instruction not to book khadi yarn for transport.

1949: Manjubhashini and Congress leader, K. Kamaraj, founded the Bala Mandir Kamaraj Trust. What is now a sprawling campus with a home, school, dispensary, laundry, carpentry unit, auditorium, research centre and resource centre, began with one cradle and one child. Manjubhashini gave the organisation all of her formidable organisational ability and under her disciplined leadership, hundreds of children, over more than three generations.

1954: Indian National Congress and its leader K. Kamaraj won its second election, and defeated its rival DMK. Due to the resignation of C. Rajagopalachari, for his controversial Kula Kalvi Thittam, the leadership of Congress was contested, between K. Kamaraj, and C. Subramaniam.

October 1956: Periyar E. V. Ramaswamy issued a statement in support of K. Kamaraj before the commencement of the election. The central executive of Dravidar Kazhagam resolved to support K. Kamaraj.

1957: To provide free meals and education to people, was for the first time in the world that a measure like this was being executed.

July 21, 1958: The Polytechnic was started. Honourable, Bharat Ratna Sri. K. Kamaraj, the then Chief Minister of Madras inaugurated the Polytechnic with his blessings.

February 21, 1962: Indian National Congress led by K. Kamaraj won the election.

1963: K. Kamaraj initiated the cunning 'Kamaraj Plan'. It called upon senior Congressmen to relinquish government positions and devote themselves to organisational work. It was meant to serve a dual purpose: purge Nehru's detractors and infuse new blood into the party.

1963: K. Kamaraj's resignation as the Chief Minister, to concentrate on party affairs, along with persistent rumours of corruption had weakened the previous Indian National Congress Government. The Dravida Munnetra Kazhagam (DMK) led coalition under the leadership of C. N. Annadurai won the election defeating the Congress.

January 6, 1964: Congress president K. Kamaraj was welcomed at a Congress Party session in Gopabandhunagar, Bhubaneshwar in Orissa.

January 10, 1964: Congress president K. Kamaraj along with Congress stalwart from Orissa, Biju Patnaik went to attend the plenary session of Congress party in Bombay.

July 27, 1965: Congress president K. Kamaraj addressed at an All India Congress Committee (AICC) session held in Bangalore.

February 10, 1966: The Subjects Committee met at Nehru Nagar, Jaipur. Shri K. Kamaraj presided. Four hundred and fifteen members attended the meeting. Consideration of the draft resolution on "Tashkent Declaration" was resumed. Shri Mohan Lal (Punjab) supported the resolution said that the Tashkent agreement had certainly reduced tension between India and Pakistan and it would benefit the people and the Governments of both the countries.

June 23, 1967: The All India Congress Committee met again at Mavalankar Hall, Vithalbhai Patel House, New Delhi. Shri K. Kamaraj presided. In all 305 members attended the meeting. The discussion on the results of the fourth general election was resumed. Shri Ram Sahay (Madhya Pradesh) said that the responsibility of the debacle was not solely that of the High Command.

1971: Its precursor, the Congress (Organisation) led by K. Kamaraj, along with the Swatantara Party, had challenged the DMK. Now, the BJP has decided to go it alone in the Assembly elections.

October 2, 1975: On Gandhi Jayanti day, Kamaraj awoke from his afternoon nap feeling uneasy. His housekeeper, Vairavan, rang up to his physician. K. Kamaraj died that day.

APPENDICES

Appendix – I

Tribute to K. Kamaraj

[Prime Minister Manmohan Singh's Speech on the Occasion of the Release Ceremony of Kamaraj Commemorative Coins on Oct. 27, 2004 at New Delhi].

It is a proud privilege to speak in honour of one of the greatest sons of our country, Bharat Ratna Shri K. Kamaraj. As a political leader, he stands out as an example for all those in public life today — a leader completely dedicated to the cause of the people, a model of rectitude and correctness, far-sighted visionary and an exceptionally able administrator. It is not without reason that today several years after his demise he is still a legend hailed and venerated as 'karmaveera'.

Bharat Ratna Shri K. Kamaraj belonged to that select breed of freedom fighters who walked the Gandhian path and contributed magnificently to making the freedom movement a truly mass movement in the country. When he was about fifteen, the Jallianwala Bagh massacre was a turning point in his life. He was barely eighteen when he heeded Gandhiji's call for non-cooperation against the British and took it to the villages. The great freedom fighter Shri Satyamurthy was his mentor and his political guru. Shri Kamaraj participated in all the Gandhian non-violent mass struggles in the three decades before independence and spent a good part of his in life various jails. He was an indefatigable political worker and a skilful organiser.

Shri Kamaraj first reluctantly accepted the office of the Chief Minister of erstwhile Madras State in 1954 and in his tenure of nine years made his mark as an exceptionally able, pragmatic and effective administrator. His administration was based on the simple advice he gave his ministers, "Face the problem. Don't evade it. Find a solution, however small. People will be satisfied if you do something".

Sound advice that holds good even today for those of us in Government and public administration. What he himself was deprived of as a child was the first focus of his attention — education. The aim was to open primary schools in all villages. Free education upto Class XI was introduced. The Midday Meal Scheme was introduced for the first time in our country and it is the forerunner of the scheme which is now attempted to be implemented throughout the country. This is one of the examples of his tremendous foresight and vision.

He also focused on irrigation and building infrastructure in the State. A number of medium and small scale industries were also set up with the able assistance of Shri Venkataraman who fortunately is present with us. His efforts in this direction have meant that Tamil Nadu today is one of the States with the least regional disparities in the country.

After being elected as Chief Minister three times consecutively, in 1963, Shri Kamaraj noticing the declining vigour in the Congress party resigned as Chief Minister and decided to take up party work. He advocated the "Kamaraj Plan" for all senior Congress leaders to resign from their posts and devote their energy to the revitalisation of the party. This became a model for sacrifice and service in our public life, abjuring the lure of power — an ideal that has now been rediscovered and re-established in the personality of our Chairperson, Smt. Sonia Gandhi.

In 1964, he was elected the President of the Indian National Congress, a post he held through the turbulent years guiding the country in the days following the death of the two illustrious Prime Ministers. The nation honoured him with the Bharat Ratna in 1976. But Shri Kamaraj is a person whose memory needs to be recalled again and again and the release of this commemorative coin is a very timely event. It is an appropriate occasion to recall what Shri Kamaraj stood for. Simplicity and humility characterised him. He was not rich and did not grow rich. He spoke, walked, ate and dressed the way the common people did. He overcame his initial handicap of the lack of formal education to acquire felicity in English and knowledge of both national and world affairs. He was correctly described as "a common man's man with an uncommon common sense".

Rising from an humble background, he was an embodiment of simplicity, honesty, courage and compassion for the poor — qualities which endeared him to the masses who reciprocated with their affection for the 'Perunthalaivar' — a great leader. The release of commemorative coins in honour of this great son of India is a humble tribute of this Government to his memory. I am sure it will gladden the hearts of millions of his admirers and followers. The real tribute to him however, would be for all his followers to follow the values he espoused in their conduct in public life.

Jai Hind.

Quotations

- "One should not accept any post to which one could not do full justice."
- "Face the problem. Don't evade it. Find a solution, however small. People will be satisfied if you do something."

- "Only hard labour will save people. Wealth should not be massed with one group. No violence is necessary to form equality in society. It is also not desirable. Gandhiji got the freedom in a peaceful way. Let us form this society in the same way."
- "A person who holds a post even if it is a honorary one, should act properly. If he is not able to function properly he should not hold that post."
- "Every person who has any intelligence, initiative or enterprise will be encouraged to engage himself in productive enterprise for the benefit of the nation."
- "All should be equal not only in life status but also in social status. Only for this Gandhiji wanted independence."

Appendix – II

Midday Meal Scheme

(One of Kamaraj's Great Achievements)

The Midday Meal Scheme is the popular name for school meal programme in India. It involves provision of lunch free of cost to school-children on all working days. The key objectives of the programme are: protecting children from classroom hunger, increasing school enrolment and attendance, improved socialisation among children belonging to all castes, addressing malnutrition, and social empowerment through provision of employment to women. The scheme has a long history especially in Tamil Nadu introduced statewide by K. Kamaraj government in 1960s and expanded by M. G. Ramachandran in 1982 has been adopted by most of the states in India after a landmark direction by the Supreme Court of India on November 28, 2002. The success of this scheme is illustrated by the tremendous increase in the school participation and completion rates in the state of Tamil Nadu.

12 crore (120 million) children are so far covered under the Midday Meal Scheme, which is the largest school lunch programme in the world. Allocation for this programme has been enhanced from Rs. 3,010 crore to Rs. 4,813 crore (Rs, 48 billion 1.2 billion) in 2006-07.

The Background

One of the pioneers of the scheme is the Madras Presidency that started providing cooked meals to children in corporation schools in the Madras city in 1923. The programme was introduced in a large scale in 1960s under the Chief Ministership of K. Kamaraj. However, the first major thrust came in 1982 when the then Chief Minister of Tamil Nadu, Dr. M. G. Ramachandran, decided to universalise the scheme for all children in government schools in primary classes. Later the programme was expanded to cover all children up to class 10. Tamil Nadu's midday meal programme is among the best known in the country.

There is an interesting story about how K. Kamaraj got the idea of a noon meal scheme. The spark is said to have occurred in a small village (now a town) called Cheranmahadevi in Tirunelveli District of Tamil Nadu. K. Kamarajar was a very simple person who used to travel in his car (even without the red lamp at the top) and was not accustomed to convoys.

On one such journey, he had to stop at the railway intersection in Cheranmahadevi and got out of the car and waited. He saw a few boys busy with their cows and goats. The Chief Minister had asked one small boy, "What are you doing with this cows? Why didn't you go to school?" The boy immediately answered, "If I go to school, will you give me food to eat? I can learn only if I eat." The boy's retort sparked the entire process into establishing the midday meal programme.

Kerala has computerised the Midday Meal Scheme in schools. All the dealings are made online and the accounting become accurate.

Several other states of India also have had midday meal programmes. The most notable among them is Gujarat that has had it since the late 1980s. Kerala started providing cooked meals in schools since 1995 and so did Madhya Pradesh and Orissa in small pockets. On November 28, 2001 the Supreme Court of India gave a landmark direction, which made it obligatory for the government to provide cooked meals to all children in all government and government assisted primary schools. The direction was resisted vigorously by State governments initially, but the programme has become almost universal by 2005.

National Programme for Nutrition Support to Primary Education

Although the programme in Tamil Nadu was initially termed as an act of "Populism", the success of the scheme made the project hugely popular. The success was so spectacular that in 1995, the then Indian Finance minister Manmohan Singh hailed the success of the project and suggested that the scheme be implemented all over the country, and thus began the "National Programme for Nutrition Support to Primary Education".

According to the programme the Government of India will provide grains free of cost and the States will provide the costs of other ingredients, salaries and infrastructure. Since most State governments were unwilling to commit budgetary resources they just passed on the grains from Government of India to the parents. This system was called provision of 'dry rations'. On November 28, 2001 the Supreme Court of India gave a famous direction that made it mandatory for the state governments to provide cooked meals instead of 'dry rations'. The direction was to be implemented from June 2002, but was violated by most States. But with sustained pressure from the court, media and in particular from the Right to Food Campaign more and more states started providing cooked meals.

In May 2004 a new coalition government was formed in the centre, which promised universal provision of cooked meals fully funded by the centre. This promise in its Common Minimum Programme was followed by enhanced financial support to the states for cooking and building sufficient infrastructure. Given this additional support the scheme has expanded its reach to cover most children in primary schools in India. In 2005 it is expected to cover 130 million children.

The Supreme Court Direction

In April 2001 People's Union for Civil Liberties (Rajasthan) initiated the now famous right to food litigation. This public interest litigation has covered a large range of issues relating to right to food, but the best known intervention by the court is on midday meals. In one of its many direction in the litigation the Supreme Court directed the government to fully implement its scheme of providing cooked meals to all children in primary schools. This landmark direction converted the Midday Meal Scheme into a legal entitlement, the violation of which can be taken up in the court of law. The direction and further follow-up by the Supreme Court has been a major instrument in universalising the scheme.

Akshaya Patra and Private Sector Participation in Midday Meals

The State of Karnataka introduced the provision of cooked meals in June 2002. Since then it has successfully involved private sector participation in the programme. One of the successful of the ventures is Akshaya Patra, which started with leadership from both ISKCON and secular leaders in the Bangalore community. The programme, now 100 per cent secular, is an independent organisation that cooks and distributes lunch to children in Bangalore Municipal Corporation schools. The Foundation gets a corpus from the State government but meets a major share of its costs with donations from private corporations and individuals in the city.

The programme is managed with an ultra modern centralised kitchen that is run through a public/private partnership. Food is delivered to schools in sealed and heat retaining containers just before the lunch break every day. The programme contains one of the best menus in school meal programmes in India with tasty sambar, rice, vegetables and some curd on most days.

Since the success of this programme private sector participation in midday meals has increased considerably. Software corporations such as Infosys, Bharti and Jindal are major donors to the programme. This model has been successfully replicated in rural Karnataka, Delhi, Hyderabad and other cities.

The foundation is now serving midday meals to almost a million children every day and hopes to feed over 20 million children by 2020.

Naandi Foundation Midday Meal Programme

Naandi Foundation, is one of the largest and fastest growing social sector organisations in India working to make poverty history. In its effort to eradicate poverty it has been working in the fields of Child rights, Education, Sustainable livelihoods, Midday meal and Safe Drinking water since last decade.

To fulfil the motto towards eradicating poverty Naandi took its first step towards banishing hunger through its Midday meal programme. In partnership with state governments and through corporate donations Naandi runs several automated central Midday Meal Kitchens across the country. These kitchens prepare and deliver high-nutrition noon meals to lakhs of underprivileged children everyday.

Naandi even delivers Midday meal in many tribal areas across its project areas in 4 states which includes Andhra Pradesh, Rajasthan, Madhya Pradesh and Orissa. With a highly sophisticated centralised kitchen Naandi delivers food to nearly 8 lakhs children (will touch a million soon) in every working days. The Midday Meal menu is decided in consultation with nutritionists from the National Institute of Nutrition.

Feedback and suggestions from respective government school teachers are taken into consideration for further improvement. For locations such as Hyderabad, Naandi uses Global Positioning System (GPS), where they identified and mapped all the schools to determine the optimum way to transport food.

Naandi in partnership with the Government of Rajasthan started the Hunger-Free programme on 1 May 2006 by providing cooked meals to the poorest of the poor at a very nominal price apart from its Midday meal programme.

Other Aspects of the Programme

The programme in Gujarat also includes regular provision of iron tablets (to counter anaemia) and deworming tablets once in six months. In Tamil Nadu also the children are dewormed at regular intervals.

School Meal Programmes in other Parts of the World

A school meal programme is now a standard welfare measure for school children in developing as well as developed nations. Even countries such as USA have it in many states. World Food Programme, among other organisations, are involved in the programme in many countries across the world.

Scams behind Midday Meal Scheme

Various scams involving Midday Meal Scheme have been unearthed since it was started.

In January 2006, the Delhi Police unearthed a scam in the Midday Meal Scheme. In December 2005, the police had seized eight truckloads (2,760 sacks) of rice meant for primary schoolchildren being carried from Food Corporation of India (FCI) godowns in Bulandshahr District of UP to North Delhi. When the police detained the trucks, the drivers claimed that the rice was being brought all the way to Delhi to be cleaned at a factory. However, according to the guidelines, the rice has to be taken directly from FCI godown to the school or village concerned. Later it was found that the rice was being siphoned off by a UP-based NGO, Bharatiya Manav Kalyan Parishad (BMKP), in connivance with the government officials.

In November 2006, the residents of Pembong village under the Mim tea estate (around 30 km from Darjeeling), accused a group of teachers of embezzling midday meals. In a written complaint, the residents claimed that students at the primary school had not got midday meal for the past 18 months.

In December 2006, The Times of India reported a scam involving government schools that siphon off foodgrains under the Midday Meal Scheme by faking attendance. The modus operandi of the schools was simple — the attendance register would exaggerate the number of students enrolled in the class. The additional students would not exist — they were "enrolled" to get additional foodgrains which were pocketed by the school staff. The scam was exposed, when P. Asha Kumari, an assistant teacher at the government model primary school, Jakkur, in Yelahanka acted as a whistleblower. She informed the Lok Ayukta, who conducted a probe and indicted four persons for misappropriation. The whistleblower was harassed by the school staff and requested a transfer. She was transferred to a government primary school at Cholanayakahalli, where she again found the same modus operandi being used to siphon off the foodgrains. She again complained to the Lok Ayukta, who issued notice to the school.

Analysis

Despite the success of the programme, child hunger as a problem persists in India. According to current statistics, 42.5 per cent of the children under 5 are underweight. This is due to simple reasons such as not using iodised salt. "India is home to the world's largest food insecure population, with more than 200 million people who are hungry," India State Hunger Index (ISHI) said, adding that the country's poor performance is driven by its high levels of child under-nutrition and poor calorie count. "Its rates of child malnutrition is higher than most countries in Sub-Saharan Africa," it noted. A report released as part of the 2008 Global Hunger Index ranks India at 66 out of 88 countries. It says that India has more people suffering hunger - a figure above 200 million - than any other country in the world, it says. The report also says "improving child nutrition is of utmost urgency in most Indian states".

Appendix – III

Kamaraj's Co-travellers

Tanguturi Prakasam

Tanguturi Prakasam Pantulu (b. 23 August 1872 – d. 20 May 1957) was a south Indian politician and Freedom Fighter and the first Chief Minister of the Madras province that was to become Tamil Nadu Andhra Pradesh. He was also known as Andhra Kesari (literally, the Lion of Andhra).

Early Life: He was born in a orthodox Brahmin family to Subbamma and Venkata Narasimham, in a village called Vinodarayuni Palem (or Vinoda Rayudu Palem) 26 km from Ongole in Andhra Pradesh. When he was 11, his father died and his mother had to run a boarding house at Ongole, a profession that was looked down upon at the time.

When E. Hanumantha Rao Naidu, his teacher at school, shifted to Rajahmundry, he took Prakasam along with him as that place had better opportunities for education. He was interested in becoming a lawyer since childhood, Prakasam failed his matriculation examination. He however managed to go to Madras and become a second-grade pleader. Returning to Rajahmundry, he eventually became a successful lawyer. He was elected as Municipal Chairman of Rajahmundry in 1904 when he was 31 years old. This election was a tough one at that point in time.

In England: During one of his professional visits to Madras on a court case, a barrister was impressed with his legal acumen and suggested that he become a barrister. As a second-grade pleader, Prakasam could not argue cases at higher courts as only barristers were allowed to do so. Prakasam took the idea to his heart and decided to go to England to pursue legal studies. It was considered a sacrilege to cross the seas during those days. However, as Mahatma Gandhi had done before him, Prakasam made a promise to his mother that he would abstain from eating non-vegetarian food, smoking and drinking. He reached England in 1904. In England, he joined the India Society and worked for the election of Dadabhai Naoroji to the House of Commons.

In the Service of Public: After completing the barrister course with a certificate of honour in London, Prakasam relocated to Madras high court. He was one of the prominent Telugu barrister to be successful; until then, most of the successful lawyers were either Europeans or Tamilians. He dealt with both civil and criminal cases. Of the latter, one of the important cases was the Ash murder case. Ash was the Collector of Tirunelveli and was shot dead in 1907. This was at a time when Bipin Chandra Pal, the nationalist leader from Bengal was touring the region, making fiery speeches on nationalism. Prakasam defended one of the accused and ensured that he got away with a light sentence. Prakasam also edited Law times, a legal magazine. The same year he presided over Bipin Chandra Pal's lecture at Madras when others were afraid to come forward, given that the government of the day considered Pal's speeches to border on sedition. He started attending the Congress Party sessions regularly after the Lucknow pact and signed the Satyagraha pledge in October 1921. He gave up his lucrative law practice. He also started and was the working editor of a newspaper *Swarajya* (literally self-rule). *Swarajya* was published simultaneously in English, Telugu and Tamil. He also ran a national school and a Khadi production centre. He was elected the general secretary of the Congress Party in December 1921 at the Ahmedabad session. Whenever there was unrest or strife such as a riot, he tried to be there so as to comfort people. He visited Punjab during Akali Satyagraha and the Hindu-Muslim riots in Multan. He toured Kerala during the Moplah rebellion despite a ban on visitors from outside the area and had his property at Ooty attached by the government as a consequence. In 1922, during the Non-cooperation Movement, he organised a demonstration by 30,000 Congress volunteers at Guntur. In 1926, he was elected to the Central Legislative Assembly on a Congress Party ticket.

Andhra Kesari Appellation and Struggle for Independence: When the Simon Commission visited India, the congress party decided to boycott it with the slogan "Simon, go back". There were a host of reasons for this boycott, the most important being that the commission did not have a single Indian in its ranks. The commission was greeted with demonstration of black flags wherever it went. When the commission visited Madras on 3rd February 1928, the police did not allow protests in some sensitive areas of Madras. Nevertheless, the crowd grew large and restive near the Madras High Court at Parry's Corner and the police resorted to firing with a view to control it. However, a young man, named, Pardha Saradhi was killed on the spot. The police warned the people that they would shoot if anyone tried to come near the body. At this, Prakasam grew enraged and tore open his shirt, baring his chest and daring the police to shoot at him. Understanding the situation, the police gave way to him and other supporters. After this incident, people respected him with the epithet of "*Andhra Kesari*" (Lion of Andhra). In 1930, when the Congress wanted all the legislators to resign, he did so but was not convinced about its alternative programme and hence contested and won the by-election. He joined the Nationalist Party led by Madan Mohan Malaviya but resigned from it as well and persuaded others to do so after Mahatma Gandhi and the Congress Party decided to break the salt tax law with the Dandi March. Prakasam also resigned as a legislator and was at the forefront in breaking the tax law at Madras. In the meantime, he had to suspend the publication of *Swarajya* due to the high deposit demanded by the government. It was revived after the Gandhi-Irwin pact of 1931 but it had to be suspended again due to cash flow problems. Unsuccessful attempts were made to restart it again in 1935. In 1937, Congress Party contested the provincial elections and achieved majority in Madras province, among others. Though Prakasam was in the running for Chief Minister's post, he made way for Rajaji, who returned to active politics as per the wishes of the Congress Working Committee. Prakasam became the revenue minister – his major contribution was the founding and chairing of the Zamindari Enquiry Committee which looked at the structural distortions in agriculture perpetrated due to the Zamindari system followed by the British Government. With the onset of World War II, the Congress ministries resigned from office as they were not consulted by the government about India's participation. Prakasam was the first prominent leader from South India to offer individual Satyagraha against the war effort in 1941. He was arrested for more than three years for participating in the Quit India movement of 1942. After his release in 1945, he toured South India to get back in touch with the masses.

Chief Minister of Madras Presidency: In 1946, after the Congress' victory in elections in Madras Presidency Prakasam became the chief minister on 30th April 1946, as he and Kamaraj, a Tamil leader, were against Rajaji — the choice of leaders such as Gandhi and Nehru — becoming the chief minister. However, the government lasted for only 11 months, as it was felt that Prakasam was not accommodating enough to various varying interests. During his tenure as Premier, Prakasam publicly declared his intention to scrap all textile industries in the province and replace them with khadi manufacturing and weaving units. In February 1947, Communists broke into a full-scale revolt. On Vallabhbhai Patel's advice, Prakasam responded with widespread arrests and tough crackdown on arsonists.

Post-independence Period: He visited Hyderabad state in 1948, while the Nizam was still in power, although Prime Minister Nehru warned against doing so because of concern for his personal safety. He met Qasim Rizvi, the leader of the Razakars and warned him about pushing his luck too far. The Razakars were impressed by his courage and accorded him a march of honour. In 1952, he formed the Hyderabad State Praja Party (Hyderabad State People's party) and ensured that all the sitting ministers of the Congress Party were defeated. However, Praja party could not come into power by its own and the coalition that he cobbled up collapsed even before a show of strength could be contemplated.

Chief Minister of Andhra Pradesh: Meanwhile, in December 1952, Potti Sriramulu died fasting for the cause of a separate state for the Telugu-speaking people. On 1 October 1953, the state of Andhra was created and Prakasam, due to his reputation, was made the first chief minister. However, due to opposition from the communists and halting support from the socialists, the government fell after a year. Mid-term elections were held in 1955 by which time Prakasam had more or less retired from active politics. On 1 November 1956, Telugu speaking parts of the erstwhile Hyderabad state were merged in the Andhra state to form Andhra Pradesh. Marathi speaking parts (Aurangabad region) of the Hyderabad state were merged with Bombay State (which later split into Gujarat and Maharashtra) and Kannada speaking parts (Gulbarga region) were merged with Mysore State. Neelam Sanjiva Reddy, a future President of India and a staunch follower of Prakasam became the chief minister. Though retired from politics, Prakasam was active in touring the state. On one such visit to Ongole, he suffered from severe sunstroke. He was admitted in a Hyderabad hospital and died on 20 May 1957.

Institutions Named after Prakasam

- Andhra Kesari Yuvajana Samiti, a Socio-cultural Organisation was formed on 30-04-1962.
- Andhra Kesari Centenary Junior College was established on 23-08-1972, the birth centenary of Andhra Kesari Prakasam Pantulu.
- Andhra Kesari Degree College was opened on 23.08.1994, by Freedom Fighter Padmabhushan Vavilala Gopalakrishnayya.
- Prakasam Engineering College Kandukur.

The Government Junior College at Yanam, named as Sri Tanguturi Prakasam Pantulu Government Junior College.

M. Bhaktavatsalam

Minjur Bhaktavatsalam (October 9, 1897 – January 31, 1987) was a lawyer, politician and freedom fighter from the state of Tamil Nadu. He served as the Chief Minister of Madras state from

October 2, 1963 to March 6, 1967. He was the last Congress chief minister of Tamil Nadu and the last to have taken part in the Indian independence movement.

Bhaktavatsalam was born on October 9, 1897 in the Madras Presidency. He studied law and practised as an advocate in the Madras High Court. He involved himself in politics and the freedom movement right from an early age and was imprisoned during the Salt Satyagraha and the Quit India Movement. He was elected to the Madras Legislative Assembly in 1937 and served as Parliamentary Secretary in the Rajaji government and as a minister in the O. P. Ramaswamy Reddiyar government. He led the Indian National Congress during the 1950s and served as the Chief Minister of Madras Presidency from 1963 to 1967. Following the defeat of the Indian National Congress in the 1967 elections, Bhaktavatsalam partially retired from politics. He died on January 31, 1987 at the age of 89.

Early Life: Bhaktavatsalam was born to C. N. Kanagasabhapathi Mudaliar and his wife Mallika in a Vellalar family of Nazareth village, Madras Presidency. His father died when he was five and Bhaktavatsalam was brought up by his uncles C. N. Muthuranga Mudaliar and C. N. Evalappa Mudaliar. He completed his schooling in Madras and enrolled at Madras Law College. On graduation in 1923, Bhaktavatsalam commenced practice as a lawyer of the Madras High Court.

Family: Bhaktavatsalam was related by marriage to some noted political families of Tamil Nadu. The Indian National Congress politician and Union Minister O. V. Alagesan and former Chief Minister of Madras Presidency, P. T. Rajan were brother-in-laws of Bhaktavatsalam. Bhaktavatsalam's daughter Sarojini Varadappan is a social activist while his granddaughter Jayanthi Natarajan is a politician of the Indian National Congress, Rajya Sabha member and Union minister.

Freedom Movement: Bhaktavatsalam joined the Indian Independence Movement even during graduation. He joined the Indian National Congress and became a member of the Madras Provincial Congress Committee in 1922. In 1926, he became a member of the Congress Working Committee. Bhaktavatsalam started the daily newspaper *India* which he managed till 1933. He was the Secretary of the Tamil Nadu Congress Civic Board during the district board and municipal elections of 1935 and 1926. He also served as the Secretary of the Madras Mahajana Sabha for sometime. Bhaktavatsalam was injured during the Salt Satyagraha at Vedaranyam. He was arrested in 1932 for conducting India's independence day celebrations and spent six months in prison. In the 1936 municipal body elections, Bhaktavatsalam was elected to the Madras City Corporation and served as Deputy Mayor.

Quit India Movement: Bhaktavatsalam stood in the Madras Assembly elections held in 1937 and was elected from the Thiruvallur Rural constituency. Bhaktavatsalam served as the Parliamentary Secretary to the Minister of Local Self-Government in the Rajaji government. Bhaktavatsalam resigned along with the other office-holders of the Indian National Congress on declaration of war by the United Kingdom. Bhaktavatsalam participated in the Quit India Movement agitations and was jailed by the British. On his release in 1944, he elected to the Constituent Assembly of India.

Indian Independence and the Kamaraj Era: Bhaktavatsalam stood in the Madras Assembly elections held in 1946 and was re-elected. He served as the Minister of Public Works and Information in the O. P. Ramaswamy Reddiyar Cabinet. In the 1952 Assembly elections, the first in independent India, Bhaktavatsalam lost.

Chief Minister of Madras State: In 1962, the Indian National Congress won the assembly elections and formed the government in the state for the fifth time in 25 years. On October 2, 1963, Bhaktavatsalam took office as the Chief Minister of Madras, after Kamaraj resigned to spend more time as an office bearer of the Congress. Bhaktavatsalam is, till date, the last Chief Minister of Madras from the Indian National Congress.

Construction of the Vivekananda Rock Memorial: In August 1963, M. S. Golwalkar, the *Sarsangchalak* of the Rashtriya Swayamsevak Sangh established a Swami Vivekananda Centenary Committee and a Vivekananda Rock Memorial Committee and appointed Eknath Ranade as its Secretary. The main function of the committee was to construct a rock memorial at Kanyakumari in order to honour Swami Vivekananda on his birth centenary. The Chief Minister Bhaktavatsam and the Union Minister for Cultural Affairs, Humayun Kabir vehemently opposed the move. However, Bhaktavatsalam yielded when Ranade presented him a letter with signatures of 323 members of Parliament in support of a memorial.

Anti-Hindi Agitations: Bhaktavatsalam's tenure as Chief Minister witnessed severe anti-Hindi agitations in Madras state. Bhaktavatsalam supported the Union Government's decision to introduce Hindi as compulsory language and rejected the demands to make Tamil the medium of instruction in colleges saying that it was "not a practical proposition, not in the interests of national integration, not in the interests of higher education, and not in the interests of the students themselves". On March 7, 1964, at a session of the Madras Legislative Assembly, Bhaktavatsalam recommended the introduction of a three-language formula comprising English, Hindi and Tamil. As January 26, 1965, the day when the 15-year long transition period recommended by the Indian Parliament came to an end, neared, the agitations intensified leading to police action and casualties. Six of the agitators (Chinnaswamy, Sivalingam, Aranganathan, Veerappan, Mutthu, and Sarangapani) immolated themselves while three others (Dandapani, Mutthu, and Shanmugam) consumed poison. One of the agitators, eighteen-year old Rajendran was killed on January 27, 1965 as a result of police firing. On February 13, 1965, Bhaktavatsalam claimed that the opposition Dravidar Munnetra Kazhagam and the Left parties were responsible for the large scale destruction of public property and violence during the anti-Hindi agitations of 1965.

The Demise: Bhaktavatsalam died at the age of 89.

Appendix – IV

History of Tamil Nadu

The region of Tamil Nadu in modern India has been under continuous human habitation since pre-historic times, and the history of Tamil Nadu and the civilization of the Tamil people are among the oldest in the world. Throughout its history, spanning the early Palaeolithic age to modern times, this region has coexisted with various external cultures. Except for relatively short periods in its history, the Tamil region has remained independent of external occupation.

The four ancient Tamil Empires of Chera, Chola, Pandya and Pallava were of ancient origins. Together they ruled over this land with a unique culture and language, contributing to the growth of some of the oldest extant literature in the world. They had extensive maritime trade contacts with the Roman Empire. These three dynasties were in constant struggle with each other vying for hegemony over the land. Invasion by the Kalabhras during the third century disturbed the traditional order of the land by displacing the three ruling kingdoms. These occupiers were overthrown by the resurgence of the Pandyas and the Pallavas, who restored the traditional kingdoms. The Cholas, who re-emerged from obscurity in the ninth century by defeating the Pallavas and the Pandyas, rose to become a great power and extended their empire over the entire southern peninsula. At its height the Chola Empire spanned almost 3,600,000 sq km (1,389,968 sq mi) straddling the Bay of Bengal. The Chola navy held sway over the Sri Vijaya Kingdom in South East Asia.

Rapid changes in the political situation of the rest of India due to incursions of Muslim armies from the northwest marked a turning point in the history of Tamil Nadu. With the decline of the three ancient dynasties during the fourteenth century, the Tamil country became part of the Vijayanagara Empire. Under this empire the Telugu speaking Nayak governors ruled the Tamil land. The brief appearance of the Marathas gave way to the European trading companies, who began to appear during the seventeenth century and eventually assumed greater sway over the indigenous rulers of the land. The Madras Presidency, comprising most of southern India, was created in the eighteenth century and was ruled directly by the British East India Company. After the independence of India, the state of Tamil Nadu was created based on linguistic boundaries.

Pre-historic Period

Palaeolithic Age: The pre-historic period during which the Palaeolithic civilizations existed in the Tamil Nadu region has been estimated to span the period from about 500,000 BCE until around 3000 BCE. For most part of the lower Palaeolithic stage, humans lived close to river valleys with sparse forest cover or in grassland environments. The population density was very low and so far only two localities of this lower Palaeolithic culture have been found in south India. One of these is in Attirampakkam valley in the northwest of Chennai in Tamil Nadu. Archaeological research has uncovered evidence of fossil remains of animals and primitive stone implements around the northern Tamil Nadu that could be dated to belong to around 300,000 BCE. Humans in South India, belonging to the species of *Homo erectus*, lived in this primitive 'old stone age' (Palaeolithic) for quite a long time, using only crude implements such as hand axes and choppers and subsisting on food he hunted and gathered instead of actively growing it according to his needs.

The ancestor of modern humans (*Homo sapiens sapiens*) who appeared around 50,000 years ago was more developed and could make thinner flake tools and blade-like tools using a variety of stones. From about 10,000 years ago, humans made still smaller tools called Microlithic tools. The material used by the early humans to make these tools were jasper, agate, flint, quartz, etc. In 1949, researchers found such microliths in Tirunelveli district. Archaeological evidence suggests that the microlithic period lasted between 6000–3000 BCE.

Neolithic: In Tamil Nadu, the Neolithic period had its advent around 2500 BCE. Humans of the Neolithic period made their stone tools in finer shapes by grinding and polishing. A Neolithic axe head with ancient writing on it has been found in Tamil Nadu. The Neolithic humans lived mostly on small flat hills or on the foothills in small, more or less permanent settlements but for periodical migration for grazing purposes. They gave the dead proper burials within urns or pits. They were also starting to use copper for making certain tools or weapons.

Iron Age: During the Iron Age humans started using iron for making tools and weapons. The Iron Age culture in peninsular India is marked by Megalithic burial sites, which are found in several hundreds of places. On the bases of both some excavations and the typology of the burial monuments, it has been suggested that there was a gradual spread of the Iron Age sites from the north to the south. Comparative excavations carried out in Adichanallur in Thirunelveli district and in Northern India have provided evidence of a southward migration of the Megalithic culture. The earliest clear evidence of the presence of the megalithic urn burials are those dating from around 1000 BCE, which have been discovered at various places in Tamil Nadu, notably at Adichanallur, 24 km from Tirunelveli, where archaeologists from the Archaeological Survey of India unearthed 157 urns, including 15 containing human skulls, skeletons and bones, plus husks, grains of rice, charred rice and Neolithic celts. One urn has writing inside, which, according to archaeologists from the Archaeological Survey of India, resembles early Tamil-Brahmi script, confirming it of the Neolithic period 2800 years ago. Adhichanallur has been announced as an archaeological site for further excavation and studies. Mentions of the political situation of Tamil Nadu before the common era are found in Ashoka's edicts dated c 300 BCE and, vaguely, in the Hathigumpha inscription dated c.150 BCE. The earliest epigraphical evidence in the Tamil country are that of the Pandya King Kadungon (c. 560-590 CE) who displaced the Kalabhras from the Pandyas country. — Nilakanta Sastri, *A history of South India*.

Ancient Period

Ancient Tamil Nadu contained three monarchical states, headed by Kings called *Ventar* and several tribal chieftaincies, headed by the chiefs called by the general denomination *Vel* or *Velir*. Still lower at the local level there were clan chiefs called *kizar* or *mannar*. During the third century BCE, the Deccan was part of the Mauryan Kingdom, and from the middle of the first century BCE to second century CE the same area was ruled by the Satavahana dynasty. The Tamil area had an independent existence outside the control of these northern empires. The Tamil Kings and chiefs were always in conflict with each other mostly over property. The royal courts were mostly places of social gathering rather than places of dispensation of authority; they were centres for distribution of resources. Gradually the rulers came under the spell of north Indian influence and Vedic ideology, which encouraged performance of sacrifices to enhance the status of the ruler.

The Dynasties: The names of the three dynasties, Cholas, Pandyas, and Cheras are mentioned in the Pillars of Ashoka (inscribed 273–232 BCE) inscriptions, among the kingdoms, which though not subject to Ashoka, were on friendly terms with him. The King of Kalinga, Kharavela, who ruled around 150 BCE, mentioned in the famous Hathigumpha inscription of the confederacy of the Tamil Kingdoms that had existed for over 100 years.

Karikala Chola was the most famous early Chola. He is mentioned in a number of poems in the Sangam poetry. In later times Karikala was the subject of many legends found in the *Cilappatikaram* and in inscriptions and literary works of the eleventh and twelfth centuries. They attribute to him the conquest of the whole of India up to the Himalayas and the construction of the flood banks of the river Kaveri with the aid of his feudatories.

These legends however are conspicuous by their absence in the Sangam poetry. Kocengannan was another famous early Chola King who has been extolled in a number of poems of the Sangam period. He was even made a Saiva saint during the medieval period.

Pandyas ruled initially from Korkai, a sea port on the southernmost tip of the Indian peninsula, and in later times moved to Madurai. Pandyas are also mentioned in Sangam Literature, as well as by Greek and Roman sources during this period. Megasthenes in his *Indika* mentions the Pandyan Kingdom. The Pandyas controlled the present districts of Madurai, Tirunelveli, and parts of south Kerala. They had trading contacts with Greece and Rome. With the other Kingdoms of Tamilakam, they maintained trading contacts and maritial relationships with Tamil merchants from Eelam. Various Pandya Kings find mention in a number of poems in the Sangam literature. Among them Nedunjeliyan, 'the victor of Talaiyalanganam', yet another Nedunjeliyan 'the conqueror of the Aryan army' and Mudukudimi Peruvaludi 'of several sacrifices' deserve special mention. Besides several short poems found in the *Akananuru* and the *Purananuru* collections, there are two major works—*Mathuraikkanci* and the *Netunalvatai* (in the collection of *Pattupattu*) that give a glimpse into the society and commercial activities in the Pandyan Kingdom during the Sangam age. The early Pandyas went into obscurity at the end of the third century CE during the incursion of the Kalabhras.

The Kingdom of the Cheras comprised the modern state of Kerala, along the western or Malabar Coast of southern India. Their proximity to the sea favoured trade with Africa. The people of the current Indian state of Kerala, which constitutes the ancient territories of the Cheras spoke the same language and had extensive interaction with the rest of the Tamil country. It was only towards the ninth or the tenth centuries CE, Due to Aryan's Sanskrit influence in Tamil their individual identity change then a new language began to evolve.

Growth of Literature: These early kingdoms sponsored the growth of some of the oldest extant literature in Tamil. The classical Tamil literature, referred to as Sangam literature is attributed to the period between 200 BCE and 300 CE. The poems of Sangam literature, which deal with emotional and material topics, were categorised and collected into various anthologies during the medieval period. These Sangam poems paint the picture of a fertile land and of a people who were organised into various occupational groups. The governance of the land was through hereditary monarchies, although the sphere of the state's activities and the extent of the ruler's powers were limited through the adherence to the established order (*dharma*). The people were loyal to their Kings and roving bards and musicians and danseuse gathered at the royal courts of the generous Kings. The arts of music and dancing were highly developed and popular. Musical instruments of various types find mention in the Sangam poems. The amalgamation of the southern and the northern styles of dancing started during this period and is reflected fully in the epic *Cilappatikaram*.

The Trade: Internal and external trade was well organised and active. Evidence from both archaeology and literature speaks of a flourishing foreign trade with the *yavanas*. The port city of Puhar on the east coast and Muziris on the west coast of south India were emporia of foreign trade, where huge ships moored, offloading precious merchandise. This trade started to decline after the second century CE and the direct contact between the Roman Empire and the ancient Tamil country was replaced by trade with the Arabs and the Auxumites of East Africa. Internal trade was also brisk and goods were sold and bartered. Agriculture was the main profession of a vast majority of the populace and *Vellalars*, the hereditary agriculturalists, owned the bulk of the land.

The Interregnum (300-600)

After the close of the Sangam era, from about 300 to about 600 CE, there is an almost total lack of information regarding occurrences in the Tamil land. Some time about 300 CE, the whole region was upset by the appearance of the Kalabhras. These people are described in later literature as 'evil rulers' who overthrew the established Tamil Kings and got a strangle hold of the country. Information about their origin and details about their reign is scarce. They did not leave many artefacts or monuments. The only source of information on them is the scattered mentions in Buddhist and Jain literature.

Historians speculate that these people followed Buddhist or Jain faiths and were antagonistic towards the Hindu and Brahminical religions adhered by the majority of inhabitants of the Tamil region during the early centuries C.E. As a result Hindu scholars and authors who followed their decline in the 7th and 8th century may have expunged any mention of them in their texts and generally tended to paint their rule in a negative light. It is perhaps due to this reason, the period of their rule is known as a 'Dark Age'—an interregnum. Some of the ruling families migrated northwards and found enclaves for themselves away from the Kalabhras. Jainism and Buddhism, took deep roots in the society, giving birth to a large body of ethical poetry.

Writing became very widespread and *vatteluttu* evolved from the Tamil-Brahmi became a mature script for writing Tamil. While several anthologies were compiled by collecting bardic poems of earlier centuries, some of the epic poems such as the *Cilappatikaram* and didactic works such as the *Tirukkural* were also written during this period. The patronage of the Jain and Buddhist scholars by the Kalabhra Kings influenced the nature of the literature of the period, and most of the works that can be attributed to this period were written by the Jain and Buddhist authors. In the field of dance and music, the elite started patronising new polished styles, partly influenced by northern ideas, in the place of the folk styles. A few of the earliest rock-cut temples belong to this period. Brick temples (known as *kottam*, *devakulam*, and *palli*) dedicated to various deities are referred to in literary works. Kalabhras were displaced around the 7th century by the revival of Pallava and Pandya power.

Even with the exit of the Kalabhras, the Jain and Buddhist influence still remained in Tamil Nadu. The early Pandya and the Pallava Kings were followers of these faiths. The Hindu reaction to this apparent decline of their religion was growing and reached its peak during the later part of the seventh century. There was a widespread Hindu revival during which a huge body of Saiva and Vaishnava literature was created. Many Saiva Nayanmars and Vaishnava Alvars provided a great stimulus to the growth of popular devotional literature. Karaikkal Ammaiyar who lived in the sixth century CE was the earliest of these Nayanmars. The celebrated Saiva hymnists Sundaramurthi, Thirugnana

Sambanthar and Thirunavukkarasar were of this period. Vaishnava Alvars such as Poigai Alvar, Bhoothathalvar and Peyalvar produced devotional hymns for their faith and their songs were collected later into the four thousand poems of *Naalayira Divyap Prabhandham*.

Medieval Period

Age of Empires (600-1300): The medieval period of the history of the Tamil country saw the rise and fall of many kingdoms, some of whom went on to the extent of empires, exerting influences both in India and overseas. The Cholas who were very active during the Sangam age were entirely absent during the first few centuries. The period started with the rivalry between the Pandyas and the Pallavas, which in turn caused the revival of the Cholas. The Cholas went on to becoming a great power. Their decline saw the brief resurgence of the Pandyas. This period was also that of the re-invigorated Hinduism during which temple building and religious literature were at their best.

The Hindu sects Saivism and Vaishnavism became dominant, replacing the prevalence of Jainism and Buddhism of the previous era. Saivism was patronised more by the Chola Kings and became more or less a state religion. Some of the earliest temples that are still standing were built during this period by the Pallavas. The rock-cut temples in Mamallapuram and the majestic Kailasanatha and Vaikuntaperumal temples of Kanchipuram stand testament to the Pallava art. The Cholas, utilising their prodigious wealth earned through their extensive conquests, built long-lasting stone temples including the great Brihadisvara temple of Thanjavur and exquisite bronze sculptures. Temples dedicated to Siva and Vishnu received liberal donations of money, jewels, animals, and land, and thereby became powerful economic institutions.

Tamil script replaced the *vatteluttu* script throughout Tamil Nadu for writing Tamil. Both secular and religious literature flourished during the period. The Tamil epic, Kamban's *Ramavatharam*, was written in the 13th century. A contemporary of Kamban was the famous poetess Auvaiyar who found great happiness in writing for young children. The secular literature was mostly court poetry devoted to the eulogy of the rulers. The religious poems of the previous period and the classical literature of the Sangam period were collected and systematised into several anthologies. Sanskrit was patronised by the priestly groups for religious rituals and other ceremonial purposes. Nambi Andar Nambi, who was a contemporary of Rajaraja Chola I, collected and arranged the books on Saivism into eleven books called *Tirumurais*. The hagiology of Saivism was standardised in *Periyapuranam* by Sekkilar, who lived during the reign of Kulothunga Chola II (1133-1150 CE). Jayamkondar's *Kalingattupparani*, a semi-historical account on the two invasions of Kalinga by Kulothunga Chola I was an early example of a biographical work.

Pallavas: The seventh century Tamil Nadu saw the rise of the Pallavas under Mahendravarman I and his son *Mamalla* Narasimhavarman I. The Pallavas were not a recognised political power before the second century. It has been widely accepted by scholars that they were originally executive officers under the Satavahana Kings. After the fall of the Satavahanas, they began to get control over parts of Andhra and the Tamil country. Later they had marital ties with the Vishnukundina who ruled over the Deccan. It was around 550 AD under King Simhavishnu that the Pallavas emerged into prominence. They subjugated the Cholas and reigned as far south as the Kaveri River. The Pallavas were at their finest during the reigns of Narasimhavarman I and *Pallavamalla* Nandivarman II. Pallavas ruled a large portion of South India with Kanchipuram as their capital. Dravidian architecture reached its peak during the Pallava rule. Narasimhavarman II built the Shore Temple which is a UNESCO World Heritage Site. Many sources describe Bodhidharma, the founder of the Zen school of Buddhism in China, as a Prince of the Pallava dynasty. During the sixth and the seventh centuries, the western Deccan saw the rise of the Chalukyas based in Vatapi. Pulakesi II (c.610-642) invaded the Pallava Kingdom in the reign of Mahendravarman I. Narasimhavarman who succeeded Mahendravarman mounted a counter invasion of the Chalukya country and took Vatapi. The rivalry between the Chalukyas and the Pallavas continued for another 100 years until the demise of the Chalukyas around 750. The Chalukyas and Pallavas fought numerous battles and the Pallava capital Kanchipuram was occupied by Vikramaditya II during the reign of Nandivarman II. Nandivarman II had a very long reign (732-796). He led an expedition to the Ganga Kingdom (south Mysore) in 760. Pallavas were also in constant conflict with the Pandyas and their frontier shifted along the river Kaveri. The Pallavas had the more difficult existence of the two as they had to fight on two fronts—against the Pandyas as wells as the Chalukyas.

Pandyas: Pandya Kadungon (560-590) is credited with the overthrow of the Kalabhras in the south. Kadungon and his son Maravarman Avanisulamani revived the Pandya power. Pandya Cendan extended their rule to the Chera country. His son Arikesari Parantaka Maravarman (c. 650-700) had a long and prosperous rule. He fought many battles and extended the Pandya power. *Pandya* was well known since ancient times, with contacts, even diplomatic, reaching the Roman Empire; during the 13th century of the Christian era Marco Polo mentioned it as the richest empire in existence.

After some decades of expansion, the Pandyan Empire was large enough to pose a serious threat to the Pallava power. Pandya Maravarman Rajasimha aligned with the Chalukya Vikramaditya II and attacked the Pallava King Nandivarman II. Varagunan I defeated the Pallavas in a battle on the banks of the Kaveri. The Pallava King Nandivarman sought to restrain the growing power of the Pandyas and went into an alliance with the feudal chieftains of Kongu and Chera countries. The armies met in several battles and the Pandya forces scored decisive victories in them. Pandyas under Srimara Srivallaba also invaded Sri Lanka and devastated the northern provinces in 840. The Pandya power continued to grow under Srimara and encroached further into the Pallava territories. The Pallavas were now facing a new threat in the form of the Rashtrakutas who had replaced the Chalukyas in the western Deccan. However the Pallavas found an able monarch in Nandivarman III, who with the help of his Ganga and the Chola allies defeated Srimara at the battle of Tellaru. The Pallava Kingdom again extended up to the river Vaigai. The Pandyas suffered further defeats in the hands of the Pallava Nripatunga at Arisil (c. 848). From then the Pandyas had to accept the overlordship of the Pallavas.

Cholas: Around 850, out of obscurity rose Vijayalaya, made use of an opportunity arising out of a conflict between Pandyas and Pallavas, captured Thanjavur and eventually established the imperial line of the medieval Cholas. Vijayalaya revived the Chola dynasty and his son Aditya I helped establish their independence. He invaded Pallava Kingdom in 903 and killed the Pallava King Aparajita in battle, ending the Pallava reign. The Chola Kingdom under Parantaka I expanded to cover the entire Pandya country. However towards the end of his reign he suffered several reverses by the Rashtrakutas who had extended their territories well into the Chola Kingdom. The Cholas went into a temporary decline during the next few years due to weak Kings, palace intrigues and succession disputes. Despite a number of attempts the Pandya country could not be completely subdued and the Rashtrakutas were still a powerful enemy in the north. However, the Chola revival began with the accession of Rajaraja Chola I in 985. Cholas rose as a notable military, economic and cultural power in Asia under Rajaraja and his son Rajendra Chola I. The Chola territories stretched from the islands of Maldives in the south to as far north as the banks of the river Ganges in Bengal. Rajaraja Chola conquered peninsular South India, annexed parts of Sri Lanka and occupied the islands of Maldives. Rajendra Chola extended the Chola conquests to the Malayan archipelago by defeating the Srivijaya Kingdom. He defeated Mahipala, the King of Bihar and Bengal, and to commemorate his victory he built a new capital called Gangaikonda Cholapuram (*the town of Cholas who conquered the Ganges*). At its peak the Chola Empire extended from the island of Sri Lanka in the south to the Godavari basin in the north. The kingdoms along the east coast of India up to the river Ganges acknowledged Chola suzerainty. Chola navies invaded and conquered Srivijaya in the Malayan archipelago. Chola armies exacted tribute from Thailand and the Khmer Kingdom of Cambodia. During the reign of Rajaraja and Rajendra, the administration of the Chola Empire matured considerably. The empire was divided into a number of self-governing local government units, and the officials were selected through a system of popular elections. Throughout this period, the Cholas were constantly troubled by the ever resilient Sinhalas trying to overthrow the Chola occupation of Lanka, Pandya Princes trying to win independence for their traditional territories, and by the growing ambitions of the Chalukyas in the western Deccan. The history of this period was one of constant warfare between the Cholas and of these antagonists. A balance of power existed between the Chalukyas and the Cholas and there was a tacit acceptance of the Tungabhadra river as the boundary between the two empires. However, the bone of contention between these two powers was the growing Chola influence in the Vengi Kingdom. The Cholas and Chalukyas fought many battles and both kingdoms were exhausted by the endless battles and a stalemate existed.

Marital and political alliances between the Eastern Chalukya Kings based around Vengi located on the south banks of the river Godavari began during the reign of Rajaraja following his invasion of Vengi. Virarajendra Chola's son Athirajendra Chola was assassinated in a civil disturbance in 1070 and Kulothunga Chola I ascended the Chola throne starting the Chalukya Chola dynasty. Kulothunga was a son of the Vengi King Rajaraja Narendra. The Chalukya Chola dynasty saw very capable rulers in Kulothunga Chola I and Vikrama Chola, however the eventual decline of the Chola power practically started during this period. The Cholas lost control of the island of Lanka and were driven out by the revival of Sinhala power. Around 1118 they also lost the control of Vengi to Western Chalukya King Vikramaditya VI and Gangavadi (southern Mysore districts) to the growing power of Hoysala Vishnuvardhana, a Chalukya feudatory. In the Pandya territories, the lack of a controlling central administration caused a number of claimants to the Pandya throne to cause a civil war in which the Sinhalas and the Cholas were involved by proxy. During the last century of the Chola existence, a permanent Hoysala army was stationed in Kanchipuram to protect them from the growing influence of the Pandyas. Rajendra Chola III was the last Chola King. The Kadava chieftain Kopperunchinga I even captured Rajendra and held him prisoner. At the close of Rajendra's reign (1279), the Pandyan Empire was at the height of prosperity and had completely absorbed the Chola Kingdom.

Pandya Revival: After being overshadowed by the Pallavas and Cholas for centuries, Jatavarman Sundara Pandyan briefly revived the Pandya glory in 1251 and the Pandya power extended from the Telugu countries on banks of the Godavari river to the northern half of Sri Lanka. When Maaravaramban Kulasekara Pandyan I died in 1308, a conflict stemming from succession disputes arose amongst his sons - the legitimate Sundara Pandya and the illegitimate Vira Pandya (who was favoured by the King) fought each other for the throne. Soon Madurai fell into the hands of the invading armies of the Delhi Sultanate (which initially gave protection to the vanquished Sundara Pandyan).

Campaign from Delhi

Malik Kafur, a general of the Delhi Sultan Alauddin Khilji invaded and sacked Madurai in 1311. Pandyas and their descendants where confined to a small region around Thirunelveli for a few more years. Ravivarman Kulasekara (1299-1314), a Chera feudatory of Kulasekara Pandya, staked his claim to the Pandya throne. Ravivarman Kulasekhara, utilising the unsettled nature of the country, quickly overran the southern Tamil Nadu and brought the entire region from Kanyakumari to Kanchipuram, under the Chera Kingdom. His inscription was found in Punaamalli, a suburb of Madras.

Vijayanagar Empire and Nayak Period (1300-1650): The fourteenth century invasion by the Delhi Sultans caused a retaliatory reaction from the Hindus, who rallied to build a new kingdom, called the Vijayanagara Empire. Bukka, with his brother Harihara founded the Hindu Vijayanagara Empire based in the city of Vijayanagara in Karnataka. Under Bukka the empire prospered and continued to expand towards the south. Bukka and his son Kampana conquered most of the kingdoms of southern India. In 1371 the Vijayanagar Empire defeated the short lived Madurai Sultanate, which had been established by the remnants of the invading Khilji army. Eventually the empire covered the entire south India. Vijayangara Empire established local governors called Nayaks to rule in the various territories of the empire.

The Vijayanagar Empire declined in 1564 defeated by the Deccan Sultans in the battle of Talikota. The local Nayak governors declared their independence and started their rule. The Nayaks of Madurai and Thanjavur were the most prominent of them. Ragunatha Nayak (1600-1645) was the greatest of the Tanjavur

Nayaks. Raghunatha Nayak encouraged trade and permitted a Danish settlement in 1620 at Tarangambadi. This laid the foundation of future European involvement in the affairs of the country. The success of the Dutch inspired the English to seek trade with Thanjavur, which was to lead to far-reaching repercussions. Vijaya Raghava (1631-1675) was the last of the Thanjavur Nayaks. Nayaks reconstructed some of the oldest temples in the country and their contributions can be seen even today. Nayaks expanded the existing temples with large pillared halls, and tall gateway towers, which is representative of the religious architecture of this period.

In Madurai, Thirumalai Nayak was the most famous Nayak ruler. He patronised art and architecture creating new structures and expanding the existing landmarks in and around Madurai. On Thirumalai Nayak's death in 1659, the Madurai Nayak Kingdom began to break up. His successors were weak rulers and invasions of Madurai recommenced. Shivaji Bhonsle, the great Maratha Ruler, invaded the south, as did Chikka Deva Raya of Mysore and other Muslim Rulers, resulting in chaos and instability. Rani Mangammal, a local ruler, tried to resist these invasions showing great courage.

Advent of European

European settlements began to appear in the Tamil country during the Vijayanagara Empire. In 1605, the Dutch established trading posts in the Coromandel Coast near Gingee and in Pulicat. The British East India Company built a 'factory' (warehouse) at Armagaon (Durgarazpatnam), a village around 35 miles (56 km) North of Pulicat, as the site in 1626. In 1639, Francis Day, one of the officers of the company, secured the rights over a three-mile (5 km) long strip of land a fishing village called Madraspatnam from the Damarla Venkatadri Nayakudu, the Nayak of Vandavasi. The East India Company built Fort St George and castle on an approximate five square kilometre sand strip. This was the start of the town of Madras. The coromandel coast was ruled by the Vijayanagara King (Aravidu Dynasty), Peda Venkata Raya, based in Chandragiri and Vellore Fort. With his approval the English began to exercise sovereign rights over their strip of land.

In 1675, a column of Bijapur army came to Thanjavur to help Vijayaraghava and retrieved Vallam from the Madurai Nayak. However the same army subsequently killed Vijayaraghava Nayak and Ekoji managed to ascend the throne of Thanjavur Kingdom. Thus began the Maratha rule of Thanjavur. After Ekoji, his three sons namely Shaji, Serfoji I, Thukkoji alias Thulaja I ruled Thanjavur. The greatest of the Maratha rulers was Serfoji II (1798-1832). Serfoji devoted his life to the pursuit of culture and Thanjavur became renowned as a seat of learning. Serfoji's patronised art and literature and built the Saraswati Mahal Library at his palace. The incursion of the Muslim armies from the north forced a southward migration of Hindus from the central Deccan and the Andhra countries to seek shelter under the Nayak and the Maratha Kings. The famous Carnatic music composer Tyagaraja (1767-1847), along with the Trinity of Carnatic music flourished in the Thanjavur district during this time.

Decline of Mughal Empire: With the demise of the Mughal Emperor Aurangzeb in 1707, his empire dissolved amidst numerous succession wars and the vassals of the empire began to assert their independence. The administration of the southern districts of Tamil Nadu was fragmented with hundreds of Poligars or *Palayakkarars* governing a few villages each. These local chieftains often fought amongst each other over territory. This turned the political situation in the Tamil country and in South India in general into confusion and chaos. The European traders found themselves in a situation where they could exploit the prevailing confusion to their own advantage.

European Colonisation (1750-1850)

Anglo-French Conflicts: The French were relative newcomers to India. The French East India Company was formed in 1664 and in 1666 the French representatives obtained Aurangzeb's permission to trade in India. The French soon setup trading posts in Pondicherry on the Coromandel coast. They occupied Karaikal in 1739 and Joseph François Dupleix was appointed Governor of Pondicherry. In Europe the War of the Austrian Succession began in 1740 and eventually the British and the French forces in India were caught up in the conflict. There were numerous naval battles between the two navies along the Coromandel coast. The French led by La Bourdonnais attacked the poorly defended Fort St. George in Madras in 1746 and occupied it. Robert Clive was one of the prisoners of war from this battle. The war in Europe ended in 1748 and with the peace of Aix-la-Chapelle Madras was restored to the British. The conflict between the British and the French continued, this time in political rather than military terms. Both the Nawab of the Carnatic and Nizam of Hyderabad positions were taken by rulers who were strongly sympathetic to the French. Chanda Sahib had been made Nawab of the Carnatic with Dupleix's assistance, while the British had taken up the cause of the previous incumbent, Mohammed Ali Khan Walajah. In the resultant battle between the rivals, Clive assisted Mohammed Ali by attacking Chanda Sahib's fort in Arcot and took possession of it in 1751. The French assisted Chanda Sahib in his attempts to drive Clive out of Arcot. However the large Arcot army assisted by the French was defeated by the British. The Treaty of Paris (1763) formally confirmed Muhammad Ali as the Nawab of the Carnatic. It was a result of this action and the increased British influence that in 1765 the Emperor of Delhi issued a *firman* (decree) recognising the British possessions in southern India.

British Government Control: Although the Company was becoming increasingly bold and ambitious in putting down resisting states, it was getting clearer day by day that the Company was incapable of governing the vast expanse of the captured territories. Opinion amongst the members of the British Parliament urged the government to control the activities of the Company. The Company's financial position was also bad and it had to apply for a loan from Parliament. Seizing this opportunity, the Parliament passed the Regulating Act (also known as East India Company Act) in 1773. The act set down regulations to control the Company Board and created the position of the Governor General. Warren Hastings was appointed the first Governor-General. In 1784 Pitt's India Act made the Company subordinate to the British Government.

The next few decades were of rapid growth and expansion in the territories controlled by the British. The Anglo-Mysore Wars of 1766 to 1799 and the Anglo-Maratha Wars of 1772 to 1818 put the Company in control of most of India. In a sign of the early resistance against the English control, the Palayakkarar chieftains of the old Madurai Kingdom, who had independent authority over their territories, ran into a conflict with the Company officials over tax collection. Kattabomman, a local Palayakkarar chieftain in the Tirunelveli district, rebelled against the taxes imposed by the Company administration in the 1790s. After the First Polygar War (1799-1802), he was captured and hanged in 1799. A year later, the Second Polygar War was fought by Dheeran Chinnamalai, by winning three wars against British after the fall of Tipu Sultan Kingdom at last he and his two brothers was illegally hanged and Dheeran Chinnamalai was the last Tamil King died in the war against Britishers and was put down by the Company after a long and expensive campaign. The end of the Polygar Wars gave the British complete control over a major portion of Tamil Nadu.

In 1798 Lord Wellesley became the Governor-General. In the course of the next six years Wellesley made vast conquests and doubled the Company's territory. He shut out the French from further acquisitions in India, destroyed several ruling powers in the Deccan and the Carnatic, took the Mughal Emperor under the company's protection and compelled Serfoji, the King of Thanjavur to cede control of his kingdom. The Madras Presidency was established so that the territory under direct Company control could be administered effectively. The direct administration began to cause resentment among the people. In 1806 the soldiers of the Vellore cantonment rebelled when William Bentinck, the Governor of Madras decreed that the native soldiers should abandon all caste marks. Fearing this act to be an attempt of forceful conversion to Christianity, the soldiers mutinied. The rebellion was suppressed but 114 British officers were killed and several hundred mutineers executed. Bentinck was recalled in disgrace.

End of Company Rule: The simmering discontent in the various districts of the company territories exploded in 1857 into the Sepoy war. Although the rebellion had a huge impact on the state of the colonial power in India, Tamil Nadu was mostly unaffected by it. In consequence of the war, the British Government enacted the Act of 1858 to abolish the powers of the Company and transfer the government to the Crown.

British Rule (1858-1947)

In 1858 the British Crown assumed direct rule in India. During the early years the government was autocratic in many ways. The opinion of Indians in their own affairs was not considered by Britain as important. However, in due course the British Raj began to allow Indians participation in local government. Viceroy Ripon passed a resolution in 1882, which gave a greater and more real share in local government to the people. Further legislation such as the 1892 Indian councils Act and the 1909 "Minto-Morley Reforms" eventually led to the establishment of the Madras Legislative Council. The non-cooperation movement started under Mahatma Gandhi's leadership led the British government to pass the Government of India Act (also known as Montagu-Chelmsford Reforms) of 1919. First elections were held for the local assemblies in 1921.

Failure of the summer monsoons and administrative shortcomings of the Ryotwari system resulted in a severe famine in the Madras Presidency during 1876-77. The government and several charitable institutions organised relief work in the city and the suburbs. Funds were also raised from Europeans in India and overseas for the famine relief. Humanitarians such as William Digby wrote angrily about the woeful failure of the British administration to act promptly and adequately in response to the wholesale suffering caused by the famine. When the famine finally ended with the return of the monsoon in 1878, between three and five million people had perished. In response to the devastating effects of the famine, the government organised a Famine Commission in 1880 to define the principles of disaster relief. The government also instituted a famine insurance grant, setting aside 1.5 million Rupees. Other civic works such as canal building and improvements in roads and railway were also undertaken to minimise effects of any future famines.

Freedom Struggle

The growing desire for independence began to gradually gather pace in the country and its influence in Tamil Nadu generated a number of volunteers to the fight against the British colonial power in the struggle for Independence. Notable amongst these are Tiruppur Kumaran, who was born in 1904 in a small village near Erode. Kumaran lost his life during a protest march against the British. The location of the French colony of Pondicherry, offered a place of refuge for the fugitives freedom fighters trying to flee the British Police. Aurobindo was one such living in Pondicherry in 1910. The poet Subramanya Bharathi was a contemporary of Aurobindo. Bharathi wrote numerous poems in Tamil extolling the revolutionary cause. He also published the journal *India* from Pondicherry. Both Aurobindo and Bharathi were associated with other Tamil revolutionaries such as V. V. S. Aiyar and V. O. Chidambaram Pillai. Tamils formed a significant percentage of the members of the Indian National Army (INA), founded by Netaji to fight the British occupation in India. Lakshmi Sahgal from Tamil Nadu was a prominent leader in the INA.

In 1916 Dr. T. M. Nair and Rao Bahadur Thygaraya Chetty released the *non-Brahmin Manifesto* sowing the seeds for the Dravidian movements. During the 1920s, two movements focused mainly on regional politics began in Tamil Nadu. One was the Justice Party, which won the local legislative elections held in 1921. The Justice Party was not focused on the Indian independence movement, rather on the local issues such as affirmative action for socially backward groups. The other main movement was the anti-religious, anti-Brahmin reformist movement led by E. V. Ramaswamy Naicker. Further steps towards eventual self-rule were taken in 1935 when the British Government passed the All-India Federation Act of 1935. Fresh local elections were held and in Tamil Nadu the Congress party captured power defeating the Justice party. In 1938, Ramaswamy Naicker with C. N. Annadurai launched an agitation against the Congress ministry's decision to introduce the teaching of Hindi in schools.

Post-independence Era

The trauma of the partition did not impact Tamil Nadu when India was granted Independence in 1947. There was no sectarian violence against various religions. There had always been an atmosphere of mutual respect and peaceful coexistence between all religions in Tamil Nadu. Congress formed the first ministry in the Madras Presidency. C. Rajagopalachari (Rajaji) was the first

Chief Minister. Madras Presidency was eventually reconstituted as Madras State. Following agitations for a separate Andhra state comprising the Telugu speaking regions of the Madras state by Potti Sriramalu, the Indian Government decided to partition the Madras state. In 1953 Rayalaseema and the coastal Andhra regions became the new state of Andhra Pradesh and the Bellary district became part of the Mysore state. In 1956 south Kanara district was transferred to Mysore, the Malabar coastal districts became part of the new state of Kerala, and the Madras state assumed its present shape. The Madras state was named Tamil Nadu (the land of the Tamils) in 1968.

Ethnic conflict in Sri Lanka during the 1970s and the 80s saw large numbers of Sri Lankan Tamils fleeing to Tamil Nadu. The plight of Tamil refugees caused a surge of support from most of the Tamil political parties. They exerted pressure on the Indian government to intercede with the Sri Lankan government on behalf of the Sri Lankan Tamilians. However, LTTE lost much of its support from Tamil Nadu following the assassination of Rajiv Gandhi on 21 May 1991 by an operative from Sri Lanka for the former Prime Minister's role in sending Indian peacekeepers to Sri Lanka to disarm the LTTE.

The east coast of Tamil Nadu was one of the areas affected by the Indian Ocean earthquake of 2004, during which almost 8000 people died in the disaster. The sixth most populous state in the Indian Union, Tamil Nadu was the seventh largest economy in 2005 among the states of India. The growing demands for skilled labour has caused increased number of educational institutions in Tamil Nadu. The widespread application of caste based affirmative action caused the state to have 69 per cent of all educational and employment vacancies to be reserved to the backward castes. Such caste-based reservations have huge public support in Tamil Nadu, with no popular protests organised against its implementation.

Evolution of Regional Politics

The politics of Tamil Nadu have gone through three distinct phases since independence. The domination of the Congress Party after 1947 gave way to the Dravidian populist mobilisation in the

1960s. This phase lasted until towards the end of the 1990s. The most recent phase saw the fragmentation of the Dravidian political parties and led to the advent of political alliances and coalition governments.

Annadurai formed the Dravidar Munnetra Kazhagam (DMK) in 1949 after splitting from Dravidar Kazhagam. DMK also decided to oppose the 'expansion of the Hindi culture' in Tamil Nadu and started the demand for a separate homeland for the Dravidians in the South. The demand was for an Independent state called *Dravida Nadu* (country of Dravidians) comprising Tamil Nadu and parts of Andhra, Karnataka and Kerala. The increased involvement of the Indian National Congress party in Madras during the late 1950s and the strong pan-Indian emotions whipped up by the Chinese invasion of India in 1962 led to the demand for *Dravida Nadu* losing some of its immediacy. Consequently in 1963, when the Sixteenth Amendment to the Constitution of India, precluded secessionist parties from contesting elections, the DMK chose to formally drop its demand for an independent Dravidistan, focusing instead on securing greater functional autonomy within the framework of the Indian Constitution.

The Congress Rule: The Congress party, riding on the wave of public support stemming from the independence struggle, formed the first post-independence government in Tamil Nadu and continued to govern until 1967. In 1965 and 1968, DMK led widespread anti-Hindi agitations in the state against the plans of the Union Government to introduce Hindi in the state schools. Affirmative action in employment and educational institutions were pioneered in Tamil Nadu based on the demands of the Dravidian movement. The leadership of the Dravidian movement had very capable authors and literati in Annadurai and Karunanidhi, who assiduously utilised the popular media of stage plays and movies to spread its political messages. M. G. Ramachandran (MGR) who later became the Chief Minister of Tamil Nadu, was one such stage and movie actor.

Rise of DMK: In 1967 DMK won the state election. DMK split into two in 1971, with MGR forming the splinter All India Anna Dravida Munnetra Kazhagam (AIADMK). Since then these two parties have dominated the politics of Tamil Nadu. AIADMK, under MGR retained control of the State Government over three consecutive assembly elections in 1977, 1980 and 1984. After MGR's death AIADMK was split over the succession between various contenders. Eventually J. Jayalalita took over the leadership of AIADMK.

Other Developments: Several changes to the political balance in Tamil Nadu took place during the later half of the 1990s, eventually leading to the end of the duopoly of DMK and AIADMK in the politics of Tamil Nadu. In 1996, a split in the Congress party in Tamil Nadu eventuated in the formation of Tamil Maanila Congress (TMC). TMC aligned with the DMK, while another party Marumalarchi Dravidar Munnetra Kazhagam (MDMK), which split from DMK aligned with the AIADMK. These and several smaller political parties began to gain popular support. The first instance of a 'grand alliance' was during the 1996 elections for the National Parliament, during which the AIADMK formed a large coalition of a number smaller parties to counter the electoral threat posed by the alliance between the DMK and TMC. Since then the formation of alliances of large number of political parties has become an electoral practice in Tamil Nadu. The electoral decline of Congress party at the national level, which started during the early 1990, forced the Congress to seek coalition partners from various states including Tamil Nadu. This paved the way for the Dravidian parties to be part of the Central Government.

Tamil History at a Glance

Pre-historic Period

- *c. 30,000 BCE:* Palaeolithic industries in north Tamil Nadu
- *c. 8000-3000 BCE:* Pre-pottery microlithic industries
- *c. 3000-1000 BCE:* Neolithic and fine microlithic industries

Pre-Sangam Period

- *c. 1000-300 BCE:* Megalithic age
- *c. 600 BCE:* Tamil-Brahmi prevalent as the Tamil script
- *c. 250 BCE:* Ashoka's inscription recording the four kingdoms (Chera, Cholas, Pandya and Satyaputra) of the ancient Tamil country

- *c. 200 BCE:* Elara, a Tamil Prince and contemporary of Dutte Gamini, rules Lanka

Sangam Age

- *c. 200 BCE-200 CE:* Sangam age during which books of Sangam Literature are created
- *c. 150 BCE:* Kharavela of Kalinga records his conquest of a federation of Tamil Kings in his Hathigumpha inscription
- *c. 130:* Chera King Udayanjeral rules in the Chera country
- *c. 175-195:* Gajabahu I of Lanka a contemporary of Chera Senguttuvan and Karikala Chola
- *c. 190:* Chera Kadukko Ilanjeral Irumporai rules in the Chera country
- *c. 200:* Writing becomes widespread and *vattezuttu* evolved from the Tamil Brahmi becomes a mature script for writing Tamil
- *c. 210:* Pandya Neduncheliyan rules in Madurai and defeats his enemies at the battle of Talaiyalanganam

Post-Sangam Period

- *c. 300-590:* Kalabhras invade the Tamil country and displace the traditional rulers
- *c. 300-500:* Post-Sangam period, Tamil epics such as Silappatikaram written

Pallava and Pandyas

- *c. 560-580:* Pallava Simhavishnu overthrows the Kalabhras in Tondaimandalam
- *c. 560-590:* Pandya Kadungon rules from Madurai and displaces the Kalabhras from the south
- *c. 590-630:* Pallava Mahendravarman I rules in Kanchipuram
- *c. 610:* Saiva saint Thirunavukkarasar (Appar) converts Mahendravarman from Jainism

- *c. 628:* Chalukya Pulakesi II invades the Pallava Kingdom and lays siege on Kanchipuram
- *c. 630-668:* Pallava Narasimhavarman I (*Mamalla*) rules in Tondaimandalam
- *c. 642:* Pallava Narasimhavarman I launches a counter invasion into the Chalukya country and sacks Vatapi. Pulakesi is killed in battle
- *c. 670-700 CE:* Pandya Arikesari Parankusa Maravarman rules in Madurai
- *c. 700-728:* Pallava Rajasimha builds the Kailasanatha temple in Kanchipuram and many of the shore temples in Mamallapuram
- *c. 700-730:* Pandya Ranadhira (Koccadayan) expands the Pandya Kingdom into the Kongu country
- *c. 731:* Succession crisis in the Pallava Kingdom. Council of ministers select Nandivarman II (Pallavamalla) (731-796) as the Pallava King
- *c. 731-765:* Pandya Maravarman Rajasimha aligns with the Chalukya Vikramaditya II and attacks the Pallava King Nandivarmam
- *c. 735:* Chaluka Vikramaditya II invades the Pallava country and occupies the capital Kanchipuram
- *c. 760:* Pallava Nandivarman II invades and defeats the Ganga Kingdom at the battle of Villande
- *c. 765-815:* Pandya Parantaka Nedunjadaiyan (Varaguna Pandyan) rules in Madurai
- *c. 767:* Pandya forces defeat the Pallavas on the south banks of the Kaveri
- *c. 800-830:* Varagunan I becomes Pandya King and extends his empire up to Tiruchirapalli by defeating the Pallava King Dandivarman
- *c. 830-862:* Pandya Sirmara Srivallabha rules in Madurai
- *c. 840:* Srimara invades Lanka and captures the northern provinces of the Lanka King Sena I

- *c. 848:* Rise of Vijayalaya Chola in Tanjavur
- *c. 846-869:* Pallava Nadivarman III leads an invasion against the Pandya Kingdom and defeats the Pandyas at the battle of Tellaru. Pallava Kingdom extends up to the river Vaigai
- *c. 859:* Pandya Srivallaba defeats the Pallavas at a battle at Kumbakonam
- *c. 862:* Sinhala forces under Sena II invade the Pandya country and sack Madurai. Srimara is killed in battle

Chola Period

- *c. 903:* Aditya Chola defeats the Pallava King Aparajita
- *c. 949:* Battle of Takkolam. Rashtrakuta Krishna III defeats the Chola army
- *c. 985:* Accession of Rajaraja Chola I
- *c. 1010:* Rajaraja completes the Brihadisvara Temple
- *c. 1012:* Accession of Rajendra Chola I
- *c. 1023:* Rajendra's expedition to the Ganges
- *c. 1025:* Chola navies defeat the King of Srivijaya
- *c. 1041:* Rajendra invades Lanka
- *c. 1054:* Rajadhiraja Chola dies in the battle of Koppam against Western Chalukyas
- *c. 1070:* Accession of Kulothunga Chola I
- *c. 1118:* Vikrama Chola
- *c. 1133:* Kulothunga Chola II
- *c. 1146:* Rajaraja Chola II
- *c. 1163:* Rajadhiraja Chola II
- *c. 1178:* Kulothunga Chola III
- *c. 1216:* Rajaraja Chola III
- *c. 1246:* Rajendra Chola III

Chola to Pandya Transition

- *c. 1190-1260:* Bana Dynasty rule Magadaimandalam with family title of 'ponparappinan' and headquarters at Aragalur
- *c. 1216:* Kadava Dynasty

Pandiya Revival and Muslim Rule

- *1251:* Accession of Jatavarman Sundara Pandiyan
- *1279:* End of the Chola dynasty with the death of Rajendra Chola III
- *1268-1310:* Maravarman Kulasekhara Pandiyan rules in Madurai
- *1308:* Malik Kafur a general of Allaudin Khilji invades Devagiri *en route* to Tamil Nadu
- *1310:* Sundara Pandian, son of Kulasekara Pandiyan, kills his father and becomes King. In the ensuing civil war he is defeated by his brother Vira Pandiyan.
- *1311:* Malik Kafur, invades Pandiya country and attacks Madurai
- *1327-1370:* Madurai under the rule of Madurai Sultanate

Vijayanagar and Nayak Period

- *1370:* Bukka, the Vijayanagara ruler and his son Kumara Kamapna capture the entire Tamil country
- *1522:* Portuguese land on the Coromandal coast
- *1535:* Achyuta Raya of Vijayanagara appoints Sevappa Nayak, who established the Nayak dynasty at Tanjavur
- *1535-1590:* Sevappa Nayak rules as the first independent Nayak ruler in Tanjavur
- *1600-1645:* Ragunatha Nayak, the greatest of the Tanjavur Nayaks
- *1609:* the Dutch establish a settlement in Pulicat
- *1623-1659:* Tirumalai Nayak rules in Madurai

- *1639:* British East India Company purchases Chennapatinam and establishes Fort St. George
- *c. 1652:* Tanjavur and Jingi fall to the Bijapur Sultan
- *1656:* Mysore army invades Salem against the Madurai Nayak Tirumalai
- *1675:* Maratha army from Bijapur marches into Tanjavur, Ekoji declares himself King
- *1692:* Nawab of Arcot established by Nawab Zulfiqar Ali Khan, a viceroy of the Mughal Emperor
- *1746:* La Bourdonnais of the French East India company attacks and takes Fort St. George

Company Period

- *1749:* British regain Fort St. George through the Treaty of Aix-la-Chapelle arising out of the War of the Austrian Succession
- *1751:* Robert Clive attacks Arcot and takes it with only 500 men
- *1756:* The British and the French sign the first Carnatic treaty. Muhammad Ali Walajah was recognised as Nawab of the Carnatic
- *1759:* French under Thomas Arthur, Comte de Lally, attack Madras
- *1760:* Battle of Vandavasi between the British and the French. Birth of Veerapandya Kattabomman
- *1767:* Hyder Ali, Sultan of Mysore attacks Madras, but defeated by the British at the Battle of Chengam
- *1773:* British Government passes the Regulating Act. The administration of Madras comes under British Government review
- *1777-1832:* Serfoji II rules in Tanjavur
- *1799:* Serfoji cedes the Tanjavur Kingdom to the British. Kattabomman executed by British
- *1803:* Bentinck appointed governor of Madras

- *1806:* Vellore Mutiny East India Company's Indian soldiers in Vellore mutiny against governor Bentinck in Vellore fort. 114 British officers killed and 19 mutineers executed.

British Rule

- *1892:* British Government passes the Indian Councils Act
- *1909:* 'Minto-Morley Reforms'. Madras Legistlative Council formed
- *1921:* First regional elections held in Madras. Justice party forms government
- *1927:* Madras Congress passes a resolution for 'Full Independence'
- *1928:* Simon Commission visits Madras. Mass protests results in several deaths
- *1937:* Congress party under C. Rajagopalachari wins provincial elections and forms government in Madras
- *1938:* Thanthai Periyar [EVR] organises a separatist agitation demanding *Dravidanadu* consisting of Tamil Nadu, Karnataka, Andhra Pradesh and Kerala
- *1941:* Indian Muslim League holds its congress in Madras. Muhammad Ali Jinnah delivers keynote speech
- *1944:* Periyar EVR and C. N. Annadurai organises Dravidar Kazhagam

Post-independence Period

- *1947:* Madras Presidency, comprising of Tamil Nadu and parts of Andhra Pradesh and Karnataka established
- *1953:* Madras state comes into being along linguistic lines
- *1968:* Widespread agitations in response to the Federal Government's directive of Hindi being the National Language
- *1969:* Madras state is renamed as Tamil Nadu (Land of the Tamils)

Bibliography

Aiyangar, Sakkottai Krishnaswami: *South India and her Muhammadan Invaders*, Oxford University, 1921.

Alexander, K. C.: *Caste Mobilization and Class Consciousness: The Emergence of Agrarian Movements in Kerala and Tamil Nadu*, Dominance and State Power in Modern India: Decline of a Social Order, Oxford University Press, Delhi, 1989.

Bakshi, S. R.: C. *Rajagopalachari: Role in Freedom Movement*, Anmol Publications PVT. LTD., 1991.

Besant, Annie: *How India Wrought for Freedom*, Adyar, Theosophical Publishing House, Madras, 1915.

Christophers, S. R.: The Indian Empire Souvenir, Executive Committee of the Congress, 1927.

Codrington, Humphry William: *A Short History of Lanka*, Macmillan & Co., 1926.

Craik, D. Alex: *Mr. Hopkins' Men: Cambridge Reform and British Mathematics in the 19th Century*, Springer, 2007.

Dutt, Romesh Chunder:, *Open Letters to Lord Curzon on Famines and Land Assessments in India*, Adamant Media Corporation, 1926.

Finnemore, John: *Peeps at Many Lands: Home Life in India*, A. & C. Black, London, 1917.

Gough, Kathleen: *Rural Society in Southeast India*, Cambridge University, 2008.

Great Britain India Office, The India List and India Office List, Harrison and Sons, London, 1905.

Gupta Om: *Encyclopaedia of India, Pakistan and Bangladesh*, Gyan Pulisher House, New Delhi, 2006.

Iyengar, Srinivasa, P. T.: History of the Tamils from the Earliest Times to the Present Day, 1929.

Kamath, Suryanath U.: *A Concise History of Karnataka: from Pre-historic Times to the Present*, Jupiter Books, Bangalore, 2001.

Kanubhai Raval: *Bharat Ratna K. Kamaraj*, Deepak Associates, 1994.

Karthikeyan, T.: *Perunthalaivar Kamaraj Kalappettagam*, Kommadikottai, 1990.

Kothari, Rajni: Caste in Indian Politics, Orient Blackswan, 2004.

Kulke, Hermann, Dietmar Rothermund: *A History of India*, Routledge, UK, 2004.

M. S. Muthuswamy: *K. Kamaraj: Socio-political Study*, Tamil Nadu Academy of Political Science, 1988.

MaClean, C. D.: *Standing Information Regarding the Official Administration of Madras Presidency*, Government of Madras, 1877.

Major MacMunn, G. F. Major, Lovett A. C.: The Armies of India, Adam and Charles Black, 1911.

Mazumdar, Amvika Charan: *Indian National Evolution*, G. A. Natesan & Co., Madras, 1917.

Mehrotra, K. Santosh: *The Economics of Elementary Education in India: The Challenge of Public Finance*, Private Provision and Household Costs, 2006.

Muthiah, S.: *Madras Rediscovered: East West Books*, Pvt Ltd., Madras, 2004.

Newell, Herbert Andrews: *Madras the Birth Place of British India: An Illustrated Guide with Map*, The Madras Times Printing and Publishing, 1919.

Nilakanta Sastri, K.A.: *A History of South India*, New Delhi, Oxford University Press, 2000.

Osborne, T. Hitch, C. Millar, A. John Rivington, Crowder, S. Law, B. & Co, Longman, T. Ware, C.: *The Modern Part of An Universal*

History from the Earliest Account of Time, Oxford University, London, 1765.

P. Kandaswamy: *The Political Career of K. Kamaraj: A Study in the Politics of Tamil Nadu, 1920-1975,* Concept Publication Company, 2001.

Palanithurai, G.: *Caste, Politics and Society in Tamilnadu,* Kanishka Publishers Distributors, Delhi, 1994.

Palayam M. Balasundaram: *Kamaraj and His Secrets of Success,* Poompuhar Pub. Trace, 1983.

Patnaik, Nihar Ranjan: *Economic History of Orissa,* Indus Publishing, 1997.

Penny, F. E. Lady Lawley: Southern India, A. C. Black, 1914.

Playne, Somerset; J. W. Bond, Arnold Wright: *Its History: People,* Commerce and Industrial Resources, Southern India, 1914.

R. Parthasarthi: *K. Kamaraj,* Publications Division, Ministry of Information and Broadcasting, Govt. of Indian, 1982.

Raghavaiyangar, Srinivasa: *Memorandum of progress of the Madras Presidency During the Last Forty Years of British Administration,* Government of Madras, 1893.

Raghu Pati Kapur: *Kamaraj, The Iron Man,* Deepak Associates, 1966.

Ralhan, O. P.: *Encyclopaedia of Political Parties,* Anmol Publications Pvt. Ltd., 2002.

Read, Anthony: *The Proudest Day - India's Long Ride to Independence,* Jonathan Cape, London, 1997.

Seal, Anil: *The Emergence of Indian Nationalism: Competition and Collaboration in the Later Nineteenth Century,* CUP Archive, 1971.

Shri Ram Bakshi: *K. Kamaraj: The Patriot and Statesman,* Anmol Publication, New Delhi, 1992.

Shri Ram Bakshi: *Struggle for Independence: K. Kamaraj,* Anmol Publication, New Delhi, 1989.

Sinha, Aseema: *The Regional Roots of Developmental Politics in India: A Divided Leviathan,* Indiana University Press, 2005.

Slater, Gilbert: *Economic Studies Vol I: Some South Indian Villages,* 1918.

Some Madras Leaders: Babu Bhishambher Nath Bhargava, 1922.

Steinberg, S. H.: The Statesman's Yearbook 1950, Macmillan and Co., London, 1950.

Stuart Mill, John; John M. Robson, Martin Moir, Zawahir Moir: *Miscelaneous Writings,* Routledge, 1996.

Talboys-Wheeler, James: *Hand-book to the Cotton Cultivation in the Madras Presidency,* J. Higginbotham and Pharoah and Co., 1862.

Tercentenary Madras Staff: *Madras Tercentenary Celebration Committee Commemoration Volume,* Indian Branch, Oxford Press, 1939.

Thangaraj, M.: *Tamil Nadu: An Unfinished Task,* SAGE, 2003.

The Northern Nadars of Tamil Nadu: An Indian Caste in the Process of Change Dennis Templeman Hardcover/Published, 1997.

Thurston, Edgar: *Provincial Geographies of India: The Madras Presidency with Mysore,* Cambridge University, Coorg and Associated States, 1913.

Thurston, Edgar; Rangachari, K.: *Castes and Tribes of Southern India Vol. I to VII,* Government of Madras, 1909.

V. K. Narasimhau: *Kamaraj: A Stury, 1967,* National Book Trust, 2007.

Vadivelu, A.: The Aristocracy of South India, Vest & Co., 1903.

Von Fürer-Haimendorf, Christoph: *Tribes of India - The Struggle for Survival,* University of California, 1982.

Washbrook, David A.: *Caste, Class and Dominance in Modern Tamil Nadu: Non-Brahmanism, Dravidianism and Tamil Nationalism,* Oxford University Press, New Delhi, 1989.

——————: *The Emergence of Provincial Politics: The Madras Presidency,* Cambridge University Press, Cambridge, 1976.

Wright, Arnold: *Twentieth Century Impressions of Ceylon: Its History,* Asian Educational Services, Industries and Resources, 1999.

Index

M

N

P

Q

R

S

T

V

W

Y

❑❑❑